ASSESSMENT IN PRACTICE

Assessment in Practice explores timely and important questions in relation to assessment. By examining the relationship between identity, culture, policy and inclusion, the book investigates the conflicted and fractured battleground of assessment, and challenges current and practiced understandings of assessment practice.

The authors encourage the reader to reconceptualise assessment as a sociocultural practice. Each chapter studies a key theme in the understanding of assessment policy and practice from a sociocultural perspective and provides questions to prompt reflection on the key assessment concepts outlined in the book. Using culture as both a lens and analytic tool, the chapters examine topics such as:

- the social order of assessment, how assessment works in the world and how learning could be assessed;
- perspectives on social justice and assessment, with a particular focus on social class and other potential inequalities on the experiences of assessment for young people;
- discussions of ability and the assessment of students with special education needs as well as the role of inclusivity in assessment practice.

Written by leading academics from University College Cork, the third volume in the successful *Routledge Current Debates in Educational Psychology* series is an essential read for researchers and postgraduate students in educational research and education psychology.

Alicia Curtin is a lecturer in the School of Education, University College Cork. She lectures and supervises students on the Cohort PhD, Masters in Education, Professional Master of Education, Sports Studies and Physical Education and BSc Science Education.

She researches and publishes in the areas of assessment, learning, literacy and pedagogy from a sociocultural perspective.

Kevin Cahill is a lecturer in the School of Education, University College Cork. He lectures across programmes in the school with responsibilities in the areas of inclusive education, sociology of education and pedagogy. He also researches, writes, and supervises doctoral students, across these areas of interest.

Kathy Hall is Professor of Education in the School of Education, University College Cork. She has researched and published in the areas of learning, assessment, literacy and inclusion. She leads the cohort PhD programme in UCC.

Dan O'Sullivan is a lecturer in the School of Education, University College Cork. He lectures on inclusion-related issues on a range of postgraduate programmes and engages in doctoral supervision.

Kamil Özerk is a Professor of Education at the University of Oslo and Sami University for Applied Sciences, Norway. His research interests are teaching and learning, curriculum development, educational counselling, bilingualism, reading and socio-emotional difficulties and autism.

CURRENT DEBATES IN EDUCATIONAL PSYCHOLOGY

Series Editor: Kieron Sheehy

Assessment in Practice: Explorations in Identity, Culture, Policy and Inclusion
Alicia Curtin, Kevin Cahill, Kathy Hall, Dan O'Sullivan, Kamil özerk

Must inclusion be special? Rethinking educational support within a community of provision
Jonathan Rix

Rethinking Learning in an Age of Digital Fluency: Is being Digitally Tethered a New Learning Nexus?
Maggi Savin-Baden

ASSESSMENT IN PRACTICE

Explorations in Identity, Culture, Policy and Inclusion

Alicia Curtin, Kevin Cahill, Kathy Hall, Dan O'Sullivan and Kamil Özerk

LONDON AND NEW YORK

First published 2020
by Routledge
2 Park Square, Milton Park, Abingdon, Oxon OX14 4RN

and by Routledge
52 Vanderbilt Avenue, New York, NY 10017

Routledge is an imprint of the Taylor & Francis Group, an informa business

© 2020 Alicia Curtin, Kevin Cahill, Kathy Hall, Dan O'Sullivan and Kamil Özerk

The right of Alicia Curtin, Kevin Cahill, Kathy Hall, Dan O'Sullivan and Kamil Özerk to be identified as authors of this work has been asserted by them in accordance with sections 77 and 78 of the Copyright, Designs and Patents Act 1988.

All rights reserved. No part of this book may be reprinted or reproduced or utilised in any form or by any electronic, mechanical, or other means, now known or hereafter invented, including photocopying and recording, or in any information storage or retrieval system, without permission in writing from the publishers.

Trademark notice: Product or corporate names may be trademarks or registered trademarks, and are used only for identification and explanation without intent to infringe.

British Library Cataloguing in Publication Data
A catalogue record for this book is available from the British Library

Library of Congress Cataloging-in-Publication Data
A catalog record has been requested for this book

ISBN: 978-1-138-83240-4 (hbk)
ISBN: 978-1-138-83242-8 (pbk)
ISBN: 978-0-429-32661-5 (ebk)

Typeset in Bembo
by Taylor & Francis Books

CONTENTS

List of illustrations viii
Acknowledgements ix

Introduction: examining the social order of assessment 1

1 Setting the boundaries in assessment: intersections of identity and value in personal spaces 10

2 Assessment as public practice: international aspects of assessment and accountability 29

3 Cultural scripts of assessment for practice: predictability, outcomes and life chances 61

4 Junior cycle reform: the negotiated nature of assessment policy in Ireland 66

5 Perspectives on social justice and assessment: testing, social class and opportunity to learn 82

6 The assessment of pupils with special educational needs: giving effect to the principles of inclusivity in practice. 103

Conclusion: disrupting normative thinking on assessment 131

Bibliography 140
Index 159

ILLUSTRATIONS

Figures

1.1	19
5.1 Elaine at school	99
5.2 Barry working at school	100

Tables

4.1 Policy actors	69
4.2 English assessment arrangements, 2014	77
4.3 Final version of English assessment arrangements, 2017	78
4.4 Grading system for junior cycle	78
4.5 JCPA grade descriptors and CBAs features of quality	80

Box

5.1 ALIAS study scenario responses	97

ACKNOWLEDGEMENTS

We would like to thank in particular our School of Education colleagues in University College Cork for their sustained interest, encouragement and support to us in our completion of this project. We would also like to thank the Irish Research Council for Humanities and Social Sciences (IRCHSS, now renamed the Irish Research Council, IRC) for funding the VIP research study and the Cambridge Primary Review for its support for the work drawn on in Chapter 2. We thank too the schools, teachers, staff and students who participated in our ALIAS and VIP research studies. Our experiences with the people in each of these settings has extended and developed our own understandings of teaching, learning and assessment practice explored in this text. Finally we would like to thank our nearest and dearest for affording us the space and time to pursue this book. It is not always easy to let us dwell in the world of assessment when the pleasures of family life lay waiting beyond the study door. Our eternal gratitude to each of you for your patience and support.

INTRODUCTION: EXAMINING THE SOCIAL ORDER OF ASSESSMENT

Introduction

This chapter introduces the central sociocultural perspective on assessment policy and practice which frames our discussion of key assessment themes throughout this text. To conceptualise our understanding of assessment as a complex sociocultural practice a central aim within this text is to investigate the personal, public, cultural, political, economic and ability driven worlds that govern it. Each chapter sets itself in one of these worlds and explores how assessment policy and practice shapes and is shaped by related concepts, discourses and contexts. Our approach is Rogoffian in this regard (as explained later in this chapter) and our intention to focus on separate arenas for assessment in individual chapters maintains always the understanding that to know the conflicted and fractured battleground of assessment is to ultimately consider how all of these worlds or layers of assessment work together to create assessment as ever unique and emergent in individual settings for individual participants.

To begin we suggest that understanding the importance of examining the social order of assessment connects context, meaning, participation and reification to assessment policy and practice, and identifies assessment as a sociocultural practice. We offer a brief theoretical justification for investigating the social order of assessment across a variety of contexts through exploring different official assessment policies and systems internationally, as we develop in later chapters. This justification entails some elaboration of sociocultural concepts that are helpful in grappling with the practice of assessment and in particular with understanding the importance of examining the social order of assessment. We use Barbara Rogoff's conceptualisation of three planes as applied to assessment policy and practice to exemplify some of our key ideas present in later chapters. Finally, we outline the remaining chapters in the book, highlighting and connecting key themes for understanding assessment policy and practice as a mediated, meaning laden, constitutive and negotiated social practice in a variety of contexts.

The individual and the collective as constitutive

It is through participation in practice, as people engage in ongoing activity using the tools of their community that understanding happens. Cultural tools or scripts are the means through which people act and make meaning of assessment practices and experiences. These tools or scripts can derive from taken-for-granted beliefs about how the world is or ought to be in terms of such aspects as education, schooling, learning, assessment, knowledge and so on. These tools or ways of thinking and acting can also be based on assumptions, for instance, how to be a boy, girl, an English teacher and so on. Chapter 1 provides a telling example of how some individuals engage and construe different meanings from school assessment practices – the lived experience of assessment. Assessment practices produce particular kinds of people or identities. Drawing on Rogoff (1998) we accept the argument that the cultural tools of assessment deployed in that setting 'serve to amplify as well as constrain the possibilities of human activity' since the tools and scripts available to us 'participate in the practices in which they are employed' (Rogoff, 1998). In other words, practices, including outcomes (in the form of identities) form and are formed by the practices of their use. In this sense policies/procedures and practices are interrelated and identity-forming.

Policies and procedures like official national policies project beliefs that shape action in the lived world (Lave, 1988; 1996). As we will show in Chapter 2 the emphasis in assessment policy and on accountability in many countries privileges a view of the learner as possessing knowledge that can be legitimately and validly assessed in a straightforward manner which then allows for comparative judgements at the level of the individual student, the individual teacher, school, neighbourhood, and nation state. Because such policies function as cultural resources and can be embedded in the consciousness of, say, teachers, they exert wide influence. Policies can change what it is to be a student in a particular context at a particular stage in life. What are the affordances and possibilities available to students and teachers in a system of relations where the political, the economic, the social and the personal are ever enmeshed? The social order is at one level outside the individual as agent, but inevitably the individual student and teacher are enmeshed in that order. The following chapters raise questions for example about the intentions of agencies such as the state as part of the lived experience of agents as they go about their learning and assessment.

Cultural tools include ideas and cultural legacies that are, to various degrees, held consciously by individuals as they act in the world. They constitute the wherewithal for human action. In this context McDermott argues that we can only learn what is available to be learned or put another way, we can only act in relation to the mediational means available to us. This means that understanding human action in relation to assessment requires reference to the cultural tools that are deployed in that process. It requires attention to the local and to the more apparently distant, to the individual and to the collective. It requires attention to the individual meaning-maker in the here and now, moment-by-moment 'everyday' interaction and it requires attention to the broader social order.

As socioculturalists, we accept that collective and individual meaning-making are inseparable. Schools are inevitably exposed to practices beyond their boundaries (Bruner, 1996) such that what and how teachers assess is mediated by the social order of what is assumed to count as success and of value. What counts as success gets specified or reified and is part of the broader social order. The broader social order of assessment incorporates beliefs and practices about for instance what knowledge is of value, how that knowledge can be represented and demonstrated, and how teachers and pupils are held to account for it. Wider policy imperatives, and their perceived relative status, generate cultural scripts that mediate, albeit in different ways, what people do and can do. Some of this mediation can be so subtle as to be practically invisible. The issue is that in curriculum and assessment enactments in classrooms, cultural scripts and their policy entailments get built, reproduced and contested in, and through, lived world interactions during moment-by-moment processes of negotiation and engagement. The enactor (e.g. the teacher, the pupil) is the agent through which the social order gets negotiated and reproduced. In this sense the teacher is never completely free to act because s/he is shaped by and is enmeshed in the social order. Put another way, the social order or external is also in the person (Hermans, 2001; Rogoff, 1995). In a sociocultural exploration of an individual's assessment practice account needs to be taken not just of that person's practice and expressed views. It is also important to seek to understand and make visible the constraining and facilitating influences of the social order on those practices and views.

Thinking about assessment with the tools and institutions of culture

In a chapter entitled, 'Thinking with the Tools and Institutions of Culture' Barbara Rogoff considers how social order emerges in practice. Though decades old, her work (1995) still offers a useful conceptual framework that captures the complexity of human learning in a way that we think has merit for our work here on assessment. We introduce and apply it here in our introductory chapter as a sociocultural and contextual frame for our discussion and analysis of assessment in later chapters. Rogoff's framework encapsulates the dynamic nature of individuals' contributions and interactions in the moment-by-moment social context, along with their social partners and the broader cultural/institutional context in which they participate. She talks about three different planes of analysis: the personal, inter-personal and institutional. The feasibility of her framework stems from the potential foregrounding and backgrounding of these different planes without losing sight of their enmeshed nature.

The social/institutional plane is where the idealised competencies, understandings, procedures and attitudes are expressed, circulated and institutionalised. The interpersonal plane with its emphasis on guided participation allows for the emergence of multiple meanings, the negotiation, contesting and sharing of meanings and the examination of sources of the multiple meanings that emerge as people interact and participate in activity of curriculum enactment. The personal plane foregrounds learners' experience through its emphasis on appropriation and identity transformation.

One can read the first chapter of this book as bearing on various elements of the personal, the inter-personal and institutional planes, although we did not make the latter explicit in that analysis. In Chapter 2 we attend almost exclusively to the institutional plane or the broader social order since it is important to recognise the imperatives at national and international level that are likely to shape and colour one's experience of assessment explored in detail in Chapter 1. The fundamental premise therefore is that assessment practices at the classroom level do not exist in isolation but are part of a wider social order of relations in which they have purpose and meaning. Practices, therefore, can be inscribed in our routines and actions, they can be taken for granted activities that are simply assumed to be a natural way to be or to act.

As we demonstrate in Chapter 2, traditional assessment approaches for measuring the progression of individuals and standards reached tend to rely on age of learners. Expectations for achievement are set around ages and stages. We invite readers to problematise this feature of international assessment. In addition, the focus of assessment is only the learner, the student, the child but by implication the individual teacher, the individual school, the individual neighbourhood. Not so much attention is paid in policy or the social order of assessment to the 'dynamic interplay' (Fleer, 2015) across those individualities. What conditions were made available to groups of learners? This is not part of the known in this analysis. We note in Chapter 1 how the assessment regime made sense or did not make sense to different participants. Drawing on Fleer (2015) we pose the question: how is the environment constituted for providing the possibilities of meaningful learning and assessment? What do we know for instance about resources available to learners and schools to support achievement? In a sociocultural take everything is subjective and meanings do not exist outside of people. If this is the case we need accounts of learners' own experiences, how these mediated their responses to assessment situations. To what extent have assessors access to what learners really know and can do, and how they know it, and who they believe themselves to be? How are assessors' interpretations of their learners limited and constrained, especially in follow-up action to further enhance learning? Jannette Elwood argues that 'assessment can only describe the relationship between the learner, the teacher and the assessment task in the social, historical and cultural context in which it is carried out' (2006, p. 230). She goes on to argue that if we look 'to within the student for their learning we are looking in the wrong place' (p. 230) and that learning can only be viewed in the context of the relationship and interactions between learner, teacher and task. With reference to accountability systems, she highlights the challenge of convincing those holding systems to account of the validity of information on learning contexts and ultimately how the social order of official policy needs to adopt 'a more humble way of considering how students come to know and how we "measure" that knowing' (p. 231). These are questions and issues we invite the reader to consider as we offer an account of policy and practice in various countries in Chapter 2 where we attend almost exclusively to the institutional plane or the broader social order in this analysis.

Engaging with assessment worlds

Adolescent Literacy Identity And School (ALIAS) is a research project undertaken by four of the authors of this book (Kevin Cahill, Alicia Curtin, Kathy Hall, Dan O' Sullivan) here in University College Cork and our engagement with experiences of assessment in this study shaped our understandings of assessment presented in this text. Some initial findings from this research have also been reported elsewhere (Cahill, Curtin, Hall and O'Sullivan, 2017; Cahill, Curtin, Hall and O'Sullivan, 2018) This research involved the collaboration of two post-primary schools and several alternative education settings where students, teachers, administrators and volunteers were interviewed and engaged with in relation to the key research questions of the project:

- How do children see themselves in relation to school and learning?
- What literacy experiences have/ have not worked for these children in terms of their in-school learning to date?
- What can we learn about their out-of-school literacy practices which would contribute to their in-school learning?
- What are the experiences of teachers and students with other literacy interventions?
- How can we collaborate with students and teachers on the design of engaging literacy-learning experiences for first year post-primary students?

These broad questions led us on a fascinating journey far beyond the intended literacy focus and indeed much of the data and findings tended to develop into stories of experience and practice in a variety of educational settings. Our thoughts and ideas strayed into the worlds of mainstream post-primary classrooms, special school settings, a Youthreach centre and a voluntary education setting providing flexible learning opportunities for young people who had dropped out of mainstream settings. Their stories and experiences helped us to condense our ideas about the entwined nature of assessment practice.

The ALIAS project drew upon a broad theoretical framework wherein the 'Funds of Knowledge' perspective on learning became an orientating concept for the research team (Moll, Amanti, Neff and Gonzalez, 1992). Relatedly, we drew upon developmental concepts growing from the Fok tree. Ideas such as Zipin's (2009) 'Funds of Pedagogy', as well as Esteban-Guitart and Moll's (2014) 'Funds of

Identity' supported our thinking throughout the project also. So much so that much of our research pointed towards possibilities around conceptualising 'Funds of Assessment', an idea that is still gestating within the research group.

Data were generated via focus group interviews with students in the post-primary schools, as well as open-ended qualitative questionnaires and group workshop activities focused on experiences of curriculum, pedagogy and assessment. The data were generated from oral, written and visual perspectives. For instance, visual representations of the participants' thoughts about school and assessment are used at various stages in this book. Data were also generated through interviews with teachers in alternative settings and this data produced findings around the key areas of curriculum innovation, learner-centred pedagogies and tensions in assessment processes (Cahill, Curtin, Hall and O'Sullivan, 2018).

The ALIAS study also produced broad findings across areas such as experiences of literacy, pedagogical practices, curriculum design, learner identities and experiences of assessment. Data pertaining to explorations of assessment are drawn upon throughout this book. Post-primary school student data revealed the central link between experiences of assessment and learner identity whilst our investigations in alternative settings constructed teacher views upon how assessment had become such a complex, contested and often problematic space for young people experiencing education beyond the gates of mainstream schools. These views are developed throughout this book, most particularly in chapters relating to issues of social justice and inclusion. ALIAS taught us, above all else, that experiences of assessment have an impact far beyond the experience and the moment of assessment itself; these experiences are important, cultural, historical, social and personal moments that shape the identity of the learner from within and without.

Oftentimes during the ALIAS project our conversations were about creating consonance between young people's *lifeworlds* and their *schoolworlds* and yet what became obvious as the research progressed was that assessment and assessment moments had a permeating influence on their experiences and thoughts about learning. This was evidenced through the use of assessment for streaming and banding purposes in post-primary schools; as well as assessment emerging as a pedagogical tool where students experiencing difficulties often found the assessment moment to be a source of failure, embarrassment, anxiety and disconnection from school. Therefore, although we set out to build connections between schools and learners in the ALIAS project, we often found assessment emerging as a most significant moment of disconnection for young people. Indeed, the research provided us with a privileged insight into the minds of learners and educators as they grappled with the dilemmas presented to them by the external pressures created by assessment as an arm (or an eye) of the state and even from within as an indicator of learning at the level of the person, ideas, of course, that are entwined within the web-like nature of practice and experience. The ideas that emerged through ALIAS have allowed to form some of our thinking around this book and around conceptualising assessment from a variety of perspectives relating to inclusion, social justice, special education, policy formation, identity, participation and culture.

To a lesser extent our experiences on The VIP (Voice, Identity, Participation) Project (Kathy Hall and Alicia Curtin, 2013) frame our discussion in particular chapters also. The VIP Project is an 18-month knowledge exchange project funded by the Irish Research Council for the Humanities and Social Sciences (IRCHSS). This project was primarily concerned with issues of inclusion and student voice, identity and participation in Irish primary and secondary schools. We aimed to explore classroom and school-based strategies for learning based on recent developments in understanding the learning process, while also developing respect for the learner's perspective and promoting learning through the integration of education and everyday experiences.

The group itself consisted of 18 primary and secondary school teachers and principals in Ireland who met once a month for approximately two hours in the spirit of knowledge exchange to have conversations about teaching and learning. Public events and conferences were also organised and one of the themes explored in these fora was assessment practice in primary and post primary schools. At one event group members were asked to each bring an artefact with them to our meeting that revealed something about their understanding of assessment. The artefacts brought in, alongside the practices they represented, were varied and insightful in relation to assessment practice in classrooms across Ireland from the perspectives of teachers and school leaders (and their understanding of their own identity in relation to assessment) and we explore these in the next chapter of this book alongside the relationship between assessment and identity for students and young people, the assessors and those being assessed.

Our story of assessment

Each chapter in this book explores what we understand to be a key world and theme in the understanding of assessment policy and practice from a sociocultural perspective, building on our definition of assessment introduced in this chapter. Understanding assessment as a complex and contested learning space, these worlds, themes and aspects within each are not always complimentary and at times oppose each other in our participation in and reification of assessment. At the end of every chapter readers will find a series of questions to prompt reflection on the key assessment concepts explored in each chapter in the context of the reader's own individual setting and assessment practice and experience.

Chapter 1 begins with the personal word of assessment and the voices of young adolescent learners, foregrounding their personal stories and the personal plane of assessment practice in a discussion of the intersecting roles of space, identity and value in the experience of assessment in a variety of formal and informal learning settings. Overlaying Rogoff's personal plane of learning with an emphasis on spatial and temporal aspects and the Wengerian concept of trajectories and boundary practices this chapter shares individual stories of assessment to highlight assessment as a social practice developing within shared and mediated histories of practice over time. We consider assessment as a bounded and binding sociocultural space offering itself in this understanding as a learning asset. We consider what kinds of sustainable assessment are required to address personal and interpersonal experiences in assessment and ask how assessment practices informed by Rogoff's concept of participatory appropriation can develop our planning, practice and experience of assessment and thus learning and teaching in and outside of classroom practice.

Chapters 2 and 3 place these assessment stories of individuals within the wider national and international context of public and cultural assessment policy and practice. This is essential to our understanding of the social order of assessment and how assessment works in the world to organise the daily individual experiences of assessment outlined in Chapter 1. Chapter 2 describes, analyses and interprets assessment as a public practice through an exploration of policies from a variety of selected countries. Our purpose here is to encourage reflection on how the social order of assessment impacts individual experiences in assessment in classrooms. We highlight the theme of accountability as central to our understanding and an organisational feature of the social order of assessment, questioning how this dominant ruling force of accountability in the public arena of assessment compares and contrasts with the previous chapter themes of space, identity and value writ large in the personal and immediate assessment space. The countries (England, Finland, Germany) and states (California, USA and Victoria, Australia) are chosen specifically to contextualise social order imperatives in assessment that shape assessment at personal and interpersonal levels for its participants, in particular national and international factors which serve to mediate what teachers do and how learners are positioned in relation to assessment. We look at Ireland in detail in this way in Chapter 4.

Chapter 3 develops directly the international case studies of public assessment explored in Chapter 3, moving to a cultural analysis of assessment using the sociocultural theme of cultural scripts to explore further the organisation and functioning of assessment in our selected countries at local levels as a result of social and policy imperatives. We discuss a number of cultural scripts we understand to mediate assessment practices in this regard and question how identities, learning trajectories and ultimately life chances are variously impacted as a result.

Chapter 4 moves to the authors' own national context and Ireland where assessment is currently undergoing (2012–2018) a pivotal point in its sociopolitical history. We investigate the revised junior cycle curriculum statement *Framework for Junior Cycle* (2015), which we term a controversial and contested cultural artifact of assessment, for the story it tells about assessment policy, practice and debate in Ireland in a moment in time. We contextualise our discussion through an exploration of the background, emergence and policy of the junior cycle curriculum, engaging also with policy analysis of the current junior cycle reform process. We focus on the subject of English in this analysis, as the first subject to change under current reforms. Connecting with Rogoff's three planes this chapter highlights through one small example and a particular focus on assessment as policy assessment as a space that is policed, politicised and fractured by policy and social opinion.

Chapter 5 is situated in the economic world of assessment and explores perspectives on social justice and assessment, with assessment being understood very particularly as testing in a variety of settings, in particular using the example of entrance examinations to secondary school for students in Ireland. This chapter sheds light on the influence of opportunity to learn, race, gender, social class, ability and other potential inequalities on the experience of assessment for young people. We argue that a social justice lens and theme is required for a sociocultural understanding of assessment as collective and individual meaning making are inseparable in a discussion of assessment as testing. Interpreting social justice issues such as reliability, validity, fairness tracking and streaming in assessment from a sociocultural perspective this chapter focuses on how social class impacts on opportunity to learn and assessment in testing settings.

Chapter 6 brings to a conclusion our developing sociocultural understanding of assessment policy and practice with a discussion of ability and the assessment of students with special educational needs, and in particular the role of inclusivity in assessment practice. Understanding assessment as serving social purpose this chapter interrogates in detail the purpose of assessment policy and practice through the theme of inclusivity on learning and assessment for students with special educational needs. As our final example of assessment processes in action in a particular context and setting, this chapter exemplifies, considers in detail and draws together many of the key themes explored in our book in a sociocultural understanding of assessment policy and practice – student identities, values and experiences; understandings of learning and assessment practices underpinning these individual experiences; the cultural scripts and fractured policies surrounding and competing in assessment practices; inequality, opportunity to learn and inclusivity in assessment practice. The chapter concludes with an inclusive model for assessment practice which prioritises assessment ideals such as inclusive values, conceptually informed assessment, disruptions of definitions of success and failure and broadening assessment outcomes.

Our concluding chapter offers some parting words from the authors on our understanding of the specified, enacted and experienced nature of assessment and how understanding assessment from a sociocultural perspective provides lessons for the planning for and negotiation of assessment as a sociocultural space for learning. We challenge the reader to reconceptualise assessment as a sociocultural practice now with a deeper understanding of the personal, public, cultural, political, economic and ability driven worlds that constitute and are constituted by assessment in one way or another. We juxtapose ideas explored in this text around assessment with large scale worldwide research initiatives on evaluation and assessment, asking questions which urge the reader to challenge dominant assessment discourses and normative thinking around assessment policy and practice. We invite readers here also to draw their own conclusions about the nature and impact of assessment policy and practice in your own particular setting, how this is mediated through broader worlds and particular agents at local, national and international levels and negotiated through social interaction in daily practice.

1

SETTING THE BOUNDARIES IN ASSESSMENT: INTERSECTIONS OF IDENTITY AND VALUE IN PERSONAL SPACES

Today Alex is getting his final year examination results. He feels a bit nervous, though you would not think it to look at him. As there is a half day today Alex has decided to come in his own clothes, black Adidas tracksuit bottoms, top and runners. His curly blonde hair is tied back tightly in a short ponytail as is required while he is on school grounds. His nose ring has had to be taken out for the return to school but small plasters hide his eyebrow and upper ear rings. Alex steps up and receives his envelope, and then takes his seat again, at a desk on his own at the back of the class. The speech begins. The principal congratulates them all on a job well done and teachers smile knowingly at certain students. Students smile back, and at each other, nervously turning the precious envelopes over and over in their hands. Rachel, the class nominated leader stands to make a presentation to the class teacher and thanks everyone in the small classroom for their help and support in completing the examinations.

Alex hits the send button on his mobile phone. Chloe had better be there at six. It was going to be a great party. With great precision and experience Alex carefully slides his mobile phone back up his jumper sleeve. The teachers did not care and for the most part ignored him anyway. He often wondered if they knew what he was doing under the cover of his jumper, he only needed a quick glance to read his messages and could type, send and save messages without ever taking his eyes off the teacher. Often he thought they did know, but were glad of the break, and as long as he was not getting in trouble, he was one less body to worry about. But the principal was different. He had challenged Alex on several occasions on dress, behaviour, manners, accessories… Alex did not want to have his mobile phone taken from him for two weeks. He would continue the conversation later.

The window. He hoped it would not rain. That could ruin the night they had planned to celebrate the results. The results. He looked at the white envelope that lay on the desk in front of him. Nobody expected him to pass. But imagine if.... Suddenly everyone is clapping. It is over. Some students tear open their envelopes and everyone is talking. Rachel is crying and is immediately surrounded by a number of teachers. Alex grabs his bag and envelope, shoves aside his chair and strolls out of the room without speaking to anyone.

Introduction

Wenger suggests that communities of practice can be understood

> as shared histories of learning. Over time, such histories create discontinuities between those who have been participating and those who have not. These discontinuities are revealed by the learning involved in crossing them: moving from one practice to another can demand quite a transformation.
>
> *(Wenger, 1998, p. 103)*

With this in mind this chapter begins our exploration of assessment with the reconceptualisation of learning and assessment within boundaries of practice. We take as our central focus young people such as Alex, introduced in the vignette, whose learning trajectories at one time or another intersect a particular academic assessment setting but who later move away from this setting. We explore how these young people position themselves in and negotiate value, boundaries and identities in a number of different formal and informal assessment settings. Considering the spatial and temporal aspects of these assessment settings through a particular emphasis on the Wengerian idea of boundaries we explore a sociocultural theorisation of assessment as a social practice within shared and mediated histories of learning. In this analysis we also consider the assessment identity of the assessor as a partner in each learning setting and the sociocultural act of assessment.

Boundaries are the spaces in practice where new ideas are developed and learning can take place. As individuals move between practices or develop competencies in particular practices they transform their identities and negotiate boundaries created as a result of shared practices. Wenger describes a boundary as a space in practice where 'competence and experience tend to diverge: a boundary interaction is usually an experience of being exposed to a foreign competence' (Wenger, 1998, p. 233). We believe that for many young people successful participation in assessment practice requires the crossing of boundaries within practices. We also believe that assessment as a setting and a practice in its own right challenges young people to take up positions in and cross over a number of boundaries in their practice of assessment to develop competencies in value-laden (assessment) enterprises.

Understanding assessment as a series of boundaries and spaces where individuals develop related identities and experience opens up assessment as a relational and creative space for 'making up people' (Hacking, 2006, p. 2). Hacking introduces this idea in his discussion of 'the looping effect' (Hacking, 2006, p. 2).

We think of kinds of people as given, as definite classes defined by definite properties. As we get to know more about these properties, we will be able to control, to help, to change or to emulate them better. But it is not quite like that. They are moving targets because our investigations interact with the targets themselves, and change them. And since they are changed, they are not quite the same kind of people as before. The target has moved. That is the looping effect. Sometimes our sciences create kinds of people that in a certain sense did not exist before. That is making up people.

(Hacking, 2006, p. 2)

Applied to assessment, this concept of looping, investigations interacting with targets and making up people, offers many opportunities for a sociocultural theorisation of assessment embedded in shared spatial and socioculturally situated practices. We define assessment here as any practices which develop patterns of participation and subsequently contribute to pupils' identities as learners and knowers in particular settings (Cowie, 2005). Within this definition relationships between learner, teacher, task and context play a central role in experiences of assessment and identity in assessment settings for all individuals involved. The consideration of these myriad relationships at the heart of assessment spaces and communities of practice is, for us, one of the central concerns of this book, as their complex and connected nature evidence the many ways in which testing and assessment construct or 'make up' the values, realities and individuals they claim to measure.

In this chapter we understand assessment as a spatial and value laden setting where nothing (knowledge, language, practice, task....) is neutral, stable or uncontested. We consider relationships between identity, learning and assessment as individuals negotiate boundaries (understood as learning assets) within and across communities of practice. Finally, we suggest the importance of understanding assessment practice presented in this chapter as temporally located, asking questions and offering implications for assessment practice.

Assessment as setting: a space for negotiating value

Mannion's (2007) work reframing participation research as research about adult child relations in socio-spatial settings aligns with our thinking and suggests that relationships should be central to understanding participation in learning. Mannion explains that our current focus on young people's voice in learning is present but in a way that values outcomes for adults as well as children and suggests that:

> by addressing the spatial alongside the dialogical and intergenerational aspects of children's participation as the main focus, we can begin to usefully move the discourse on children's participation on. Reframing voice and participation research as the study of and in the spaces of the child

adult relations is not only a better reflection of the lived experience of children and adults, but it opens up new important and fertile territory for this expanding field.

(Mannion, 2007, p. 406)

We believe a beginning focus on spatial, dialogical and intergenerational aspects of assessment, developed in this chapter, facilitates a deeper understanding of assessment a sociocultural space for the development of experience, learning and identity.

Nind, Curtin and Hall (2016) define space as providing:

> interactive scripts, shared resources and points of intersection for teachers and learners. It has physical, social, temporal, experiential (and possibly virtual) dimensions.... Space is 'not a receptacle, a vessel that can be filled and emptied of its contents ... space exists only as it is inhabited – it is created by the act of occupancy' (Buchanan 1992, p. 1).

(Nind, Curtin and Hall, 2016, p. 269)

Understanding space in this way as socially practiced places (Agnew, 2005) we can infer that these spaces are experienced differently at different times by their inhabitants. In our vignette presented at the beginning of this chapter we see some of the feelings Alex and Rachel experience as they negotiate boundary practices in relation to assessment. Receiving examination results recreates the classroom space as a setting where particular and differential assessment practices, emotions and experiences are writ large in current participation and reifications of practice.

Ivinson and Murphy (2003) explore in more detail this idea of classroom as a space and setting for learning and reveal how knowledge, social and gender values and identities become constructed in and through classroom practice and interaction. The relational nature of knowledge, identity, success and failure all become clearly visible as the teacher in this study recontextualises subject knowledge, pedagogy, task and feedback dependent on classroom setting and student gender. The authors conclude that the classroom itself is a social setting where experience is actively constructed through a range of social possibilities and constraints and where unfortunately, it is not appropriate for boys to write romance. This is because the boys in the study do not reconstruct romance in their writing in the style conventionally recognised by teachers, focusing more on romantic events rather than authentic feelings and emotions. As the work produced is not valued by the teacher or others in the assessment space as legitimate it is left to the side, passed over in favour of more suitable textual examples and not seen itself as an authentic text for assessment and development. In this study and, similar to the experiences of Alex in our vignette, this results in students devaluing of and simultaneous devaluation by academic assessment practices.

O'Sullivan (Minister for Education and Skills in Ireland, 2015) recognises this complicated relationship between assessment and value when she states in relation to current curricular and assessment reforms in Ireland:

> In reality, what is assessed is valued. School-based assessment will promote a learning culture in schools …Assessment should assist students in the quality of their learning and not be regarded as the end point. Research shows that unless assessment changes, little else will.
>
> *(O'Sullivan, J. 2015, p. 1)*

Most significant for us is O Sullivan's assertion that our understanding of assessment needs to change before anything else (teaching, learning, pedagogy…) can. This speaks to the creative and recreative aspects of assessment practice. Assessing the individual in any context or setting assumes a shared understanding of what is valued and requires the creation of what is to be measured, how it is to be measured and what the outcome will mean. Thinking about assessment in this way as a creative space reveals its power in the shaping of identities and ultimately, learning for Alex, Rachel and the young people introduced throughout this chapter.

Considering these student experiences of assessment we need to ask questions about how each individual is positioned in relation to assessment within every unique assessment setting/moment. Who has access to what kinds of participation and knowledge and in what ways? What are the relationships between individuals, experiences, identity and assessment as they differentially engage in participation across a variety of assessment settings. Gee (2003) for example suggests that if ' two children are being assessed on something they have not had equivalent opportunities to learn, the assessment is unjust' (Gee, 2003, p. 28).

There are times in our lives when assessment becomes problematic and requires close attention, for example for young people like Alex and Rachel in school or college examinations, but there are also times when learning and assessment work together, for example when through practice, trial and error in non-formal assessment settings a new skill is learnt. In every day and informal spaces for learning and assessment even when an individual fails to learn what has been set out, this does not mean that they fail to learn. That is to say every situation holds valuable opportunities for learning and identity development – value from the perspective of the learner/ individual as well as all those involved.

Within boundary spaces in these non-formal assessment and learning settings learning results from practice valued however not everyone has to value the same practice in the same way. Learning and knowledge are more fluid than in formal assessment contexts and individuals can choose to learn in a way that aligns with their past experiences and present identity trajectory. Non-formal assessments of learning opportune negotiation of what is valued in learning and assessment in ways formal settings do not.

In more formal academic assessment settings problems arise when what is learnt (or valued at an individual level) does not match what is valued or expected in a given situation. Within these fixed and more confined academic assessment spaces young people who fail to succeed in socially constructed and differentially valued practices are identified as failures – unable to complete the task at hand to the same level of ability as their peers. As Stobart (2008) makes clear these individual and contextual failures in particular tasks and ways of representing knowledge and experiencing assessment spaces become representational of the individual and over time come together to act as a metaphor for what a person can or cannot do.

A sociocultural understanding of assessment challenges this conception of testing which can reliably stand in and for an individual and provide a stable and true representation of an individual where they may be absent. In his sociocultural study of the learning biography of one young student McDermott argues that we can only ever learn for what is around us to be learnt, claiming success and failure as definitive of each other with failure understood 'as an absence real as presence, and it requires its share of the children' (McDermott, 1996, p. 295). For a much more detailed discussion of constructions of success, failure, ability and talent in learning and assessment see Hall, Curtin and Rutherford (2014).

From a sociocultural perspective formal and informal assessment settings do not measure individual ability, achievement or even potential, but rather evidence how individuals negotiate and mediate boundaries and relationships between learning, identity, task and context in different assessment settings. Lantolf (2000) suggests we can conceptualise this mediation as mediation by others, mediation by self through private speech, and mediation by artifacts (e. g. tasks and technology). Positioned very differently in relation to assessment by their own actions and the actions of those around them Alex and Rachel experience different opportunities and constraints in relation to their shared mediation of assessment practice and identity in one assessment moment outlined at the beginning of this chapter.

In assessment moments, such as the one shared by one community of practice presented as a vignette at the beginning of this chapter identity, space, values and practice intersect and transform in dynamic and social processes that change for an individual their understanding of assessment and learning. These changes occur as individuals negotiate boundaries of this practice in a variety of different ways and for many different reasons, with each negotiation including as a part previous experiences and histories of learning.

Looking at learning across these boundaries of practice offers insight into how individuals are positioned in relation to learning valued and the implications this may have the development of their identities and experiences of assessment. In our vignette Alex teeters on the periphery of the assessment practice as valued by other members of the community of practice. There is a moment where he can imagine joining the community in a 'valuable' identity by achieving the desired results (interestingly passing the examinations rather than being knowledgeable of the content) but this moment is fleeting and lost before it can take root in any meaningful identity development for Alex. Unsupported by the teachers and community members who surround Rachel in her moment of celebration or need Alex leaves the room and the practice never quite sure of its purpose. He has not managed to make the transformation required of him through crossing the boundaries enabling him to move from one practice to another.

Assessment as identity: 'There's no point in knowing about stuff that's not going to come up in exams'

Wenger-Trayner *et al.* (2015), exploring academic-workplace boundaries for health care support workers, use the term 'visitors' (Wenger-Trayner *et al.*, 2015, p. 44) to describe individuals whose learning trajectories at one time or another intersect a particular academic setting but who later move away from this academic setting. For Wenger-Trayner *et al.* (2015) these visitors to academic practice differ in their participation. 'Tourists' of particular practices 'have low levels of participation engaging only in superficial ways with local practices; their identities are hardly changed by the experience and the academic world remains a foreign country to them' (ibid., p. 44), while 'sojourners have a higher level of participation, engaging with the meaning of local practices in ways which have implications for their own identity, while nonetheless recognizing that they are passing through and unlikely to become fully assimilated' (ibid., p. 44). We believe this framework can also be applied to assessment settings to provide unique insight on the nature of relationships between assessment, space and identity.

This section borrows its title from a quote from an Irish Leaving Certificate student who was interviewed by Louise Holden in the *Irish Times* having achieved maximum points in her Leaving Certificate Examination. At time of print (2005) this interview received very mixed reviews from media and academic sources, however Ruth throughout remained honest and unwaivering in her discussion of her approach to this very important terminal examination.

> I learned over the course of the year that doing well in the Leaving is about learning the formula for each exam and practising it endlessly. I got an A1 in English because I knew exactly what was required in each question. I learned off the sample answers provided by the examiners and I knew how much information was required and in what format in every section of the paper. That's how you do well in these exams.... If you know the formula you can perform well in any subject, whether you're naturally good at it or not.
>
> *(Ruth (Student), 2005)*

Like Alex, Ruth very clearly sees herself as a visitor to this academic setting we call assessment however, unlike Alex, Ruth displays a high level of participation and engages with the meaning of assessment practices in ways which have implications for her own identity. Ruth is a sojourner to this practice and recognises the value of participation here lies not in knowledge learnt but grades achieved. Negotiating the boundaries of assessment practice in a way meaningful to her identity development

Ruth focuses on the end results rather than the knowledge shared in the here and now. In this she recreates the assessment space for herself and others and deftly mediates this formal assessment setting to a practice that is meaningful to Ruth – learning become a practice of tips and tricks, shortcuts in the here and now that will allow Ruth achieve her goal of high grades in the future. These grades will allow Ruth move forward with her education to college, something central to Ruth's identity. In her positioning towards assessment practice Ruth does not understand past, present and future learning and assessment practices as related, rather present classroom experience is a means to an end but learning trajectories and assessment careers remain disconnected in space and time.

> I chose not to fight the system but to play with it. I did what I had to do to achieve my goals, I played the game, if you will. I would not call this attitude 'utilitarian' but realistic. I got to college to study the courses I enjoy. I will have 'the pleasure of discovery' in business and economics courses.
> *(Ruth (Student), 2005)*

Ruth's experience, just like Alex's, is typical of many students' experiences of assessment. She explains how she is frustrated by teachers who move away from exam questions and material in classroom practice and cannot see the point in discussing material that will not come up in exams. From a sociocultural perspective Ruth has learnt how to do well in exams, the formula for success rather than any in depth subject knowledge or critical understanding of concepts. This is the boundary of practice that Ruth chooses to inhabit. This practice of assessment aligns with Ruth's own identity trajectory but just as for Alex, in a very different way than has been intended. From her own admission Ruth has learnt and adapted a formula for success for how to do exams. She is successful but as Dore (1997) in his publication *The Diploma Disease* warns:

> in the process of qualification…the pupil is concerned not with mastery, but with being certified as having mastered. The knowledge that he gains, he gains not for its own sake and not for constant use in a real life situation…but for the once-for-all purpose of reproducing it in an examination.
> *(Dore, 1997, p. 17)*

Wenger's (1998) sociocultural theory of learning introduced elsewhere in our book suggests that membership in a community of practice translates into identity as developing competence in practice. Taking this sociocultural definition of learning calls into question traditional assessment practice and the kinds of competencies learnt by Ruth in the various home, school, peer and media assessment (and non-assessment) communities of practice of which she is a part. Ruth has gained competency in taking exams and her practice evidences this. What she has learnt in terms of rich content knowledge and application of subject concepts in later communities of practice outside of the immediate assessment question is less clear. A sojourner to practice Ruth experiences belonging and success in her assessment practice and developing identity and her membership is validated, like Rachel's, by her own actions and the actions of those around her. Her participation in assessment can be understood as meaningful insofar as it allows her develop her identity and move to the next step in her educational career, however once the moment has passed it is left behind Ruth as she moves to new challenges and communities of practice.

Just as membership shapes our identity in particular ways, for Ruth moving her towards an understanding of assessment as playing the game, non-membership confronts individuals with the unfamiliar and also has a profound influence on identity development in assessment settings. Seeing ourselves as incompetent within certain (assessment) practices excludes us from ever becoming members of these practices as it leads to a notion of our identity as a failure, an identity which may even follow us to future practices. For Alex his own practices and the practices of those around him serve to mediate his experience of assessment in particular ways and cut him off from meaningful participation in assessment boundary settings.

Munns and Woodward (2006) suggest five key areas in which students negotiate positions and identities within the classroom through curriculum and assessment practices. These are:

1. Knowledge: What counts as knowledge and who has access to really useful knowledge?
2. Ability: Who has ability?
3. Control: Who controls the teaching space?
4. Place: Who is valued as an individual and a learner?
5. Voice: Whose voice is given credence within that space?

Considering particular assessment settings in relation to these questions resonates with our sociocultural theorisation of assessment as settings where individuals negotiate identity, space and value in temporally linked moments of change and development. Applying these questions to the experiences of the young people explored in this chapter is telling and reveals some of the social, spatial, temporal and constructed aspects of learning in the boundary spaces of assessment practice. It also begins to suggest some of the implications of mediating boundary spaces in assessment for the development of individual learning and identity. Attention to these five aspects of practice facilitates the pedagogical use of boundaries as learning assets which, over time, contribute to individual identity development and learning.

Revisiting assessment spaces: boundaries as learning assets

RESEARCHER: So tell me about your picture?
CHILD: Well this is me ...
RESEARCHER: In the purple? That is a nice colour.
CHILD: Yes. And these are the other people in my class.
RESEARCHER: They are all in pink?

Setting the boundaries in assessment 19

FIGURE 1.1

CHILD: Yes. They have a very bright colour. They are all friends. Even this guy over here who sits in the back on his own in the opposite side to me. He has to sit on his own because he talks to everyone.
RESEARCHER: And why do you have a different colour?
CHILD: I am faded.
RESEARCHER: What do you mean?
CHILD: Everybody has a bright colour except me. Purple is a dull colour for me. I sit on my own in the back and I don't talk to anyone.
RESEARCHER: And what are you all doing now?
CHILD: We are working on a test. I am thinking about the test.
RESEARCHER: What are you thinking?
CHILD: I don't like tests. They make me sad because they might judge.
RESEARCHER: The people in your class?
CHILD: And the teachers and my mom. And I won't get a good job. Tests are for your future. I stay on my own.
RESEARCHER: But do you work with other people in class? Or answer questions? … What helps you to learn?
CHILD: I keep doing it over and over. I keep repeating it… Then when I can do it myself I know it.
RESEARCHER: And then your teacher gives you a test? And you do well?
CHILD: No. Not really. Sometimes I forget. I don't get the right answer. Then I like being in the back on my own. Sometimes the teacher is very busy with the others. And then it is good to be a dull colour.

[Child smiles]
   She might forget to see you.
(Cahill, O'Sullivan, Hall and Curtin (ALIAS Project) 2018)

Building on the work of Wenger-Trayner *et al.* (2015) we understand boundaries in communities of practice as learning assets and a rich site for the development of learning and assessment practice. We believe a focus on differential practices and meaning making processes in boundaries of assessment settings (through asking questions such as those posed by Munns and Woodward, 2006) is essential to a sociocultural understanding of assessment as it 'confronts explicitly the problematic nature of boundary crossing and the potential tensions or conflicts between practices as sources of accountability' (Wenger-Trayner et al., 2015, p. 18) (identity) and makes problematic the at times presumed 'unproblematic applicability of knowledge across practices' (ibid., 2015, p. 18) (value).

We pause here to invite the reader to consider the exchange presented above in light of Munns and Woodward's (2006) questions, included in the previous section. Answering these questions makes clear the role of assessment as a space that both recreates and carries meaning and significance continuously for each individual involved in practice. The stories of student experiences presented in this chapter overall carefully exemplify the power of assessment practice to work first and foremost as a messaging system. This aligns with a sociocultural understanding of assessment as a social practice and makes essential the development of spaces in assessment practice which align more closely with the values and identities of students.

Hattie's (2012) study of classrooms reveals that teacher talk dominates classroom interactions taking up 70–80 per cent of classroom time. In an average day teachers ask approximately 200–300 questions. 60 per cent of these focus on recall of facts, 20 per cent are procedural while less than 5 per cent focus on meaningful ideas for discussion. Around 70 per cent of all answers given by students are shared in less than five seconds and are three words or so in length. These statistics resonate with our understanding of value as presented in this chapter.

In everyday classroom assessment practice teacher talk, experience and values dominate over more spatial, dialogical and intergenerational aspects. The better alignment of student and assessment values and identities necessitates an understanding of assessment as pedagogy which moves beyond traditional summative and formative distinctions to look closer at the features of the interactions between learners in boundaries of practice themselves, understanding these interactions as learning assets and exploring how they connect over time in the development of an identity for all individuals involved.

Taking the above interaction between a young student, Chris, and one of the authors reveals how despite being able to complete certain tasks in classroom practice Chris fails in the formal assessment setting (albeit a simple teacher question asking exercise). This results in a message for Chris, his teacher and every other student in the classroom which, in a traditional understanding of assessment, translates as a marker of Chris's abilities and disabilities in practice. Over time these messages add up to become more than the sum of their parts and like the learning biography of Adam in McDermott (1996), previously discussed, can be understood from a sociocultural perspective on assessment to make up and stand in for the individuals themselves. The opportunity to employ dissonances in practice as learning assets is lost as success and failure acquire their 'fair' share of young people in academic assessment settings.

To understand these dissonances or practice boundaries as learning assets requires the reconceptualisation of different assessment settings as linked temporally for the individual in a learning trajectory (Wenger, 1998) or career (Bloomer, 2001). That is to say if we are to understand boundaries in assessment practice as learning assets we must also understand learning and assessment processes as temporally as well as spatially located. In this section we develop our argument that encounters with assessment in boundary settings across a significant period of time are powerful identity experiences for an individual and can have far reaching effects.

According to Wenger as we move through successive forms of participation our identities form trajectories within and across communities of practice. These trajectories incorporate past and future in the negotiation of present identities and provide a context for individuals to determine what is important and what is not.

Connecting individuals, practices and settings Rogoff develops in more detail the temporal aspects of practice, explaining that 'the present extends through the past and future and cannot be separated from them' (Rogoff, 1995, p. 68). She continues:

> when a person acts on the basis of previous experience, his or her past is present. It is not merely a stored memory called up in the present; the person's previous participation contributes to the event at hand by having prepared it.
> *(Rogoff, 1995, p. 68)*

For Rogoff, within her concept of participatory appropriation, identity development is dynamic and learning is an aspect of ongoing events. Experiences in boundaries of practice stay with us as learners as we both change and are changed by these boundaries in the process of learning. Drawing an analogy to a child's leg Rogoff states:

> the size, shape and strength of a child's leg is a function of the growth and use that are continually occurring; the child's leg changes, but we do not need to refer to the leg accumulating units of growth or of exercise. The past is not stored in the leg; the leg has developed to be as it is currently.
> *(Rogoff, 1995, p. 68)*

Other theorists such as Lewis, Enciso and Moje (2007) also understand the temporality of identity development and learning as dynamic and an act of power (Hall, 1996). This is evident in the above exchange between Chris and our researcher where the young participant already understands well the different positions available to him in classroom and assessment practice and actively and with agency seeks out a particular position, the position of someone unseen negotiating assessment spaces and boundaries in accomplished, covert and sophisticated ways. His delight in not being seen at certain times in classroom practice and assessment reveals many things about his experiences in school and has many implications for his identity development and assessment trajectory or career. Should he continue experiencing assessment in the borderlands he so carefully has cut out for himself with the help of his teacher and classmates we can but wonder how he will be positioned in assessment settings in future practices and at the end of his formal schooling. Like Ruth he is able to manipulate the assessment setting to hide the misalignment of his identity with assessment and classroom values, however, unlike Ruth, Chris's identity and learning trajectory will perhaps not emerge as positively as Ruth's in the process.

In and across assessment settings agency, or the strategic making of the self within relations of power (Lewis, Enciso and Moje, 2007, p. 24) distinguishes between participation and learning. Learning is always situated in participation but agentive learning goes beyond this participation to conceive of current activity within a past and future participation placing the learner in an active and agentive role as they share in their own learning (Emirbayer and Mische, 1998). Thus teacher, learner, task and context all unite in the notion of agency as within participation identities are made available and learning occurs in the space between doing and knowing, between making a choice and knowing what choice to make. For a sociocultural understanding of assessment this means the development of assessment processes which are authentic and provide meaningful points of connection between the learner and the task at hand. Rather than understanding assessment as having a summative (looking back) or a formative (looking forward) function we should see assessment, practice and the individual as a function of the present, unfolding in a social and specific place and time.

Agency as it occurs in learning does not then stem from an internal process but is a way of positioning oneself so as to allow for new ways of being, new identities. This ability to position oneself in different settings and practices over time is controlled by both the individual and the group through relations of power, as defined by Foucault (1980) as productive and the result of interactions and relationships. It is socially produced, rather than individually possessed. Encouraging young people to think about assessment as an experimental repositioning or the development of new identities linked closely to their own rather than as testing or measurement of what they are or have may in a sociocultural understanding of assessment create space for agency and boundary crossing in assessment settings.

Wenger asserts that being a student is only one part of the identity of the individuals in our classrooms, and for some it is a very small part of their identity indeed. In the small snapshots of assessment practice presented in this chapter it is clear that this is the case for Alex, Rachel, Ruth and Chris. It is also clear that their understanding of assessment settings and associated successes or failures link closely with the past (previous experiences as evidence of their assessment ability) or the future (assessment as a means to an end). But an identity is not simply a single trajectory and cannot be turned on and off at will. Our forms of participation are not merely sequences of time. Each individual in this chapter and in our classroom develops their identities and their selves through a nexus of multimembership, where identities simultaneously challenge and reinforce each other as they are both multiple (past and future) and one (present) in many complimenting and contrasting communities of practice.

Partners in assessment practice: teacher identity, innovation and integrity

Understanding assessment as we do as social practice we conclude this chapter with a brief exploration of the impact of assessment policy and practice on the other social actor in these assessment settings – the assessor, usually and in our examples a teacher. To understand assessment as social practice this focus is central for educators in their negotiation of assessment policy and practice. We, alongside the reader in this section, consider our own definitions of assessment, how we position our selves and our identities in practice as a result and ultimately how our own understanding of and evolving identities as assessors in assessment settings and resulting enactment of assessment may come to bear on student experiences of assessment. We draw here on data and experiences of some of the authors (Curtin and Hall) on the VIP Project introduced in our previous chapter.

While this text will suggest that the many worlds surrounding the shaping of and being shaped by assessment policy and practice juxtapose and oppose a variety of ideas, practices and agenda, the values teachers invoke in speaking about their position as assessors, those of integrity, fairness, the centrality and importance of the student and their experiences, are very close to her own definitions of ideal assessment practice. If Jan O'Sullivan's assertion of 'what is assessed is valued' is true, teachers in our research study agree on what should be assessed with the student and their identity, histories and experiences remaining central. Issues arise for teachers however, when they move from a discussion of idealised but understood definitions and specifications of assessment, to a consideration of their enacted role as assessor in the classroom or other educational setting, where identity and practice does not quite line up with previous ideals. Emerging from this research project and an exploration of teacher assessment identity is that the question at the heart of the current assessment debate in Ireland may not one of value but one of power. Even within this huge era of reform and change in Irish education (explored in detail in Chapter 3) the importance and public nature of the Junior Certificate examinations remains writ large on the experiences of students and teachers. Discussions within this research study with principals and teachers suggest that if a change in assessment practice will in turn facilitate a change in curriculum, teaching and learning and the student experience, then the very first step must be a reconsideration of our understanding of the purposes of assessment writ small at the local level and in which teachers engage in their classrooms every day. Presently it remains, even for those from a student perspective who are perceived to control it, as complex, conflicted and conflicting in terms of their own understanding of assessment function, purpose and emerging identity, as a brief discussion of one experience on the project will now exemplify.

At one of our knowledge exchange meetings where the focus remained on assessment practice in schools, participants and researchers were asked to bring with them an artefact which they felt linked to their understanding of their own identities in relation to assessment. Despite claiming inclusive and rather nuanced understandings of assessment a number of the items brought in by teachers and principals representing their identity as assessors defined assessment clearly within the realm of the state written examinations and included curricula, marking schemes, standardised tests and newspaper/online articles and league tables discussing top schools and achievers in Ireland. One teacher made reference to her 13 years correcting Leaving Certificate examinations and the recording of this and the marks of all students in a single notebook she had kept since beginning correcting the examinations. Items such as these dominated in the beginning of our two-hour knowledge exchange, but then moved to other considerations and conceptions of assessment in practice. While we cannot share all the artefacts here, we would like to share a few examples, which connect to our developing sociocultural definition of assessment and provide examples which may ask interesting questions about assessment policy and practice across a variety of settings.

One teacher who teaches in an Irish language school held up a sheet of paper which she explained was an invisible sheet of paper she uses in her classroom to assess her students use of the Irish language. This sheet was invisible in the sense that it was never seen by anyone other than the teacher herself. Nor was it made reference to in report cards, parent teacher meetings or any interactions with other teachers. The teacher simply used it to record for herself where and when students spoke in Irish, what they spoke about and what problems they had speaking Irish. This document was later used in her planning to connect the curriculum to the identities and interests of her students as they themselves talk about. This example speaks to a nuanced understanding if assessment which reflects that much of what teachers do as assessors every day in practice remains invisible to anyone else outside (and in this example even within) the primary assessment setting. Discussion around this on the project explored the contradictions inherent in this very simple and common but rich example of assessment practice that is integral to a teacher's daily practice and assessment identity but has no profile, position or connection to other assessment arenas or worlds (for examples those taken as themes for chapters in this book).

Another teacher brought a digital camera, to symbolise the innovative ways in which she asks her students to assess themselves and make records and evidence of their learning and learning journeys at various times in the school term. Understanding the assessment of learning as shared and incremental she encourages students to manage and partly assess their own work through projects and group work. Other artefacts such as portfolios and paintbrushes also echoed this active and creative approach to assessment. These kinds of artefacts exemplified well assessment as a practice of negotiation between assessor and those to be assessed, all social actors and positioned in very obvious way in relation to assessment policy and practice across a variety of educational settings.

A pen was shared with the group by a principal and for him, there were a number of reasons for his choice. First, he spoke about how as a teaching principal he uses a pen to write down and record his observations of students across a variety of criteria in his classroom. He felt the informal nature of these daily observations allow teachers the autonomy to make informed decisions about teaching methods, classroom participation etc. in a diagnostic and formative way, while not being intimidating for the learner. In this way he understands his assessment identity as involving mediation of practice between what is idealised and what can be actualised. Second, he explains how he uses the pen every day to make records on students for files, parent teacher meetings and other class teachers. He raises here a question about who assessment is for and how necessary recording for files and folders pushes students further and further down the line. Finally, he suggests that his students themselves need to be given materials (such as paper and pens) so that they can themselves participate in the processes of teaching and learning as they often do not come prepared to school with what they need to engage in learning.

This last artefact and indeed the many different artefacts shared in relation to assessment within this study represent the many complexities inherent in understanding assessment policy and practice. It cannot be understood in and of itself completely, perhaps because it does not exist or indeed sustain itself in this way. Assessment in all of the stories in this chapter always exists as a part of and in relation to something else, that which is other and not immediate, existing in the past or the future, but ever present in assessment as enacted and experienced in individual settings.

The many faces of assessment in public policy and private practice explored in this chapter reveal that assessment exists across a number of sites and between a number of actors - teachers, students, principals, college admissions officers, potential employers. It is at once local and global. Recognising this and talking through the implications of this for assessment policy and practice, as we did in the VIP Project, creates spaces for the redefinition of assessment policy and practice as one teacher participant explains:

> through my participation I was defining and redefining my identity as a teacher. When left to our own devices in the classroom for years, I think it is very easy to slip into a routine where we forget to question and assess our practices. Being part of this project gave me the time and opportunity to reflect on my own practices and the beliefs that lie behind them.
> *(VIP participant, 2013)*

Concluding our brief exploration of assessor identity in the assessment relationship, the VIP project suggests that many of the difficulties experienced in assessment planning and practice for teachers revolve around the contradictions between the proposed state and accepted status of assessment in policy. Discussions around these issues such as those engaged in on the VIP Project could, we believe, better align assessment policy and practice by allowing a shared redefinition of assessment so that new assessment policy and planning directives are not measured against old definitions of assessment practice. Changing our practices of assessment involves changing how we plan for and represent it in policy and other literature documents and vice versa. In this analysis our worlds and our words become one and central to teacher and student identity development in relation to assessment.

What does this mean for our understanding of assessment?

What we claim to know and what we claim to not know over time in a landscape of assessment practices become a part of our identity. Wenger-Trayner et al. suggest that 'we cannot be competent in all of the practices in a landscape, but we can still be knowledgeable about them, their relevance to our practice, and thus our location in the broader landscape. When considering an entire landscape, claims to knowledgeability are an important aspect of learning as a social practice.' (Wenger-Trayner et al., 2015, p. 19). The stories of Alex, Rachel, Ruth and Chris however fleeting evidence this. Assessment can be seen to stand in for us when we are absent or silent. Developing our sociocultural understanding of assessment in light of theory and research explored in this chapter the situated and temporal aspects of assessment as setting become central to our theorisation of assessment.

Stobart (2010) in his lecture *Assessment fit for the future* at the IAEA Annual Conference shares his understanding of a sustainable assessment process that offers a reliable assessment of current learning as well as helping students develop their own assessment resources. Taking Boud's definition of sustainable assessment which states that 'any assessment act must contribute in some way to learning beyond the immediate task...assessment that meets the needs of the present and prepares students to meet their own future needs.' (2000, pp. 8–9). Stobart explains that 'simply assessing for the here-and-now [assessment as a 'snapshot'] is insufficient if nothing is carried forward, so too is process-based learning [for example, 'learning to learn', 'critical thinking'] if there is no substantive learning in the here-and-now' (Stobart, IAEA lecture, 2010).

Thus to achieve sustainable assessment we need assessment practices which, like Rogoff's participatory appropriation, just are, focusing simultaneously on past, present and future in an engagement of individual experience and identity. One way to achieve this aim is to reconsider an individual's participation across a number of assessment settings as making up not people as suggested by Hacking but learning and assessment careers (Bloomer, 2001). Considering assessments as dynamic and connected through learning careers facilitates exploration of the inherent relationships between teacher, learner, task and context developing over time and existing in time for learners.

Within this understanding of learning and assessment as ever present in every assessment moment or setting we return to the idea presented at the beginning of the chapter of boundaries as learning assets. In their publication Wenger-Trayner et al. (2015) suggest that this focus on boundary encounters draws out particular questions for learning (ibid., 2015, p. 18). We include them here as also most useful to a consideration of assessment.

1. What kind of boundary activity, joint project, visit, mutual storytelling or learning partnership can serve as a productive encounter for negotiating and exploring a boundary?
2. How can boundaries be used systematically to trigger a reflection process about the practices on either side?
3. What kind of boundary objects and activities can support this boundary-oriented pedagogy and create points of focus for engaging multiple perspectives?
4. Who can act as brokers to articulate regimes of competence across boundaries?

We would invite the reader to carefully consider these questions, along with other questions posed across this chapter, in relation to the experiences of the students explored here, Alex, Rachel, Ruth and Chris as you move through this text. Thinking of assessment practices as boundary activities, visits, storytellings and partnerships offer rich opportunities for a reconceptualisation of assessment forms and functions. As evidenced in this chapter the conversations we have about assessment can also be just as important as the assessments themselves for individual learning and identity development in a sociocultural understanding of assessment and this also has powerful implications for pedagogy and classroom practice. A sociocultural understanding of assessment as itself an identity trajectory incorporating past, present and future in each assessment moment highlights the important role of assessment in learning and complicates our understanding of knowledge, participation, success and failure in assessment settings. As Wenger-Trayner (2015) suggests:

> As a trajectory through a social landscape, learning is not merely the acquisition of knowledge. It is the becoming of a person who inhabits the landscape with an identity whose dynamic construction reflects our trajectory through that landscape. This journey within and across practice shapes who we are. Over time it accumulates memories, competencies, key formative events, stories and relationships to people and places. It also provides material for directions, aspirations, and projected images of ourselves that guide the shaping of our trajectory going forward. In other words, the journey incorporates the past and the future in our experience of identity in the present.
>
> *(Wenger-Trayner* et al*., 2015, p. 19)*

Conclusion

This chapter introduces assessment as a complex and problematic site of identity development. Our focus on the spatial and temporal aspects of assessment aligns with a sociocultural perspective on learning. We explore in detail the Wengerian concept of boundaries in practice and suggest how we might understand these boundaries (spatially and temporally) as learning assets (Wenger-Trayner et al., 2015) in assessment practice. We present assessment settings as spaces for the negotiation of value, suggesting that in traditional assessment settings spatial, dialogical and intergenerational aspects of present practice are ignored in favour of a past- or future-oriented approach. We suggest that assessment practices which better align with the identities and values of young people in the present offer a more sustainable approach to assessment practice.

We return to Stobart's (2010) IAEA lecture to conclude our chapter on assessment as setting and the quote he offers from Garrison Keillor in his publication *Lake Wobegon Days*, a mythical town where all students are above average. Though written to exemplify rather than describe it aligns closely with contemporary assessment settings where:

> the reputation of a school, its principal, its teachers…depends largely on test scores, schools are devoting less time to reading real books, writing essays, and discussing current events and more and more time teaching kids strategies for filling in blanks and choosing the answers to multiple choice questions. This destroys much of the value of these tests, which only tell you something if they are an independent measure of what the student knows.
>
> *(Shanker, 1988, p. 7)*

We include it here to provoke final thought on the complex relationships between assessment, value, identity and space considered in this chapter.

> For years, students of the senior class were required to read ['Phileopolis'] and answer questions about its meaning etc. Teachers were not required to do so, but simply marked according to the correct answers supplied by Miss Quoist, including: (1) To extend the benefits of civilization and religion to all peoples, (2) No, (3) Plato, and (4) A wilderness cannot satisfy the hunger for beauty and learning, once awakened. The test was the same from year to year, and once the seniors found the answers and passed them to the juniors, nobody read 'Phileopolis' anymore.
>
> *(Keillor, 1985)*

Questions

1. What implications could understanding assessment as a boundary encounter hold for teaching and learning pedagogy and practice?
2. How can we understand and develop boundary spaces (including spaces where learners do not participate in valued practices) for learning and assessment in and beyond the classroom as learning assets?
3. How might we develop our understanding of assessment as summative (looking back) and formative (looking forward) to include a deeper focus on the present learner in a more sustainable assessment practice?

2

ASSESSMENT AS PUBLIC PRACTICE: INTERNATIONAL ASPECTS OF ASSESSMENT AND ACCOUNTABILITY

Introduction

The intention in this chapter then is to allow a perspective on assessment by describing, comparing and contrasting policies on assessment and accountability in various selected countries. More particularly, the intention is to show how paying attention to the social order of assessment itself has significant implications for the individual experiences in classrooms. We have chosen to look at England in some detail since we suggest that assessment and its associated accountability developments here project a highly salient frame of reference for both teachers' and learners' experience of assessing and being assessed. We also examine other parts of the UK but more briefly. We consider developments in assessment in Finland, Germany, the state of California in the US and the state of Victoria in Australia. (We examine the situation in the Republic of Ireland in a separate chapter.) We have chosen these countries/states as we believe they offer a useful lens through which one can begin to consider possible social order imperatives that shape local and individual levels, including the inter-personal and personal planes.

Our chosen comparator countries (states) vary in educational standards and equity as revealed by international metrics e.g. Programme for International Student Assessment (PISA), and OECD analyses (OECD, 2013). Some are 'close to home' as the four parts of the UK while the state of Victoria in Australia, though distant geographically, is English-speaking and is currently pursuing reforms similar to those in England. The state of California was chosen as illustrative of policies and practices in the US, although we are not suggesting California is necessarily representative of the entire US. It is important to include the US here since so many other countries including, England and increasingly Ireland, tend to be influenced generally in the social policy sphere by the individualism and meritocracy characteristic of that country. A small country population-wise, Finland was chosen, not only because it tends to come out on top in educational performance tables, but because its approaches are frequently discussed and examined by countries across the world with a view to understanding educational success, in itself an interesting dimension of the social order. Germany as a large EU country with a population of 81 million also offers a worthwhile point of comparison.

Our methodological approach in each case was to access policy documents through official websites and throughout we have tried to be up-to-date in our reporting although it is noteworthy that arrangements appear to be in flux nearly everywhere due to ongoing reforms and the sometimes rapid changes on assessment policy. This makes our task challenging as the themes are far from stable but our main purpose is not necessarily to describe in minute detail the policies of different countries, rather the purpose is to understand something of the broader social order so the mediational means and cultural scripts that we find in local enactments of assessment can be better understood.

We begin by describing the case of England, paying attention to the key vehicles for assessing and holding education to account and for highlighting *inter alia* the emphasis on and nature of assessment and teacher autonomy in its policies. We follow this by a brief description of policies in the other parts of the UK where we identify similarities and differences with England. We then describe and discuss the situation in Finland, Germany, California and Victoria highlighting at the end of that section continuities and discontinuities across countries.

Assessment and accountability in England

In England there has been agreement and continuity across official policy documents for a long time that schools should be 'properly accountable to pupils, parents and the taxpayer for the achievement and progress of every child, on the basis of objective and accurate assessments' (DfE, 2010). The notion of 'accuracy' here in assessment is telling and we return to it below as a salient feature. The rationale offered by officials for linking assessment and accountability includes reference to OECD documents. For instance, in 2010 the DfE reported that OECD has concluded that external accountability is the key driver of improvement in education standards and particularly important for the least advantaged children in society. In 2013 the Department for Education (DfE, 2013, p. 1) said that 'international evidence shows that greater autonomy drives up education standards, and is most effective when coupled with accountability'.

In England summative assessment of student learning is a key vehicle for holding the education system to account. It provides data on outcomes. Another related vehicle is the inspection system which provides data on outcomes and processes. We describe both as they are inter-related. The system overall is highly complex and is largely centralised insofar as the administrative authority is vested in central government rather than locally. It is decentralised insofar as, within specified parameters, some financial and some curriculum and assessment decisions have been delegated to schools.

A most significant piece of educational legislation in England was the Education Reform Act of 1988 which at once gave increased powers to schools over resource allocation and, crucially, introduced a prescriptive national curriculum with an associated assessment system based on external testing at the end of key stages (KS) in pupils' school careers – at ages seven, 11, 14 and 16. Since then curriculum and assessment have been dictated centrally with the assessment dimension highly influencing the nature of the enacted curriculum and the pedagogic decisions taken by teachers. Over this period various reforms have occurred but the emphasis on assessment for accountability has continued and deepened in terms of impact and consequences.

The legislative and policy context is central to understanding assessment and accountability in England. The above Act introduced formula funding which determined budgets on the basis of the number of pupils attending the school. It also introduced the publication of school performance tables which came to be called 'league tables'. Schools were incentivised to maximise their results and their funding by means of a system that created a quasi-market, the assumption being that on the basis of information available to them, parents would select the 'best' school for their children (evidenced by test results) eventually raising standards and eliminating 'low performing' schools. The notion of 'the failing school' was born. Local management of schools was also introduced in England (and Wales) through this legislation, and headteachers with their governing bodies became responsible for its expenditure.

Assessment and reporting of attainment

A new national curriculum (NC) was introduced into primary schools in September 2014, setting out the programmes of study for the various subjects. What is deemed essential has not been without criticism (see Vasagar and Shepherd, 2011) but we will not discuss this here. The NC sets out the expectations for the end of each KS and schools are free to develop a curriculum relevant to their pupils that teaches that content. This 'freedom' in relation to pedagogy is presented as an indication of autonomy to schools: 'Schools improve most when teachers have the autonomy to decide how best to teach their pupils, while being properly held to account for their pupils' education' (DfE, 2013, para. 6.1). Schools are expected to have an assessment system that checks on what children have learned and the extent to which they are on track to meet the externally set expectations associated with the end of the relevant KS.

There are attainment targets in the form of performance descriptors. These are described as frameworks to support teacher assessment and alongside external tests are intended to provide evidence of learners' achievement. The descriptors are for indicating how a child is performing at the end of a KS and are in the form of three categories: 'working towards the national standard', 'working at the national standard' and 'working at greater depth within the national standard' from which one is selected to describe the learner's performance. In the case, say, of writing at KS1 for seven-year-olds 'working at the national standard' incorporate 12 criteria which have to be demonstrated through a writing narrative that involves attention to a range of skills and knowledge in spelling, punctuation, grammar and handwriting. Already it becomes clear that assessment in the English system is highly prescriptive, externally determined and precise in its requirements.

Tests based on the new NC for English, maths and science were implemented in the summer of 2016. The KS2 test results are reported as scaled scores where the expected score is 100. The policy is that pupil progress is measured in relation to the average progress made by children with the same baseline i.e. the same KS1 average point score. The 2013 consultation response on reforming assessment and accountability in primary schools in England refers to a 'floor standard' which includes 85 per cent of pupils being expected to reach the expected standard. For 2016 the attainment component of the floor target is set at 65 per cent of pupils in a school reaching that level. This is how 'floor standards' is defined:

> ...schools will be above the floor if pupils make sufficient progress across all of reading, writing and mathematics or more than 65% of them achieve the national standard in reading, writing and mathematics. According to the Government's Association for Achievement and Improvement through Assessment (AAIA) website schools will be above the floor if they meet either the progress or the attainment threshold.
>
> *(www.aaia.org.uk)*

To explain further, the attainment aspect is to be based on the proportion of pupils reaching the expected standard in all of reading, writing and maths. They will need a scaled score of 100+ in reading and maths to have met the expected standard in writing. A school will be considered below the floor standard if two conditions apply: less than 65 per cent of pupils meet the expected attainment standard in reading, writing and maths combined (reading and maths assessed by external tests; writing via Teacher Assessment, TA) and pupils have not made 'sufficient progress' in any one of reading, writing and maths.

The 'progress' element is a value added measure to be compared against KS1 results throughout while developments continue around an alternative to this approach. The precise level of 'sufficient progress' was established in the light of analyses of KS2 results but apparently is based on value added from KS1 to KS2 in the areas of reading, writing and maths compared with the scores of pupils with the same KS1 results. Overall the specification of and emphasis on expected age-related standards constitutes a very significant and high stakes accountability measure in English education.

Performance assessment tables remain central to accountability in England. The performance measures that are relevant for each primary school are all of the following:

- average progress in reading, writing and maths;
- percentage reaching the expected standard in reading, writing and maths at the end of KS2;
- average score of pupils at the end of KS2 assessments;
- percentage of pupils who achieve a high score in all areas at the end of KS2.

The above measures are described by the AAIA as 'headline' measures and all schools are required to publish them in a consistent, standard format on their websites from 2016. Thus, each school must post on its website a profile of itself telling parents about pupil performance, progress and other priorities (see required assessment reporting arrangements for 2019 at Standards and Testing Agency, 2018).

An intriguing feature of accountability in England is the language used to describe schools and their work. There is a strong sense of schools being policed and the discourse is frequently punitive in style. In various official documents and on the AAIA website there are references to 'floor targets' as described above but in addition there are references to 'standards for coasting schools'. In 2015 the DfE conducted a consultation on 'interventions relating to coasting schools' (DfE, 2016, p. 12). The intention is to identify schools which have 'consistently not stretched their pupils sufficiently over a number of years'. Coasting schools are defined as those schools which are below a particular standard for three consecutive years.

Another indication of the punitive nature of the accountability language is in relation to the incorporation of progress scores. A spokesperson for the DfE (BBC News, 2015) commenting on the need to raise standards says 'this work (identifying progress made by schools) begins at primary level and that is why we are introducing ambitious new accountability measures and introducing a proper measure of progress so there is no *hiding place for under-performing schools*' (our emphases).

Schools are required to report to parents of pupils in Years 2 (at the end of KS1, usually age seven) and 6 (end of KS2, usually age 11) the results of their Teacher Assessments (using the framework described above). In addition, schools are required to report the results of the KS2 externally set and marked tests. KS1 test results are not necessarily reported to the Local Education Authority (LEA) or to the DfE or parents. School test results are published on their websites and in the form of league tables in the media and are commented upon extensively by journalists. It is this element of publication and ranking that fundamentally colours the policy and practice of accountability in England. The consequences for schools of assessment results are both grave and controversial. We return to this below as these have a huge bearing on the practices and experiences of pupils and teachers.

School inspection: external judgements and assessors

It is important to note that there is a vast range of school types in England, variously funded through Government, charities, and private industry. Schools vary by denomination and specialisation and the fundamental assumption on the part of successive governments in promoting such diversity is that competition between schools for the market of pupils will drive up standards. School choice remains part of the rationale for the particular version of accountability that exists in England's education system.

England has had a system of school inspection for many years but since 1992 when the Office for Standards in Education (OFSTED) was formed school inspection became much more frequent, consequential, interventionist and data-oriented. OFSTED's own remit is to 'raise standards and improve lives'. The governing work of OFSTED is primarily regulatory, enforcing centrally set standards across a very diverse school system.

Inspection follows a published framework (*Framework for the Inspection of Maintained Schools in England*). Inspectors visit schools and report on achievement of pupils, the quality of the teaching, the quality of leadership and the management of behaviour and safety of pupils. Inspectors also report on the spiritual, moral and social development of pupils and the extent to which the school meets pupils' needs, including those with special educational needs. A school's overall performance is judged as one of the following: 'outstanding', 'good', 'requires improvement', 'inadequate'. Schools whose results are declining would trigger a re-inspection and schools deemed to be 'good' are re-inspected after five years. Along with school visits, the inspection process involves the distribution of questionnaires to parents, pupils and school staff. Schools submit a self-evaluation template in advance of the inspection and during the inspection interviews are conducted with the headteacher, school staff, and members of the governing body. A key element is the observation of teaching. Meetings with inspectors and staff discuss observations but there is little or no scope for negotiation of the outcome/determination of the inspectors' decision and judgement.

In line with the policing discourse noted above in relation to test performance data, the language used in OFSTED's own website suggests a hierarchical and market-oriented accountability (www.gov.uk/government/organisations/ofsted/about). It intends to focus its inspection on schools that are 'less than good or whose performance has slipped' and on 'the performance of the most disadvantaged' and 'identify and report on issues of concern'. A negative OFSTED inspection can have serious consequences for the viability of a school. A warning notice may be issued to a school when the standards are deemed to be too low resulting in the appointment of additional governors or indeed the dismissal of the existing school board and the establishment of a new executive board or the closure and setting up of a new school (see next section). Such sanctions ('naming and shaming') inevitably result in reputational damage to a school.

School autonomy and new school types

In the past two decades or so new types of schools have been encouraged in England. 'Free schools' could be established by parents or other groups and be funded directed by government thus adding to the wide range of faith and specialist schools already in the system. Since 2000 so-called 'free schools' have been brought under the umbrella of academy schools (DfE, 2011). The policy developed in 2015/16 is that schools deemed to be failing will be obliged to convert to an academy and even schools who are not failing but coasting (see above) could also be obliged to convert to academy status. In his 2016 research report for the Cambridge Primary Review Trust, Warwick Mansell refers to cases of 'hostile takeovers' where the DfE forced non-academy schools into academy status under a chosen sponsor, despite local opposition. Becoming an academy involves leaving the auspices of the local education authority and handing over power to an external sponsor (often a wealthy businessperson) who would 'sit at the top of the new school's governance structure' (Mansell, 2016, p. 5). The assumption on the part of the government is that such a structure would revitalise practices and inject new energy into its management.

The option of academy status was extended to primary schools in 2010 and while today only 17 per cent of all primary schools in England are academies, the radical possibility is that the number will grow under the current Conservative government. Evidence to date suggests that one of the attractions for converting to academy status is greater funding, greater control over curriculum matters and admission policies, all of which imply greater autonomy. However, since such schools have little or no autonomy when it comes to assessment and the publication of league tables, the promised freedom may be more notional than real (see Mansell, 2016 for a full discussion). We mention this initiative here in the context of an international comparison of assessment and accountability systems because it is such a radical departure from the status quo of state-funded schools that has obtained in the country since the Second World War. We mention it also because it aligns with a particular version of accountability and autonomy – market-oriented and hierarchical – concepts which are highly significant in understanding assessment practice in classrooms. Unsurprisingly, the initiative has been deeply controversial and heavily criticised by various groups not least because of its undermining of democratic processes (see Mansell, 2016; Ball, 2009; Keddie, 2016). Typically criticism of academies includes concern about the impact of diverting funding away from other needy areas of the education system and of increasing social segregation through a process that allows academies manipulate admissions to select 'easy-to-teach' pupils, if they wish. The fragmentation of the school system indicated in general by the introduction of academies and 'free schools' has been criticised for leading to inconsistency in the quality of necessary support to schools (e.g. Glatter, 2012; 2014).

Ongoing concerns about the nature of assessment and accountability in England

There is now a considerable empirical literature on the nature and influence of the overall practice of summative assessment and accountability in England, including the impact of the publication of inspection reports, pupil performance data and league tables. Given its high stakes nature, a major concern would appear to be the dependability and consistency of judgements especially in relation to the observation of teaching and learning (Waldergrave and Simons, 2014) while another is the extent to which equity may be compromised (Lingard and Sellar, 2012). It is beyond our scope here to document this literature but it is worth referring to some concerns that have an influence on some groups and individuals in society. Work by Vincent *et al.* (2010) for instance would suggest that some societal groups, specifically middle class parents, are better placed to access, interpret and use the vast amount of information now made publicly available about school performance. Of major concern is the evidence in many studies showing the negative impact of ranking and league tables on the enactment of curriculum with a narrowing of student experience to a disproportionate focus on the areas that are externally tested and published (Whitby, 2010; Wiggins and Tymms, 2002; Luginbuhl *et al.*, 2009; Courtney, 2016) and several studies of practice (e.g. Hall *et al.*, 2004; Harlen and Deakin Crick, 2002) showing how pedagogy too is negatively impacted due to 'teaching to the test'.

In their review and synthesis of the impact of the mechanisms of school inspection internationally, Nelson and Ehren (2014) list a number of consequences for teaching that are pertinent to the English case. Consequences include window-dressing, fraud, gaming and misinterpretation. Other consequences, as already noted, include the narrowing of curriculum, the use of pedagogies that are assumed to be 'inspection-approved', and the rigid application of performance measurement schemes, all of which minimise innovation and contextual responsiveness. In the case of the high stakes nature of the accountability system in schools in England, where the outcome can be grave for schools and individuals working in them, one might not be surprised that the system is prone to a range of manipulation and gaming practices.

Because the assessment system is 'high stakes', decisions about curriculum and pedagogy are severely limited in practice. Even aspects of funding designed to extend decision making of headteachers are heavily circumscribed from the centre. For instance, the Pupil Premium – a funding strategy introduced in 2011 to support poorer pupils (those registered for free school meals) – is to be spent on interventions from a list which has been approved by OFSTED (2012; 2014). Thus, the available autonomy is a highly constrained one and, in this case, questionable as to its positive impact on the promotion of inclusion (Ainscow *et al.*, 2016).

A key message from our account so far is that the system of accountability in England is data-heavy, focussed on regulation, comparing and exposing underperformance. It is an external, largely punitive, form of assessment and accountability that is 'high stakes' and controversial because a school's profile and reputation is based on it. Overall, it is a system which, it would appear, has not enjoyed the endorsement of either the professional or research communities.

Other parts of the UK

Before we look at other countries with a view to offering a comparison, we consider very briefly the policy context in other parts of the UK.

Scotland

The systems of education in Scotland (and Northern Ireland) have historically been distinct from that obtaining in England.

There are no standard assessment tests (SATs) in Scotland but new compulsory standardised assessments in literacy and numeracy commenced in 2017 which are designed to provide diagnostic information to support teachers in planning learning (https://standardisedassessment.gov.scot/). Scottish schools continue to have access to a bank of materials to support assessment – the National Assessment Resource (NAR) which is an interactive computerised assessment system (InCAS). These resources align with the curriculum (see Education Scotland, 2016, *Assessment for Curriculum for Excellence*) and attempt to help teachers integrate their teaching and assessment. They also include moderation guides with exemplars of children's assessed work designed to help teachers interpret and cross check their own assessment of their pupils' work. Teachers and schools decide when to administer these tests to their pupils but it is noteworthy that the obligatory standardised assessment in literacy and numeracy from 2017 may have implications for the take up of these resources. At the end of their primary schooling, a pupil profile is prepared for each pupil summarising their achievements in the various curriculum areas with a summative category indicating whether the achievement is 'developing', 'consolidated' or 'secure'. National standards in literacy and numeracy are monitored through representative sampling procedures. Thus, unlike England, individual schools are not held to account through comparative achievement data and there are no league tables of performance.

In essence the tests available to Scottish schools are not substantially different to those used in England but crucially they are not 'high stakes' because there is not an emphasis on ranking and comparing. Performance tables are not compiled and published. Research by Wiggins and Tymms (2002) showed that there were fewer negative effects arising from the use of testing in Scotland with far more evidence in England of teachers teaching to the test and overly concentrating on 'borderline' learners who had the greater potential to perform at the expected level and thus enhance the overall achievement profile of a school.

Scottish schools are inspected and evaluated using quality indicators (Education Scotland, 2015, *How good is our school?)* focusing on leadership and change; learning, teaching and assessment; raising attainment and achievement; and ensuring wellbeing, equality and inclusion. A six-point scale is used in negotiation with schools ('excellent', 'very good', 'good', 'satisfactory', 'weak' and 'unsatisfactory').

We already noted how England's accountability system is centralised. Scotland also has a centralised inspection system. However, there are some important differences. The main difference is that the Scottish inspectorate places far more emphasis on schools evaluating themselves (self-evaluation) and is more directive in promoting school improvement through collaboration and sharing good practice. With devolved powers to a Scottish parliament in 1999 for education plus the Scottish National Party's formation of government since 2007, Scotland has pursued a very different philosophy of educational accountability compared to its near neighbour. Publicly-funded, free state education and opposition to privatisation remain hallmarks of the system and to a large extent this philosophy could be deemed to be the basis of its increasing divergence from England in terms of its mechanisms for school accountability and quality assurance, both at the level of inspection and the monitoring of standards.

In aligning itself with school improvement and development, Scottish inspectors see themselves as guides and enablers of quality assurance who are partners with teachers (see Education Scotland website). Providing support and fostering schools' capacity for self-evaluation are emphasised which means they are less confrontational. Thus, authority and power are far less autocratic and 'distant' than is the case in England (see Clarke et al., 2013). Clarke and Ozga (2011) attribute this to the fact that in Scotland inspectors, policy makers and senior teachers occupy 'a partially shared milieu that implies a reduced social distance'.

Wales

Up until 1999 the English and Welsh school systems were aligned. Since then Wales has opted for quite a different approach especially in matters of assessment for accountability purposes.

Wales ceased to externally assess seven-year-olds through SATs in 2006 and abandoned external testing for 11-year-olds in 2014 but Teacher Assessment is mandatory at the end of KS2 (age 11). There are changes occurring in relation to the introduction of reading and numeracy assessments from age seven as part of the new national literacy and numeracy strategy. The situation in Wales is changing in the light of the review of its curriculum and assessment framework under Graham Donaldson (Learning Wales website; Donaldson, 2015). The recommendation from that review is that Key Stages should be removed in favour of a more coherent and holistic approach to assessment where 'progression steps' or points of learning on a continuum should be viewed as a staging post for a child's development, not a judgement. The Welsh government does not publish primary performance data through which league tables can be compiled. There is a 'national school categorisation system' which ranks schools based on hard and soft measures including self-evaluation. This is designed to highlight a school's capacity to improve and the overarching value would appear to be collaboration rather than mistrust (Power, 2016). Relations between schools and Government tend to be based on trust and collaboration.

Wales has a school inspection system the starting point of which is school self-evaluation. The Welsh Assembly says that the main purpose of its inspection system is to identify which schools are in most need of support and insists that it is not about labelling or creating league tables. However, the Assembly's website, mylocalschool, is regularly updated with descriptions of individual schools incorporating contextual data, performance data and information benchmarking a school against schools with a similar profile (see also learning.gov.wales). Schools fall into one of four categories: green (the best schools); yellow (good schools); amber (schools in need of improvement); and red (in need of greatest improvement).

Following the publication of the *Donaldson Review* (2015) accountability procedures are intended to address teaching and learning and school improvement and not to compare one school with another. This perspective aligns also with the OECD (2014) report on 'Improving Schools in Wales' which complimented Wales on its comprehensive school system which emphasises equity and inclusion – student performance being less dependent on a student's socioeconomic background than the OECD average. However, the OECD report concluded that assessment and evaluation arrangements lacked coherence in Wales and struggled to obtain a good balance across accountability and improvement.

Schools are encouraged to use Estyn's Common Inspection Framework for with its focus on standards/outcomes, provision and leadership. (The word 'estyn' is a welsh word meaning 'to stretch' or 'to reach out'). Inspections occur every six years following a notice period of 20 days. Grading of schools is on a four-point scale: excellent, good, adequate, and unsatisfactory. Inspections are posted on the Estyn (inspection) website.

Northern Ireland

The Education Training Inspectorate (ETI) inspects schools in Northern Ireland and in many respects the format is very like the OFSTED approach in England with similar criticism levelled against it including consistency and validity. The inadequacy of the appeals process is another point of criticism. In April 2016 one of the largest teacher unions passed a motion of no confidence in NI's chief inspector of schools and in the entire ETI organisation. Questions are being raised in NI about the purposes and functions of the ETI, including who, if anyone, is tasked with its own evaluation.

While the ETI has similar powers to OFSTED, the title of its framework (*Together Towards Improvement*) and *Every School a Good School* suggests collaboration and enhancing provision rather than merely monitoring it in a punitive way. Classroom observation is a central feature of school inspections and there is a strong emphasis on self-evaluation but this is not mandatory. Reports are published on the ETI website within 30 days of an inspection.

Literacy and numeracy tests are implemented in Years 4–7 via InCAS (see above in respect of Scotland). Teacher assessment is based on levels of achievement allocated for cross-curricular skills of communication, using and applying maths and using IT.

Key comparator social order messages

Key messages to note so far in relation to our comparative work are:

- Unlike England, 'league tables' of performance in Scotland, Wales and NI are not compiled and published.
- As in England, individual school inspection reports are published, including the grades awarded.
- In all three cases there is a strong emphasis on collaboration, school improvement and teacher support and this emphasis is stronger than in England.
- There is not a high stakes culture in these parts of the UK compared to that evident in England.
- The emphasis on competition between schools, school choice and parents as consumers is not a central plank of the policy discourse.
- Scotland, Wales and NI have Teaching Councils which regulate the teaching profession and which is a form of peer review since the vast majority of the membership in each case consists of teachers. Professional accountability, in this sense, is privileged arguably over market or hierarchical accountability.

Assessment and accountability in Germany

Background

Germany is a federal state consisting of 16 States (Bundesländer). It has a decentralised education system, with responsibility for education in each state shared between the Federation, the Bundesländer and local authorities. Education policies differ from state to state but generally pupils must attend Grundschule (primary schooling covering grades 1–4) between the ages of six and ten and education is compulsory for nine or ten years overall. The aim of the Grundschule is to provide its pupils with the basis for the next educational level and lifelong (formal, non-formal and informal) learning. Language, mathematics and science remain central to curriculum and assessment but consideration is also given to independent thinking and interaction. Media, aesthetic, environment, health, attachment to places of origin and intercultural education are also important.

Tracking from an early age

In his consideration of autonomy in the German education system Martin Heinrich suggests that we need to explore the concept of autonomy in relation to schooling on a number of levels – the autonomy of the child, the autonomy of the teacher and the autonomy of the school as an institution (Heinrich, 2015). Heinrich raises concerns for the autonomy of the child in German schooling as a result of Germany's focus on early tracking of primary school students. The purpose of this tracking is to allocate particular pupils to particular school types, mainly academic or vocational. While this eases the transition from school to work for many pupils, there are issues concerning equity surrounding the early tracking of pupils to one or other of these types of secondary schooling, particularly as generally tracking decisions are reached by schools by the time a pupil is ten years old. School decisions can be overridden by parents but this is more likely where the pupil comes from a more advantaged socioeconomic background. Socioeconomic background of students is a key factor in performance in schooling (Entorf and Minoiu, 2005) and the selection of secondary schooling (Dustmann, 2004) and may reproduce issues of social inequalities and immobility for certain groups of people in Germany (Walsh, 2008).

A highly regulated system with low autonomy for teachers and pupils

Traditionally schools in Germany are understood to have little autonomy operating in highly regulated environments. For example primary school curricula in the main continue to be published as regulations of the Ministry of Education and Cultural Affairs. Though these curricula require teacher adherence they are broad and allow some teacher freedom and autonomy, particularly in relation to pedagogical decisions and responsibilities.

Evaluation and assessment

In October 2010 the Standing Conference and the Federal Ministry of Education and Research (responsible for coordinating education across the Bundesländer) established the Centre for International Large-Scale Assessment (*Zentrum für Internationale Bildungsvergleichsstudien* – ZIB) in Munich. Responsibilities of the ZIB include the implementation of PISA studies in Germany, drafting national reports and promoting and coordinating Germany's participation in any number of international academic committees and international comparative research studies. The ZIB is jointly funded by the Federation and the Bundesländer and one of its main aims is to increase the profile of German educational research in the context of international educational comparative studies. Germany is a frequent participant in the publishing of anonymised school reports, school profiling and national and international comparisons.

A focus on market accountability (at the macro and national level) is supported by structures of hierarchical accountability in German schools. The Basic Law governing schooling in Germany outlines how the entire German school system remains under the supervision of the state (Art 7, Paragraph 1) and schools are evaluated by a number of external quality and evaluation agencies. A number of

Education Acts offer further detail and legal regulations for external evaluations of schools and in addition to this the school legislation of most Bundesländer provide measures of external and internal evaluation beyond this state supervision. Evaluation and assessment frameworks exist in each of the 16 Länder, and the Standing Conference of Ministers of Education and Cultural Affairs (KMK) aims to provide an overarching strategy. Across all Bundesländer a highly structured legal framework exists around external school supervision.

At a local level school supervisory authorities also provide academic, legal and staff supervision to evaluate schools within the education system while institutes for school pedagogy (vocational education and training committees) provide advice and recommendations to further the development of German primary schools. Academic supervision is carried out by school inspectors who visit schools, observe lessons and offer advice. Legal supervision ensures that school management and maintenance adhere to the law while staff supervision of teachers and head teachers by school supervisory authorities appraise staff and ensure that every staff member carries out their duties. With increased self-responsibility for schools, inspections and evaluations work as a further basis for accountability. School evaluations in many Bundesländer are summarised and anonymised to provide quality profiles of schools in Germany and there is a sharing of knowledge across states.

Regular assessment of pupil achievement is also understood as a part of educational monitoring and accountability in schools. From grade two (age seven) onwards schools issue half-yearly reports on pupil progress which includes comments and marks (a six-mark system: very good = 1; 'good' = 2; 'satisfactory' = 3; 'adequate' = 4; 'poor' = 5; 'very poor' = 6). These reports compare performance with that of other pupils in the class. Students do not complete any final primary schooling examination and these reports are used to track students and decide on the secondary school they will attend.

In 2008 Germany introduced comparative examinations for grade three students to provide a national grade-based evaluation of pupil achievement (VERA 3). The main purpose of this testing is to ask teachers to use their pupils' performance outcomes in a data-driven development cycle to further develop teaching. It is interesting to note then that in international studies Germany ranks below the OECD average (ranked 54 of 64 countries) with regards to the use of achievement data for accountability purposes.

Within this framework teachers also adopt a child centred approach and encourage each child to achieve all that they can, making monitoring performance and progression throughout the school year central to practice. Grades one and two rely largely on observation and talk to assess pupils with more standard written examinations being introduced from grade three onwards. Assessment is carried out by the teacher responsible for the pupil lessons. Pupils experiencing reading and writing difficulties are generally subjected to the same assessment standards that apply for all pupils. Current trends in assessment policy and practice in Germany reveal a move from a focus on developmental norms to understanding individual abilities and their developmental stages in individual pupils (Klumpp, 2014).

Environmental aspects are also a focus in impacting pupil assessment. Together these developments around assessment thinking are pushing German educators to understand that there is no such thing as a normal child and individual and that environmental factors need to be considered in assessment practice. It is interesting to note that an issue for teachers surrounding these recent trends towards autonomy and self-accountability for schools in Germany is that these trends have not been developed by schools themselves, but rather called for by school administrations and external institutions. This has resulted in a 'top down' approach to encouraging autonomy and local accountability in individual schools but schools themselves have not had a large say on how this process might function.

Setting standards: quality assurance

In the wake of poor PISA results the Federation introduced in 2003 an output-oriented quality assurance – Bildungsstandards (education standards) – which describe in detail the subject specific competencies pupils should have acquired up to certain educational milestones. Interestingly, these standards describe the average rather than the minimal levels of competence required and clearly establish significant and high achievement goals for students.

Quality assurance of assessment and progression in schools represent central issues in the development of education policy in Germany. According to the Standing Conference of the Ministers of Education and Cultural Affairs current assessment policy and practice are designed to capture good evidence on pupils' strengths and weaknesses in key areas of competence which can serve as a basis for targeted measures leading to the improvement of efficiency and learning. Studies and national and international comparisons of this assessment and also classroom practice are understood as a measurement of quality control in German schools. Examples of Germany's involvement in international comparative studies of pupil achievement include the Trends in International Mathematics and Science Study (TIMSS), the Progress in International Reading Literacy Study (PIRLS) and the OECD project entitled Programme for International Student Assessment (PISA) as a means of establishing pupils' performance.

Germany: key social order messages

- Some societal groups experience more privileged access to and experience of education than others and tracking of pupils through primary school reporting is high stakes and contributes to this in Germany.
- Teachers experience autonomy in relation to pedagogical choice and mediation of curricular documents.
- While accountability through assessment and school inspection features, it not 'high stakes' in the sense that this applies say in England.
- Hierarchical and market accountability is a feature but it is far less externally oriented than is the case in England.

- The emphasis on competition between schools, school choice and parents as consumers, present in England, does not feature strongly in Germany.
- Quality assurance is high on the agenda in Germany – output oriented education standards combine with international country wide comparisons function to provide a framework for quality assurance.

Assessment and accountability in Finland

Background

Success in the education system as a collective responsibility

School is compulsory and free of charge for children aged seven to 16 years and education is seen as an individual human right. Each school is funded based on the number of its students and of note is that funding is not dependent on the SES of the school catchment. Education is viewed as a national project involving national responsibility and support. While accountability has a long history in other jurisdictions chosen for this study, accountability is not a key part of the educational discourse in Finland (Sahlberg, 2011).

Each school district in Finland is governed by locally elected school boards and superintendents. Finland does not have private schools, and it has only a small number of 'independent' schools and these are state financed. All schools in Finland are 'public comprehensive schools'. Children are not only provided with the opportunity to learn and have access to education funded by the state, they also receive 'support' in the educational system in order to achieve expected results. According to Itkonen and Jahnukainen (2007), 'success' in the Finnish system is a 'collective responsibility'. Finnish education is equality oriented and seeks equity.

In the 1990s OECD (not necessarily OECD countries) incorporated in its discourse a strong emphasis on competition between schools and the setting up of markets to encourage competition. Privatisation was another feature of this discourse in the 1990s and several OECD countries, e.g. England, Sweden and Norway, were influenced by this new wave of thinking. The assumption was that education systems would become more competitive, that standards would rise, that efficiency would be enhanced, and that bureaucracy would reduce. Finland is one country that did not subscribe to this vision.

Approaches to assessment and publication of results

Over many years and cycles of international assessments Finnish children have tended to out-perform their counterparts in other countries. PISA results show that Finnish 15-year-olds perform better than their peers in most other countries in reading literacy, mathematics literacy, and science literacy. In addition (and importantly, given the long tale of under-achievement in other countries especially

England) between-school variance in student achievement is lower in Finland than most other countries.

Ranking schools on the basis of student achievement is prohibited in Finland. Student achievement in tests is considered a mechanism to enable schools to improve the instructional conditions for teaching and learning. Mandatory national testing for the whole age cohort is not part of the Finnish education tradition. Finland does not have a system of school inspections. It does not allow school league tables (Varjo and Kalalahti, 2015).

We can better understand the Finnish approach to assessment, testing and comparing (compared to other countries) by attending to its conception of achievement. Hochschild and Scovronick (2003) distinguish between several types of achievement in educational systems, each implying a different approach to evaluation and accountability. Take the notion of absolute achievement. The state and local authorities may either consider achievement as one's 'individual responsibility' and not provide one with more help when/if one needs it or it may provide one with support on the basis that 'Children are different and different children need different types and amount of help to achieve equitable results'. Now consider the notion of 'relative achievement'. Here individual or group/school achievement is compared to that of other individuals or groups. A further type of achievement is 'competitive achievement' where one's results are subject to comparison, ranking and categorizing which results in a discourse of 'successful students', 'failing students', 'successful schools', 'failing schools' and may be based on national or international 'standardised test results'. Ranking is an inevitable result in this conception of achievement. Itkonen and Jahnukainen (2007) say the underlying assumption here is that as a 'failing student', one had the capacity but one simply did not work hard. As a 'failing school', the staff and administration had the capacity to succeed, but they did not work hard, in other words, they did not do the job they were supposed to do. So, they must be sanctioned. In the light of these different approaches to evaluation and achievement, the Finnish education system operates on the basis of and privileges 'absolute achievement' and the need to offer students and schools the opportunity and resources to 'catch up' and improve rather than sanctioning them for any kind of under-performance. Different orientations toward achievement result in different feedback to schools about their performance. Finland is inclined to increase support rather than punish, sanction or hold to account in a public, punitive way.

The Finnish comprehensive school system

The Finnish comprehensive school system is based on the idea of providing equal educational opportunities, regardless of gender, social class and geographical origin. Based on several studies Varjo and Kalalahti (2015) assert that until the late 1980s, the Finnish comprehensive systems consisted of universal, non-selective basic education, generally provided by the public authorities. As a rule children have always had the opportunity to attend publicly-funded schools near where they live. This is known as the 'neighbourhood school principle' in Nordic countries.

Decentralisation of the power structure in the educational sector was increased in 1980s. To ensure equity and equality Finland made several important juridical changes and clarified the mandate of the local educational authorities and introduced a predictable financing system for free public education (Musset, 2012; Page and Goldsmith, 1987). According to several studies (Bogason, 2000; Varjo and Kalalahti, 2015) these decentralisation-oriented reforms represented new approaches to public sector management. On the one side they increased local autonomy but on the other side they caused some disparities among municipalities and to some degree weakened the unified structure of the Finnish comprehensive school system.

The Finnish discourse of fostering the comprehensive system is based on the ideology of equality of educational opportunities. It is constructed upon the traditional, universal, non-selective features of the comprehensive school. Within the frame of this 'comprehensive school system', the country tried to open a space for school choice. The legitimation of school choice in Finland is built on acceptable, but strictly limited, reasons for choice. Opportunity for school choice can be, and must be, locally controlled, even restricted, if needed, in order to prevent a vicious circle of 'failing schools' in deprived neighbourhoods.

The Finnish basic school law of 1999 and school choice

In 1999 a new law for Finnish basic education was introduced. The Basic Education Act made it mandatory for the municipalities to provide each elementary school aged child 'a neighbourhood school' or some other appropriate place where education is given. On the one hand this legislation strengthened the Finnish 'localism-based' approach to school choice. On the other hand the legislation removed the term 'school district' from the legislation. Varjo and Kalalahti (2015) consider this change to be very important because it means that the right to enrol in a public school in your 'school district' abolished. By the new law, 'neighbourhood school' means that municipalities have to provide and children are obliged to attend a designated school defined in terms of proximity, but the municipalities are empowered to develop distinctive policies and practices in order to allocate children to their neighbourhood schools in an equitable manner. This basic school law enables parents to choose between schools on the grounds of each school's particular character and associated curriculum. But, all the education providers and their comprehensive schools are still required to follow national curriculum guidelines. This means that they are allowed to specialise in certain areas within a given framework. In other words schools can develop and market a distinctive pedagogical profile to be attractive for different groups and to meet the different demands of parents and be able to accommodate children with different aptitudes and interests. Varjo and Kalalahti (2015, p. 316) define this educational policy as 'sub-national construction' and describe this approach as 'educational diversity inside the traditionally homogeneous national curriculum'. After the introduction of this new law and new approach to 'local institutional spaces for parental school choice', many municipalities and schools started to develop a distinctive 'profile' by 'offering a specialization in particular subjects in the curriculum or by placing an emphasis on some more general themes such as the environment or communication, for instance'. Furthermore, the researchers assert that 'classes with special emphasis' function as separate streams within regular municipal schools. Those with a music profile for example offer more lessons in music per week. Those with a sport profile, science profile or art profile offer more lessons in the core profile subject than the National Core Curriculum requires.

Selection of pupils for these specialist classes is based on aptitude tests, not academic achievement. The Basic Education Act states the following: 'If education is given according to a curriculum with special emphasis on one or several subjects, the admission of pupils may also be based on a test showing aptitude for said education' (Law 628/1998: 28§). We can therefore say that school choice in Finland takes place within the public school system. Parental choice is provided and governed by public authorities through classes with a special emphasis. Thus school choice in the Finnish system is not between the schools or between public comprehensive schools and market oriented 'free schools' or 'charter schools' as is the case in England and elsewhere (see California below). Opportunity to choose a school is to a great extent in the hands of municipalities. Each municipality can create opportunities for interested schools to specialise, that is to say, to develop its pedagogical and subject profile. In all cases consideration has to be given to matters of selection and admission so that equity is never compromised.

Though limited and on a small scale currently, the trend towards 'profilisation' of schools in Finland is a cause for concern in some respects and, like the move towards Academies in England, is important to note because it constitutes a break with tradition. According to Varjo and Kalalahti (2015), the Finnish egalitarian-oriented educational policy and tradition however is facing some threats. Several big cities, particularly the Helsinki Metropolitan Area are facing particular challenges. One can observe a growing segregation in relation to socioeconomic differences, neighbourhoods, and schools. The result is that in several Finnish cities there is considerable variation in PISA test scores and differences between schools are on the increase and the association between urban segregation and educational outcomes is quite clear (Bernelius and Kauppinen, 2011; Kupari *et al.*, 2013; Varjo and Kalalahti, 2015). Researchers are beginning to detect the emergence of 'failing schools' due to 'sociospatial segregation' in Helsinki, a feature of schooling that, to date, has been more common in metropolitan areas in England and California, than in Finland.

Key social order messages: Finland

Key messages to note in relation to Finland:

- Success in the education system is a collective, rather than an individual responsibility with a very strong traditional emphasis on matters of equity and support for learners and schools and this principle has shaped its low emphasis on external accountability frameworks.

- Accountability occurs through school-based, internal assessment and unlike England, there is no cohort-based external testing programme in primary schools; ranking of schools is prohibited, and there is no inspection system.
- Hierarchical and market accountability is not a feature of the Finnish system and in this regard Finland resisted new public sector management measures that emphasised competition between schools, school choice and external accountability.
- School choice and parents as consumers is not a evident in Finland although 'profilisation' of schools whereby schools can specialise is beginning to slightly weaken the old order of all children attending their local neighbourhood school.

Assessment and accountability in California

Current context and background

One of 50 states in the US, California is the most populous at 39 million (United States Census, 2010). The Republic of California is the sixth largest economy in the world. It is linguistically diverse with some 57 per cent having English as a first language, 30 per cent Spanish, 3 per cent Chinese, 2 per cent Tagalog and 8 per cent speaking several different native languages. Education at K-12 is free of charge in public schools. Pre-school or early childhood education is not universal. Only children in low-income families are eligible for free early childhood education and such services are organised as early intervention programs, i.e. Head Start which is a highly effective programme (California Head Start Association and CCR Analytics, 2015) of the US Department of Health and Human Services that provides comprehensive early childhood education, health, nutrition, and parent involvement services to low-income children and their families.

In the US many states, including California, do not have a national curriculum. Recently, an American education initiative was taken to establish the Common Core State Standards Initiative which outlines quantifiable benchmarks in English language arts and mathematics at each grade level from kindergarten through high school. Forty-two states, the District of Columbia, four territories, and the Department of Defense Education Activity (DoDEA) have adopted the Common Core State Standards. The California State Board of Education adopted the standards on 2 August 2010. Full implementation was set to be achieved in the 2014–2015 academic year (Common Core State Standards Initiative, 2010).

To understand assessment and how it is used for accountability purposes in California's school system, we feel it is important to track briefly its emergence and change over recent times. Like many cases, California's policies are under reform and this section seeks to provide an account of the recent, the current and the changing accountability landscape in elementary schools in California.

Accountability has a long history in Californian education. At the beginning of the last century, the American public education was built around four policy assumptions (Boyd, Kerchner and Blyth, 2008; and Özerk, 2014):

1. School policy and governance would be primarily a local concern. Locally elected school boards would raise needed revenue and provide wise guidance.
2. Education was removed from partisan politics. Schools, for example, were governed separately from cities, and school board elections were not connected to political parties.
3. The operation and major influence on education policy was primarily the preserve of the educational professionals.
4. The whole system enjoyed what became known as 'a logic of confidence' in which the public was assured that schools were well run and teachers, school heads, and superintendents were generally given wide latitude in performing their roles.

Over the last 40 years, these assumptions have been severely challenged. Now the state and national governments, rather than local school boards, initiate most education policy, and in California most of school tax funds are raised by the state, which relies heavily on income and sales taxes. Californian K-12 public schools are run by revenue from the following funding sources: 9 per cent from the Federal Government, 60 per cent State funding, 25 per cent local taxes, 5 per cent miscellaneous taxes, i.e. property tax and 1 per cent Californian Lottery (Californian Educational Data, www. ed100.org., accessed 04.09.2016).

The publication in 1984 of *A Nation at Risk* initiated a strong wave of accountability measures all based on the belief that education can be improved through constant collection, analysis, comparison and publication of the results of standardised tests at national and state levels (Hansen, 1993; Powers, 2004). The basic shift in thinking was that the federal and state governments should provide legislative mandates to stop the 'rising tide of mediocrity' in public education and that strict federal mandates would be based on the results of accountability systems in each state, all of which would include student achievement tests. The focal point for accountability, it is assumed, is the individual school and district.

Californian Accountability Act of 1988 and NCLB Act 2002

In 1988 California passed the Classroom Instructional Improvement and Accountability Act to 'enable Californians to once again have one of the best public school systems in the nation'. The Accountability Act requires '…every local school board to prepare a School Accountability Report Card to guarantee accountability for the dollars spent'. The Accountability Act guarantees a minimum, annual, and ongoing level of State support for public schools.

In 2002, President George W. Bush signed Public Law 107–110, the No Child Left Behind Act of 2001 (NCLB, 2001). This law required that schools implement an annual testing programme for every child in Grades 4 through 8 in reading and maths. The results are reported as a whole annual cohort and also by subgroups. The law mandates that all children should be proficient in reading and maths by the year 2014. Each state is allowed to determine how it uses student achievement results to report annual progress toward the 2014 goal. The NCLB reporting requirements were in addition to any existing state-level reporting requirements. As a result, accountability systems at the state level included results on meeting the NCLB requirements and on meeting the state requirements.

The Accountability Act of 1988 together with the No Child Left Behind Act (NCLB, 2001) intensified state level testing, the specification of standards, evaluation and comparison of student performance, monitoring of student progress, and generally measuring school performance (Powers, 2004). These acts along with OECD's international comparisons through PISA were highly influential in changing the discourse of accountability in California and in America in general. Indeed one of us has argued that as a result of the international achievement comparisons conducted with OECD countries, PISA became 'the second minister of education in all participating countries' (Özerk, 2010). In sum the result was a decentralisation of budgets, competition between schools, pressure on schools to improve test results because of the publication of league tables, information to allow parents choose schools for their children. The consequence of this new wave of accountability is the categorisation of schools as 'failing', 'successful', dependent on test scores.

Sanctions also became part of the rhetoric and the reality which varied from the provision of extra resources for tutoring to moving the staff and administrators of a school to other schools (Itkonen and Jahnukainen, 2007). Privatisation of educational services and the growth of charter schools increased. Currently almost 1 in 10 schools in California is chartered or private. (California Department of Education, 2016). The underpinning American, and therefore Californian, ideology is: the state gives you the opportunity to education, but it's your responsibility to work hard and learn what the standards expect from you. 'Success' is your 'individual responsibility' (Hochschild and Scovronick, 2003). A number of consequences of the accountability regime in California have been highlighted in the professional and research literature (Herman and Ing, 2008; Blume, 2016; Nichols and Berliner, 2008; Education Week Research Center, 2016).

The mandate for student achievement testing and the consequent publication of the results set the stage for all citizens to become public critics of the effectiveness of their schools. Greater transparency, while helpful, to the citizen is problematic since evidence is so heavily and exclusively based on test scores in narrow curriculum areas and on a snap shot of one day in the life of a learner. Also, the types of tests being used in the accountability programs were primarily multiple-choice in format. Not only is a multiple-choice test an inadequate measure of higher-level thinking, but it transpired that the state tests were not well aligned with the state standards. Thus the most intellectually challenging aspects of the standards were missing because those standards do not lend themselves well to multiple-choice test items. The validity of the tests on which the system is held accountable is a major theme in the research literature (e.g. Ellison, 2012).

Every Student Succeeds Act: move to a broader view of learning and accountability

A recent report in the US (Education Week Research Center, 2016, p. 1) summaries the situation of education in the American schools during the last 16 years in this way:

For many, the very term 'accountability' has become synonymous with testing, particularly the type of mandatory standardised assessments at the centre of federally driven school accountability under the No Child Left Behind Act. But now that the NCLB era has ended and the successor Every Student Succeeds Act has become law, America's schools stand at a crossroads. The path chosen in the near future may shape the course of education accountability for years to come.

As mentioned above, The California State Board of Education adopted the Common Core State Standards (CCSS) in 2010 with full implementation from 2015. A central argument is that adaptation and implementation of CCSS represents a broader view of learning and teaching. As a member state of Common Core Standards Initiative, schools in California aimed to:

a   '… build upon the most advanced current thinking about preparing all students for success in college, career, and life';
b   work for school improvement based on '…internationally benchmarked standards from top-performing countries…in the development of the maths and English language arts/literacy standards';
c   improve their teaching-learning focus and address not only development of narrow skills but also content knowledge;
d   provide students with learning opportunities for achieving the English language arts standards that require certain critical content for all students, including classic myths and stories from around the world, America's founding documents, foundational American literature, and Shakespeare.

By adopting CCSS Californian schools are expected to make crucial decisions about what content should be taught. In addition to content coverage, the CCSS require that students systematically acquire knowledge in literature and other disciplines through reading, writing, speaking, and listening. This new orientation in post-NCLB-era by Common Core Standards Initiative (2010) puts a strong emphasis on mathematics and asserts that CCSS will lay a solid foundation in whole numbers, addition, subtraction, multiplication, division, fractions, and decimals. Taken together, these elements support a student's ability to learn and apply more demanding maths concepts and procedures. The middle school and high school standards call on students to practise applying mathematical ways of thinking to real-world issues and challenges.

As a result of these recent reforms, California is beginning to better align the state standard tests to the curriculum and it is tempering the status it accords to multiple-choice test formats. All the new standards are better aligned with the CCSS. Although CCSS has been controversial in some states, it is less controversial in California, largely because the California Department of Education has not connected test results to the accountability regime of NCLB and thus standards are not any longer means for punitive actions against schools and teachers. This seems like a major shift in policy and practice compared with what obtained in the past.

Importantly in terms of professional accountability, this new orientation at the state level in California was developed in close collaboration with the California Teachers' Association (CTA) and therefore CTA (2016) argues for the importance of CCSS in their webpage (CTA, 2016, accessed 09.09.2016). The main points in CTA's support for CCSS arise from the teachers' view that CCSS has the potential to deepen problem-solving skills and critical thinking, to promote greater opportunities for children, and to return to greater flexibility and creativity. CTA asserts that 'unlike the "drill and kill" test preparation associated with NCLB, CCSS only provide the framework of what should be taught – teachers get to decide how they'll teach them based on their expertise and judgment. Educators can find more creative, hands-on applications that are more engaging for everyone.' Moreover CTA, as probably the strongest teacher trade unions in the US, believes that the CCSS invites greater collaborative decision-making and that its implementation will be the key to success.

This CTA support to the new developments in Californian education is undoubtedly of importance in the move away from the narrow view of language skills, testing and the punitive-oriented accountability legislations and NCLB's accountability logic of earlier times. The positive attitude and support by CTA toward the new educational thinking necessitates collaboration between all the 'stake holders'. CTA put it in this way:

> We must work together with parents and community members to demand a plan that makes sense to transition to the new standards and to ensure next generation assessment systems are fair and include multiple, appropriate and valid measures of student success.
>
> *(CTA, 2016, p. 1)*

With this background, one can conclude that this new approach to education in California differs significantly from the older one in which the individual schools and teachers were accountable for 'delivering' outcomes. To a great extent the new orientation is a move in the direction of a more collective and egalitarian approach. But there is a risk that the Californian ideas and aims will meet obstacles due to underfunding of schools or scarce resources for the schools due to the above mentioned revenue sources of the schools.

Key social order messages

- The use of externally set standard 'pencil and paper' tests in specified areas of the curriculum are used as the major basis of accountability, the results of which are published in the form of league tables and thus are high stakes. However, in very recent years there has been a tempering of the use of such tests for accountability purposes and there is currently a far less punitive style being adopted in Californian state policy.
- There has been a strong emphasis on the specification of outcomes/standards, evaluation and comparisons of student performance at school level.
- Again as in England, but unlike say Finland and Scotland, accountability and quality assurance tends to be hierarchical and market-oriented; there is an emphasis on competition between schools, decentralisation of budgets, privatisation of educational services, and evaluation of teachers, and sanctioning of 'under-performing' schools.
- Like England, school choice and parents as consumers is very evident and the numbers of private (charter) schools has risen in the past decade.
- Recent changes in the planned implementation of the Common Core State Standards adopted in California are welcomed by teachers as they are not linked narrowly to accountability thus indicating a potential shift towards greater professional autonomy and internal professional accountability.

Assessment and accountability in Victoria

Background, current reforms and curriculum issues

Primary schooling for pupils in Victoria exists from preparatory year to Year 6 (ages five to 12). Government schools are free to attend and exist alongside low fee-paying religious schools and independent fee-paying schools. Funding responsibilities for non-government schools comes mainly from the Commonwealth and from student fees, while the Victorian Government provides most of the funds for government schools. School governance and decision making in Victoria schools is shared between the Minister; the central office of DEECD, led by the Secretary; DEECD's regional offices; school councils; and principals. Currently Victoria is implementing a series of education reforms focusing on school autonomy and accountability.

At present Victoria is in a state of transition in the development and implementation of a new curriculum. AusVELS (Australia Curriculum F-10) is the current and newly developed Australian Curriculum Framework for government and Catholic schools in Victoria. The AusVELS understands curriculum as a developmental learning continuum rather than a series of distinct learning blocks and takes a disciplinary approach to learning. It uses an 11-level structure to reflect the design of the new Australian Curriculum while maintaining Victorian priorities to teaching and learning. Knowledge and skills are categorised as capabilities. The curriculum content is mandated through the highlighting of learning areas and capabilities but the pedagogical decision making occurs at school level. The AusVELS curriculum is structured into strands, domains and dimensions (VCAA, 2013). The three strands are Physical, Personal and Social Learning; Discipline-based Learning and; Interdisciplinary Learning.

School choice in Australia and disadvantage

Australia has the highest degree of school choice in any OECD country. Australia also has a stronger concentration of disadvantaged students in disadvantaged schools than any other comparable OECD country and Australian student achievement is significantly and disproportionately affected by the impact of social background factors. The 2012 Report AEU (VIC) SUBMISSION to the Victorian Competition and Efficiency Commission: *Inquiry into School Devolution and Accountability* cites school choice as operating to differentially distribute high and low SES students across sectors. Non-government schools had a significantly higher density of high SES students and a lower density of low SES students than government schools located in the same area.

In addition to this, national research reveals big gaps in achievement across years in Victorian schools. In an Australian Council for Educational Research study, Meiers reported that 'the top 10 per cent of students in … each year [a]re working at approximately five year levels ahead of the bottom 10 per cent' (p. 12). This was more recently confirmed by a Grattan Institute report which asserted that 'at any given year level there is a five to six year difference between the most advanced and the least advanced ten per cent of students'.

Moving towards a devolved system with high(er) autonomy?

Victoria's public education system is the most devolved education system in Australia and Victoria schools are consequently the most autonomous. The 2012 Report AEU (VIC) Submission to the Victorian Competition and Efficiency Commission: Inquiry into School Devolution and Accountability suggests that 'evidence-based policy would dictate that greater school autonomy in itself has been found wanting as a means of improving student performance' (p. 2). This report also suggests that the current focus on autonomy for Australian schools (under the banner of raising student achievement and improving student learning) hides another agenda of increased accountability that goes hand in hand with the push for school autonomy. This report also highlights that autonomy means different things for non-government and public schools. For non-government schools autonomy facilitates the raising of selection barriers (e.g. fees or religious denomination) but for public schools it is essential not to discriminate on these grounds.

Schools in Victoria experience high autonomy in relation to the flexibility around reporting to parents on student achievement as schools are free to determine the timing, format and frequency of reports. In these reports however, schools are accountable for reporting against the content of the curriculum while also being encouraged to allow some self-assessment (from the pupils themselves) in this reporting process. Students themselves receive an individual report on the completion of the state-wide NAPLAN assessment and this provides both standards and norm referenced information about student achievement.

School accountability and improvement framework

The Accountability and Improvement Framework for Victorian Government Schools 2011 have been developed around the principles of focusing on student outcomes, differentiating accountability and compliance, using an inquiry-based approach, recognizing school difference, increasing transparency, aligning resources to support improvement, strengthening collaboration, sharing responsibility, minimizing the administrative workload and applying rigour. Victoria has also committed to a set of nationally agreed principles and protocols for reporting on schooling. In terms of market accountability, Victoria schools are accessed on performance and benchmarked for achievement against all Australian schools. In 2012 it achieved below average in all testing areas – reading, maths and science and market accountability and comparison studies are seen as very important indicators of school success.

The School Accountability and Improvement framework for Victorian schools outlines a four-year planning and review cycle of hierarchical accountability, along with an annual cycle of implementation and reporting. Within the framework schools engage first in self-evaluation (including students, parents and all staff). A school review by an external reviewer immediately follows the self-evaluation step and may take the form of negotiated (flexible and focussed examination of a specific area for improvement identified from the self-evaluation), continuous improvement (schools with satisfactory outcomes but room for improvement) or diagnostic (where student outcomes or other key indicators are below expected levels) review. A school strategic plan is developed as a living and working document as a result of this process. Schools also have to engage in annual planning on progression and targets from year to year. Peer reviews are also built into this system as a part of the external evaluation procedure. Interventions and support post review are also understood as central to the success of the review process.

Public accountability through transparency is presented as a strong feature of the Victorian education system: 'a culture of excellence in Victorian education is underpinned by publicly available information which identifies high performance and where improvement is necessary.' (Department of Education and Early Childhood Development, 2013, p. 13). This public accountability is tracked in a number of different ways as summarised in the above document, including:

1. Victorian State Register (all schools' annual reports available online).
2. Intake adjusted measures of school performance in government schools (considering whether a school, taking into account its students, is performing higher than, similar to or lower than other schools, taking into account their students).

3. Victorian School Performance Summary across all sectors (these reports, consistent across all schools in Victoria, provide a means for comparing a Victorian school's performance with 'like schools' composed of similar student populations).
4. ACARA website (The Australian Curriculum, Assessment and Reporting Authority (ACARA) publishes nationally comparable data on all Australian schools).

Assessment for accountability and the National Assessment Program

School assessment is nationally recognised as an integral part of quality assurance and system evaluation and as such, is a large part of each state and territory's system evaluation practices. School assessment is a high priority. In school teacher assessment has also been made more public with the recent launch of *My School* where assessment and other policies and practices used in schools are shared. Victorian Essential Learning Standards are used to assess success, achievement and learning of students.

Under the Australian Education Act 2013 (Cth.), schools are required to participate in the National Assessment Program and results play a role in both school accountability and quality assurance. The National Assessment Program (NAP) consists of international and national sample assessments as well as a full cohort national literacy and numeracy assessment in all schools. The National Assessment Program (NAP) is run at the direction of the Standing Council on School Education and Early Childhood (SCSEEC). It includes:

- the National Assessment Program – Literacy and Numeracy (NAPLAN);
- three-yearly NAP Sample Assessments in Science Literacy, Civics and Citizenship, and Information and Communication Technology (ICT) Literacy;
- international sample assessments.

The results from this National Assessment Program allow schools to be reported and measured against nationally comparable data and is how achievement and progress of Australian students are tracked. Results are not used to track students or allow entry to other courses but to indicate areas of interest for education research, analysis and policy. The NAPLAN is an annual assessment for students in Years 3, 5, 7 and 9. The assessments are undertaken nationwide, every year, in the second full week in May. Every year all students are assessed using national tests in reading, writing, language conventions (spelling, grammar and punctuation) and numeracy. Individual student reports show each child's results in comparison with all other children in Australia at the same year level who took the test, including:

- national average;
- national minimum standard;
- range for the middle 60 per cent of students nationally;
- indication of whether the child has achieved the national minimum standard;

- school average for the same year level (for some states and territories); and,
- the items the student successfully responded to and those s/he did not (for some states and territories).

Key social order messages from Victoria

Key messages to note in relation to Victoria are:

- Autonomy and accountability are treated in relation to and with each other in current reforms in Victoria.
- Student achievement is significantly and disproportionately affected by the impact of social background factors in Victoria.
- Teachers experience autonomy in relation to pedagogical choice and mediation of curricular documents.
- Accountability through assessment and school inspection features strongly and plays a high stakes role in the education systems and an externally oriented hierarchical and market accountability is a major feature.
- Australia has the highest degree of school choice in any OECD country and has strong concentrations of disadvantaged students in disadvantaged schools compared to any other comparable OECD country.
- Quality assurance is central to education reforms in Victoria with a focus on the publication of school profiles, data and results alongside national and international benchmarking and comparison across a wide variety of fora.

Cross-case comparison of social order messages and conclusion

Assessment for comparing: independence over interdependence

Far from exceptional among our chosen comparator countries, England would appear to be at the high end of a continuum, along with California and Victoria, in relation to an almost obsession with collecting and publishing performance data and comparing schools. The emphasis on school choice and a quasi-market in education is strongest in these three jurisdictions. Along with the associated emphasis on competition is the disproportionate impact of socioeconomic status on pupil achievement. We should not be surprised therefore that experiences of students, teachers and those leading schools in these places would be coloured by this strong emphasis.

Accountability would appear to be synonymous with accountancy in these jurisdictions. Measures, indicators, data targets, assessment of outputs for comparison and competitive purposes dominate the conceptualizing of accountability and indeed the discourse of teaching and learning in policy documents in these settings. In Finland and Scotland there is much stronger emphasis than in England on partnership, collaboration and sharing of good practice, there is far less emphasis on comparisons and competition in those jurisdictions. What we see as distinguishing

England, for instance, from some other countries is the relative emphasis on independence over inter-dependence.

Success and ability are concepts that in England (and California, Victoria and, to a lesser extent, Germany) could be said to be largely individual possessions and personal attributes for which individuals are personally accountable and almost exclusively responsible. The orientation in Finland and Scotland especially, and to a lesser extent, Wales, is manifestly more collaborative and focused more explicitly on distributing resources where they are most needed in the system. The key question for Finland would appear to be: do all schools ensure sufficient and equitable resources in order to provide good teaching and learning conditions that enable each student to make progress compared to her/his starting point? It is not surprising then that in Finland socioeconomic background accounts for only 3 per cent of the variance in PISA achievement while the corresponding statistic in the US and California is about 20 per cent. The within and between school variance and impact of socioeconomic status are well above the OECD average in England – in 2010 the UK as a whole was second in terms of the between-school performance variance that is explained by socioeconomic status (OECD, 2010, para. 23).

Predominance of performance/assessment data in narrow curriculum areas

Others have argued that England is overwhelmingly concerned with 'datafication' (Roberts-Holmes and Bradbury, 2016; Courtney, 2016) in narrow curriculum areas which ultimately functions to render school improvement secondary to the less important purpose of comparing and differentiating one school from another. This approach means that ideals of education are undermined accordingly. Energies inevitably tend to be devoted to distinguishing one's school from neighbouring ones in a system that is based on competing for parental attention as a 'chosen' school. As Keddie (2016) has observed – schools can no longer be ordinary. A similar claim could be made in relation to California and Australia. We have noted that Australia has the highest level of school choice in among OECD countries and very wide gaps in achievement occur as a function of SES.

Although England has been a keen follower of neoliberal accountability in education in general and is not vastly different in this regard to Victoria in Australia or California in the US, it is important to observe the very recent shift in thinking in California to seek to work with the teaching profession and to temper the link between narrow test results and teacher accountability. Enhancing the quality of the complex area of teaching, learning and assessment for broader and deeper educational outcomes are more likely to pay greater dividends to society.

Cultural legacies

The accountability approaches across our different contexts can be seen to link with fundamental cultural values about education. To the extent to which education is a commodity that can be bought and traded – school choice being a key indicator of this – so the accountability system appears to be hierarchical and market-oriented rather than peer/professional-oriented and humanistic. Finland easily exhibits the strongest valuing of education as a public good and human right where wellbeing and a cohesive, inclusive society are privileged over other priorities or are at least equal in status to achieving high academic standards. It demonstrates faith in the power of public education and according to one analyst exhibits an 'intelligent accountability' (Sahlberg, 2011).

To differentiate and distinguish one school from another in the name of transparency and school choice needs to be questioned as a mechanism since it most certainly distorts and severely detracts from the broader purpose of education. OECD's study of more than 200 research studies of the impact of markets in school education would seem to challenge the current emphasis in some countries– it concluded that, in contrast to the rationale frequently offered for competition, such an emphasis does not enhance teaching and learning and would seem to increase social segregation (Waslander et al., 2010). The challenge for such countries is to design an accountability system that promotes high standards and equity.

Almost a decade ago an OECD-commissioned study (McKinsey, 2007) concluded that one of the factors that matters most in 'best-performing school systems' is getting the right people to become teachers and once achieving that, developing them into the most effective instructors. As so frequently claimed by policy makers, the quality of an education system cannot exceed the quality of its teachers. If this is the case the continued reforms of structures like externally-set performance tests and the publication of their comparative results are unlikely to deliver the kind of high quality education system that apparently exists in Finland. Such approaches are bound to deter prospective candidates from entering the teaching profession and alienate those already in the profession, challenging both recruitment and retention. It is worth noting that the top 10 per cent of the cohort in Finland are recruited into the teaching profession and that their training is intensive, at master's level, and involves a strong integration of theory and practice. Teachers once trained are well paid, tend to remain in the profession, have good opportunities for continuing development, and are highly valued by society. Accountability in Finland is based on a different frame of reference: on responsibility and trust, professionalism and collaboration. It is not performance and data-driven but is absolutely clear about its remit of upholding standards of achievement on the one hand and equity on the other. Accountability in such a system can avoid an externally-imposed, test-based approach and can be grounded instead in expertise and the professional accountability of teachers who are knowledgeable, skilful and highly committed.

The next chapter acts as an extended conclusion to this one by teasing out the value of cultural script as a conceptual tool for thinking about assessment practice.

Questions

1. What might be the unintended consequences of privileging assessment for comparing individuals and systems?
2. What aspects of assessment are prioritised in your setting? How does assessment function to extend and constrain the agency of learners in your setting?
3. On the basis of the analysis in this chapter what changes would you want to make to the social order of assessment in your country?

3

CULTURAL SCRIPTS OF ASSESSMENT FOR PRACTICE: PREDICTABILITY, OUTCOMES AND LIFE CHANCES

Introduction

In this chapter we make a number of key points in relation to how we see assessment functioning across the countries represented in the previous chapter and we highlight key cultural scripts that would be expected inevitably to shape local practices. As we demonstrated, cultural scripts about assessment and accountability differ between countries and draw on different traditions in relation to understandings, priorities, and values to do with knowledge or subjects, learners, and curriculum as well as society more broadly.

Cultural scripts of assessment

Among the cultural scripts that are likely to mediate assessment practices are:

- assessment for ranking schools and individuals;
- assessment for holding systems to account and promoting efficiency;
- assessment for promoting achievement;
- assessment as accountancy/measurement and an accurate enterprise;
- assessment outcomes as individual / collective responsibilities.

Additional and associated cultural scripts include: education as a human right/private enterprise, school choice and the consumerist positioning of individuals, and notions of effective pedagogy. What 'forms of meaning' do these scripts legitimate? What do they offer that may mediate practice? How are practitioners being positioned or how might they experience themselves as positioned given these cultural scripts?

The fact that assessment functions to rank schools and individuals, as is the case in England, enables people to act on the world in a particular way and, as such become part of ongoing activity. One instance of this enactment arose for one of us during a research project on assessment many years ago (Hall, et al., 2004). Having conducted in-depth case studies in two Year-6 classrooms in urban schools and having agreed with some teacher participants to discuss some initial insights and share some video material we had recorded, the research team duly arranged a meeting at the local university. Coincidentally, the test results were out on the same day as our planned meeting. One of the teachers checked her pupils' results that morning before coming to the university. She was ecstatic in telling us that no pupil in her class had obtained less than a level three in any subject area, that the vast majority had attained the expected level for end of Key Stage 2 (level 4), and that a substantial minority had exceeded this level, obtaining a level 5. These results filled her with joy and, as far as she was concerned, totally vindicated her pedagogic style. However, the pedagogic style in question was one that privileged 'the test' to such an extent that little or no time was devoted to areas of the 'broad and balanced' curriculum that were not the subject of the testing regime. Moreover, the whole-class, competitive ethos of the classroom ensured that little space and time were available for students to exert much control or agency in terms of dialogue, peer-peer interaction or self-assessment. There was minimal negotiation of meaning or discussion of personal experiences or interpretations. Rather knowledge was assumed to be something inert that needed to be acquired and possessed and represented according to pre-determined summative assessment criteria.

Not only was there huge emphasis on 'teaching to the test' but teaching the test itself (as in past tests) consumed much of the teaching day during the months of April and May each year. This teacher was very enthusiastically compliant and utterly seduced by the desire of obtaining 'high standards' in the SATs. She was in no way resistant to the policy emphasis on assessment of 11-year-olds. Arguably she subscribes to an acquisitionist discourse: the kind of learner that is shaped and valued by the external assessment process in England is one who possesses the specified knowledge and who can reproduce it independently under traditional test conditions. It is highly likely that other teachers in her school differently emphasise assessment practices and confer different interpretations on the partiality of the assessment results which in turn would have consequences for individual children's learning and their experience of themselves as successful in school. It is likely that some teachers did devote time to allowing learners negotiate the meaning of assessment tasks perhaps in small groups with strong emphasis on dialogue and interaction and agreeing targets for their future learning. Since interpretations of individual assessment tasks cannot be anticipated, in other words it cannot be assumed that all those assessed will interpret the demands of the assessment task in the same way, then opportunities to talk about the task and to negotiate meaning would be crucial and would not constitute a threat to the validity of the process. On the contrary it would arguably enhance it because what students bring to the test in terms of beliefs and values would become part of the assessment process.

While this example may not be typical of practice, we use it to illustrate the rigidity with which the broader social order and this version of accountability exerted in one particular setting with consequences for the identities of both learners and teacher. In the research publication we were careful not to criticise the teacher's practice, rather the intention was to understand and explain the observed practice. It was important to appreciate that the teacher while certainly having agency was also shaped and constrained by the social order in various ways. The teacher's identity as a 'successful' teacher was enhanced and affirmed through her pupils' test results, gaining her status and respect certainly from her head-teacher and others in her community of practice.

Taking this example we can see how the social order and the individual are constituted. At the level of the social order you might imagine how in response to such lived representations about pedagogy and assessment, the school might adopt a policy of encouraging more test-oriented work given the high stakes nature of the assessments. At the level of the experienced world the cultural script taken up by schools might influence who is hired, who gets to teach the classes in the year the assessments occur. So at the level of practice this cultural script may emerge as the way the world ought to be. In this way the social order is affirmed and reproduced but it is important to note that this is not an inevitable process. What happens in practice depends on the lived experience of all the actors, and their previous histories of participation. Cultural scripts can be resisted and emerge in ongoing practice in various ways. cultural scripts can be resisted and emerge in ongoing practice in various ways. The teacher brings her experience of the world to bear on her practice so that the pedagogy, incorporating assessment, that is enacted is mediated by her subjectivity. And practice is further mediated by her learners' subjectivities and how they position themselves and are positioned in the moment-by-moment unfolding of human action.

Cultural scripts or theories about say inclusion (in the case especially of Finland) may restrict participation in some activities and enhance participation in others. Cultural scripts are useful for understanding how practice is organised and how people may be differently positioned to participate in a practice and so experience themselves as developing competence in it. Different positioning of course does not imply fixed positioning but rather that they afford and constrain particular ways of participating. The way ideas are taken up in communities of practice will influence people's opportunities to participate and belong to those communities.

We take on board Bruner's perspective that 'a choice of pedagogy inevitably communicates a conception of the learning process and the learner. Pedagogy is never innocent. It is a medium that carries its own message' (Bruner, 1996, p. 63). A sociocultural perspective on assessment recognises individual agency and history and that the enactor and the learners are enmeshed. The possibilities for learning are not limited to those made available by the enactor. Therefore, to understand assessment and pedagogy more generally we have to reflect on and study the way experience is organised and authorised, produced, reproduced and transformed in actual settings.

Those tasked with evaluating teachers and schools implicitly draw on theories of pedagogy and assessment. As symbolic tools that carry messages, official policy and frameworks are part of the ongoing political, social and economic structuring of meanings - versions of assessment are manifest in these texts, and these manifestations are variously negotiated, reproduced, and recreated as agents interpret and apply them in the present in their different settings and activities. We can think of inspection reports, in various countries, as reifications that project meanings about what effective pedagogy is, through portrayals of practice. As reifications, they seek to capture experiences and practices and pin them down in a fixed form which is used to guide and change practices (Wenger, 1998). Policies and evaluative accounts of schools draw on 'idealised' notions of effective and 'best' practice and implicit theories of assessment and pedagogy. However, as reifications they, inevitably, are incapable of capturing the richness of lived experience. We still have to focus on the lived realities of actual people, students and teachers, to appreciate the inter-personal and personal dimensions of assessment.

In a sociocultural perspective, participants (learners, teachers/mentors) act and negotiate their meanings in the course of engaging with particular tasks within particular sets of relations, roles, interests and expectations, and broader institutional practices and imperatives. This makes a universal notion of say 'effective pedagogy' or 'best practice' untenable and challenges the assumed direct connection between specified, prescribed or so-called effective teaching methods and learning.

A cultural phenomenon in recent times associated with the dominant cultural script of pedagogy is the enormous attention to raising standards in narrow aspects of literacy and numeracy which have been shown to influence what teachers emphasise and how they interact with learners (e.g. Brown *et al.*, 2003; Hall *et al.*, 2003) and have been shown in national and international statistics to result in increased levels of achievement in some assessed aspects (Mullis *et al.*, 2003). With reference to the enacted curriculum, a preoccupation with raising standards has also been shown to conflict with other Government agendas particularly that of inclusion. This highlights the gap between intentions and unintended effects of policies. There is, for instance, evidence pointing to some children's reduced participation when placed in whole-class or groupings by ability and assessment-dominated learning settings (where teaching to the test prevails) that characterise how some teachers and schools respond to the demands of raising standards (Hall *et al.*, 2004; Benjamin *et al.*, 2003) while there is a wealth of evidence documenting how schools negotiate alignments with the demands of external inspections (Gewirtz, 1997; Troman, 1997; Jeffrey and Woods, 2002). Research by Harry Torrance, in the context of workplace learning, at Manchester Metropolitan University shows that opportunities for participation, for moving deeper into practice are constrained by the explicitness of assessment criteria and learning objectives. Torrance's evidence would imply that matters of pedagogy are by-passed in the workplace in similar ways to schools in the rush to get the tick against competency criteria.

Conclusion

The main point from our analysis is that the social order mediates in various ways, but not necessarily always predictable ways, local actions and beliefs. Consequences arise for the identities of learners and teachers as well as for the perceptions of valued knowledge and its nature. If the goals of learning and the assessment criteria are predetermined allowing little (perceived) negotiation for those charged with their enactment, so how identities and how learning trajectories are shaped are variously impacted with consequences for life chances.

Question/task

How does the social order mediate assessment practice in your setting? Are assessment criteria handed over and not negotiated or are there opportunities to establish what learners see as salient? Boud *et al.* argues, that in sustainable assessment learners need to be able to establish their own goals for learning if they are to imagine themselves as lifelong learners, and therefore, need to be engaged in this through assessment rather than being given standards which separates the locus of control from them. How might different practices and views of assessment produce different kinds of learners? How might the handing down of standards without negotiation impact the notion of knowledge and learning as a commodity?

4

JUNIOR CYCLE REFORM: THE NEGOTIATED NATURE OF ASSESSMENT POLICY IN IRELAND

This chapter will address assessment through the specific context of Ireland during the period of 2012 to 2018 as this time represents a pivotal point in the socio-political history of the development of assessment in Ireland. We will provide a brief history of curriculum and assessment reform at junior cycle level in Ireland as it provides a contemporary prism for debate around assessment of learning in a post-primary context. The process of revising the Junior Cycle (12–15-year-olds) post-primary curriculum is an example of just how entrenched education is within the social, cultural and political milieu of a place. Assessment, and most particularly summative assessment, has become ingrained into the sociocultural fabric of many countries. Assessment has contributed to considerable tensions in terms of the purpose of assessment within education systems and the wider socio-political sphere. In this chapter, we will examine the process of curricular reform in Ireland at the level of the state, and how assessment became a political battleground that provides an example of how policy is never just written. We will show how policy is negotiated, advocated for by some, opposed by others, and evolutionary in nature. We will then focus specifically on the subject of English as this was the first subject to be reformed and therefore at the centre of much of the public and political debate. Stephen Ball's work on policy analysis, amongst others, will be used here as an orientating device to inform the discussion of junior cycle policy reformation (Ball, 1993; Ball, Maguire and Braun, 2012).

In Ireland, the revised junior cycle curriculum statement, *Framework for Junior Cycle* (2015), has emerged as a controversial and contested cultural artefact of assessment. Indeed, it is this cultural status as a rite of passage, and the position as a pre-cursor to the highest of high stakes Leaving Certificate Examination, that has contributed to resistances in terms of shifting towards a perceived low stakes assessment at the midpoint of post-primary schooling. In order to interpret the significance of this summative assessment, it is necessary to understand the cultural and historical development of the examination. In this chapter, we will outline the background and emergence of the junior cycle curriculum (lower secondary school). We will also engage with some policy analysis of the current junior cycle reform of assessment in order to interrogate its significance in terms of national and international practices in assessment at post-primary level. The subject of English, being the first subject to change under the current process of junior cycle reform in Ireland, will be a later focus of this chapter as it is within this space that the contested and political nature of assessment bubbles to the surface of public debate. As Ball, Maguire and Braun (2012, p. 3) have stated:

> Policy is done by and to teachers; they are actors and subjects, subject to and objects of policy. Policy is written onto bodies and produces particular subject positions.

Ball *et al.*'s point is well-made. Policy is not distinct from any particular population but rather entwined within the fabric of our worlds. We make and do policy as much as it is made and done upon us. In the instance of junior cycle reform in Ireland the 'subject positions' taken up during the period of reform extending from 2012 to 2018 (the time of writing) have often been polarised in opinion, not always entirely on the issue of curriculum change, but most particularly on the issue of assessment change. Indeed, assessment of the junior cycle has proven to be one of the most disputed curricular reforms in Irish education history. This chapter offers some perspectives on the assessment debate as it rages on in Irish post-primary education with the intention of throwing some light on the politicised and fractured nature of opinion and voice on this issue. It is intended that this discussion, although specific to Ireland, holds relevance internationally as education systems throughout the world experience educational change and reform on a continuous basis. It is also our intention to focus on the culturally-specific context of Ireland as education, and most particularly summative assessment moments at post-primary level, have come to be significant moments on media, educational and political calendars. Indeed, O'Donoghue, Gleeson and McCormack (2017) make a specific study on the growing centrality of summative examinations, primarily the Leaving Certificate but also the Junior Certificate, instantiated by the media maelstrom surrounding these events. They point to how it is not only the reporting of results that is a focus of attention but examination content fuelled by 'expert' analysis on a daily basis during the examination period (the month of June in Ireland). It is difficult to pinpoint the reasons for this developmental curve towards the media hysteria that now exists around the Leaving Certificate but it is certainly entwined within the contemporary *zeitgeist* of education as a marketised, individualised and commodified space where success is bound up with representations of school quality and individual achievement. Indeed, young people, and most particularly post-primary school-leavers, have so much of their externally interpreted identity bound up in school performance and perceptions of success and achievement.

Stephen Ball's (1993) policy analysis toolbox consisting of *policy as text, policy as discourse* and *policy effects* are useful here in our endeavours to understand the intricacies of policy change. These tools will help us to unpack the 'localised complexity' of post-primary school assessment policy enactment in twenty-first century Ireland (Ball, 1993, p. 10; Ball, Maguire and Braun, 2012). *Policy as text* refers to the production and existence of an artefact, a document, a set of guidelines that have their own history of negotiation and production. Policies are produced in multiple iterations with inputs and negotiations from various policy actors who are deemed important voices in the policy construction process. For our purposes here, policy can be taken as the wider junior cycle framework as well as the particular artefacts of the English curriculum specification and the associated assessment documents. *Policy as discourse* then refers to the ongoing interaction and negotiation between the policy actors as curriculum reform passes through the muddied waters of public and political territory. Ball (1993) drew on Foucault to emphasise that discourses 'are not about objects; they do not identify objects, they constitute them and in the practice of doing conceal their own invention' (Foucault, 1977, p. 49). Ball continued to emphasise that policy is open to destabilisation, opposition, acceptance, ridicule and the imposition of confusion. The interesting aspects of the current reform experience in Ireland is that it seems to provoke all of the above responses. There is as much diversity of opinion and practice emerging as there is opposition to change. This recognition of the innately social, cultural, political and illusory nature of policy construction is important here as we map the emergence of the junior cycle as it now stands. Of course, our view of the policy change arena is very much dependent upon our metaphorical angle of sight upon it. Our view of it as a teacher may differ significantly from that of an academic, whose view may differ still from the perspective of the Inspectorate or the Department of Education and Skills. Indeed, Ball, Maguire and Braun (2012) have developed a useful typology of policy actors that might help us to navigate these viewpoints; a typology that has been usefully deployed and developed by Golding (2017) in her study of curriculum and assessment change of the General Certificate of Secondary Education (GCSE) in England. Indeed, Golding's work provides some useful insights that help in the development of this analysis of assessment change in Ireland. Ball, Maguire and Braun's (2012, p. 49) typology is extended below to apply to the Irish context of junior cycle reform.

Golding (2017) suggests the addition of policy 'survivors' to the typology as many teachers, most particularly, survive policy change through their endurance and adaptability in the face of the challenges of change. We would suggest that *resistors, adopters* and *adapters* would also be useful additions to the typology. The recent Irish experience has shown that there is certainly resistance to policy change and the act of resistance becomes an embodied identity. This position of the *resistor* has become largely associated with the stance of the teaching unions, and most particularly the Association of Secondary Teachers of Ireland (ASTI). Similarly, some teachers promoted, accepted and adopted the new curriculum and they could be described as *adopters*. Others still, found a middle ground as they negotiated change, they may have accepted curriculum change and yet made many, or indeed

TABLE 4.1 Policy actors

Policy actors	Policy work
Narrators	Interpretation, selection and enforcement of meanings
Entrepreneurs	Advocacy, creativity and integration
Outsiders	Entrepreneurship, partnership and monitoring
Transactors	Accounting, reporting, monitoring/supporting and facilitating
Enthusiasts	Investment, creativity, satisfaction and career
Translators	Production of texts, artefacts and events
Critics	Union representatives: monitoring of management, maintaining counter-talk
Receivers	Coping, defending and dependency
Survivors (Golding, 2017)	Endurance, adaptability
Resistors (our addition)	Resisting, obfuscating, objecting, refusing
Adopters (our addition)	Accepting, using, complying
Adapters (our addition)	Changing, adapting, compromising

Source: adapted from Ball, Maguire and Braun, 2012; Golding, 2017

few, adjustments in terms of the transaction of the curriculum in the classroom. In other words, they are adapters of both the curriculum and their practice to make change manageable and accessible for them in the cultural microcosms of their classrooms and schools. These positions will be discussed further below.

It would appear that at least two opposing camps that emerged in relation to assessment in this instance were formed, ostensibly, on ideological grounds. The teaching unions led a campaign of resistance based on the foundational belief that externally administered state assessment of students was the fairest, most valid and reliable form of assessment available. This view takes knowledge as an internalised and individual possession that can be readily examined and graded as a representation of a student's attainment that is both measurable against, and comparable to, the individualised performance of one's peer group. The comparable aspect of the state examination process in Ireland is open to critique in terms of representing a bell-curve approach to marking and grading, although such arguments are open to contestation. It is the case that year-on-year grade bands stay largely within the range of previous years, although some evidence of grade inflation also exists in this regard. It could be argued that this position has been culturally produced as the previous generations experienced and promoted the state examinations as the pinnacle of educational achievement throughout the decades since the introduction of free post-primary education in 1967. Donagh O'Malley, as the then Minister of Education in Ireland, opened up the promise of opportunity through the promise of meritocracy where all citizen-children were free to compete for educational credentials through the state examinations system. Little did Minister O'Malley know of how far that competition would inscribe itself upon the psyche of an Irish population hungry now for self-improvement and opportunity as the emerging nation-state struggled to make real the post-colonial promise of economic freedom and independent thought. Leaving aside for a moment the innate inequalities of any assessment system that favours particular knowledges (in this case classical academic knowledge and skills), external and seemingly unbiased state assessment of achievement appealed to our burgeoning sense of equality of opportunity in a post-colonial state that still remembered what it meant to be of lesser value and to exist in servitude to a foreign master in our role as colony in the globalising British Empire. Assessment was indeed seen as a gateway to freedom and even escape from poverty as well as, possibly, a chance to throw off the ideological shackles of church and state. However, as Ireland developed through the late twentieth century, increasing mobility through the opening of economic and physical borders shaped schooling into a highly competitive space where the credentials of the state examinations (dominantly, the Leaving Certificate) promised third level entry and the ensuing earning power to enable survival in the maelstrom of global capitalism sweeping through global western society. The state examinations then, as the catalyst for the individual to achieve and succeed, become detached from the more holistic and ideological aims of education, and more closely aligned with discourses around skills, competencies, comparability, employability and marketability.

Simultaneously, there was (and continues to be) a growing responsibilisation of the learner, the teacher and the school to perform in the comparative realm of the state examination. Torrance (2017) makes particular reference to the connections between neoliberalisation of education and the responsibilisation of learners where the individual is responsible for their own success/ failure in the education game. Torrance (2017 cites Lemke (2001, pp. 199–201)) who describes students as 'entrepreneurs of themselves' who are forging their own individual routes to personal success through the school and the state examination system. Similarly then, as day leads on to night, failure is also the responsibility of the individual child, their family and their school. Indeed, Torrance (2017, p. 89) points out that long-standing deficit views of populations (such as the working class) often marginalised by the examination system are being repositioned whereby '(lack of) responsibility has replaced (lack of) intelligence as the key explanatory variable in educational success and failure'. This responsibilisation transfers to teachers and schools in the macro-marketplace of international educational comparisons and the various micro-markets of school league tables, competitive third level entry systems and connecting 'good exam results' with being a 'good person', as if in some way being successful in school confers the learner with respectability, morality and an innate goodness of middle-classness (Sayer, 2005). It is not now a case of what one has learned in terms of skills and knowledge but rather what one has learned in comparison with one's peers. It would appear that debate about a continuing reliance on bell-curve marking ensures that success is a comparative and competitive entity, rather than something that is available to everyone (Murray and Herrnstein, 1994). This epitomises neoliberal principles of the market which presupposes that winners require losers in order to reify their position on top of the pile. Diane Reay (2017) makes it clear that competitive testing and assessment regimes are inherently classed and that they serve to disadvantage the working-class student body. Any analysis of student performance here in Ireland contains similar indicators (Smyth *et al.*, 2015). The assessment regimes here in Ireland are distinctly classed artefacts in terms of the outcomes for students. Students from middle-class homes consistently outperform their working class peers in the Irish state examination system (as they do elsewhere in the word also). Smyth *et al.* (2015), drawing upon the work of Weir, McAvinue and O'Flaherty (2014) identified a consistent achievement gap in the performance of students in school serving less-advantaged communities in comparison to their equivalents in more advantaged communities. Their study calculated Overall Performance Scores (OPS) based on junior certificate examination results from 2002–2011. Despite there being a significant rise on performance across all students, Weir *et al.* (2014) recognised a significant performance difference between DEIS and non-DEIS schools. However, they also recognised a significant impact in terms of improving OPS for schools benefitting from the School Support Programme (SSP) for schools serving less advantaged communities. Nevertheless, the achievement gap remains and the complexity of narrowing the gap between educational performance, and the inextricable link to the wealth and poverty indexes, remains a challenge to education systems across the globe.

It is against this cultural backdrop of competitive individualism, so heavily reliant on the external state assessment, that junior cycle reform would sail into choppy waters with its revolutionary ideas around school-based and teacher-graded assessment. Of course, there are problematic possibilities here also with regard to fairness and reliability but more of that later. Let us turn to the detail of junior cycle reform as it has emerged since its inception in 2012.

A brief history of reform

Prior to 2012, all post-primary school students in Ireland undertook a summative assessment at the end of their third year. Each subject they studied was assessed through an examination set and marked by the State Examinations Commission in several core compulsory subjects (English, Irish, Mathematics, History, Geography, Civic Social and Political Education (CSPE), Social Personal Health Education (SPHE), Science and a modern foreign language) and any elective subjects that students chose to study during their three years in junior cycle. Most subjects deployed a final examination, conducted in June of each year, that accounted for one hundred per cent of the student's achievements in that subject area. However, several subjects have been employing partial project-based assessments. For instance, Art, Home Economics and CSPE all contained tasks that were pre-submitted and completed during the school year. These assessment artefacts would then either be sent to the State Examinations Commission (SEC) for assessment or an assigned external examiner would visit the school and mark the work *in situ*. Therefore, the proposed shift towards classroom-based assessments (CBA) is not as large a leap as is sometimes intimated in the wider arguments on the issue. Indeed, the largest leap would seem to have been that presented to the teaching profession as they were moving from a position of supporter and ally against the 'big brother'-type representation on the State Examinations Commission (SEC). The shift to teacher as assessor, as will be discussed later, was the leap at which communication broke down in the brokering of policy.

Historically, the junior cycle assessment moment may have been more significant as it would have signalled the last opportunity for some students to gain a state-awarded statement of achievement and therefore it was used to delineate minimum requirements for some career choices. It is still the case that junior cycle achievements are used as a requirement for some career courses such as apprenticeships (plumbing, electricians, bricklayers, etc.). However, given recent trends in Ireland, for students to progress to senior cycle and indeed to complete post-primary education, the junior cycle has become less significant as a summative assessment moment in terms of its place on the educational trajectory for many young people. There are still, however, a significant cohort of students who do not progress to sit the Leaving Certificate (terminal post-primary examination) and leave formal schooling with the penultimate post-primary award that will be known into the future as the Junior Cycle Profile of Achievement (JCPA). The latest known statistics from Irish Department of Education and Skills reveal that 90.2 per cent of students complete the Leaving Certificate (terminal school-leaving examination) and that almost 10 per cent of students do not reach this final hurdle. This 10 per cent is also skewed significantly towards students from lower socio-economic groups. For instance, if we look at schools serving less advantaged areas the retention rate falls to 82.7 per cent and of course there are many areas and schools whose rate would be far below that figure. This class-based inequality is a very significant concern and it is also something worthy of consideration in the context of assessment reform. In Ireland, as in other countries, there has been a consistent and enduring achievement gap in post-primary state examinations mirroring social class inequality.

In October 2012, then Minister for Education and Skills in Ireland, Ruairi Quinn TD, launched *A Framework for Junior Cycle* (DES, 2012; 2015). This document provided the structures for the reform of junior cycle post-primary education in Ireland. It also heralded the beginning of one of the most turbulent periods of industrial relations in the history of state-teacher union relations in Ireland. Junior cycle reform was not the only contributing factor to these industrial disputes, however it has continued to feature as one strand of the argument, along with opposition to the severe austerity impositions placed on teachers (and public servants broadly) in the aftermath of the economic crash of 2008. Indeed the manner of change, as it was perceived, as a top-down ministerial dictum also contributed to the oppositional nature of change right form the very beginning. Minister Quinn chose to impose rather than negotiate reform and as such the battle-lines had been drawn between the teaching unions and the state. Given the one-way nature of the instigation of junior cycle reform policy, perhaps we could add *policy dictator* to our earlier typology. Quinn, ostensibly a Labour party Minister for Education, has proven to be quite controversial in terms of his own ideological stances. Most recently (as of 2017) Minister Quinn was announced as a member of the advisory board of the Nord Anglia International School in Dublin, a fully private school offering an alternative to state assessment through the International Baccalaureate at the princely fee of €8,000 per term. Such a move would be considered surprising for a stalwart of the Labour party which would declare itself (on paper at least) as a left-leaning political entity where one might imagine private forms of elite schooling would go against the over-arching political philosophy of inclusive democracy and equality.

Nevertheless, in Quinn's wake, Junior Cycle reform in Ireland continued to be a contentious and contested space in political and educational arenas with contrasting positions being taken on several issues, not least of which is assessment. The *A Framework for Junior Cycle* has instigated teacher-led assessment where there was once an external state examination. This has caused some difficulty for teachers in terms of a re-orientation of role from advocate for, and ally with the students in their engagements with the state examinations to a role of assessor. Teacher unions have argued, some more vehemently than others, that this changed role will ultimately be detrimental to the teacher-student relationship. In this sense the post-primary teacher unions took up the role of *policy resistors* and *policy critics* throughout the process. For example, the following comments from some of the teacher unions in relation to the changed assessment practices in English exemplify the ferocity of opposition to policy change in this instance.

In March 2017 one post-primary teaching union issued a position statement outlining opposition to junior cycle reform and most particularly assessment, where they stated that:

> under the new Junior Cycle your child will be, in part, assessed by their teacher, not an independent, transparent system.
>
> Teachers should be teachers, not judges.
>
> Every student is entitled to a fair, impartial and transparent evaluation of their learning efforts. Your child's teacher's role is to champion, coach and support your child to maximise their potential. If the teacher participates in the Junior Cycle exam, assessment and grading processes, the child-teacher relationship is fundamentally damaged. As part of the new Junior Cycle, students must complete Classroom Based Assessments which are assessed by their own teachers and feed into the Junior Cycle Profile of Achievement. The ASTI believes teachers should have no role in their students' formal Junior Cycle assessment and grades. It will change relations between teacher and student from supportive to judgemental.
>
> *(ASTI, 2017)*

These statements construct a clear separation between the role of the teacher as 'champion, coach and support' in opposition to the role of the assessor, previously an external *other* in the guise of the State Examinations Commission (SEC), as the judge of student learning. These are strong and emotive statements and indeed ones that could draw empathy and agreement from many quarters. We would all like to imagine teachers as the supports, scaffolding and allies of our children as they encounter the joyous challenges that formal education offers them through their school experiences. It is in these words and statements that the position of teacher union as *resistor* is most firmly evidenced. The ASTI, in particular, developed other arguments against the orientation of junior cycle reform in terms of the curriculum-as-product approach inherent in the development of a *learning outcomes* approach to curriculum. Indeed, there is significant international debate around the learning outcomes approach and what can be lost in the enactment of curriculum. Brancaleone and O'Brien (2011) suggest that the shift towards the language of learning outcomes represents a commodification and materialisation of the educational relationship that they trace back through the 'Bologna process' where higher education began a transition towards a Europe-wide shift outcomes-based framing and specification of education. This position on the constraining nature of the outcomes frame has also been described by Priestley and Drew (2016, p. 3) as the 'pervasive output regulation of teachers' work'. There may well be an important message in the resistance position of the union here around guarding against the neoliberal materialisation of perceiving education as an input-output exchange that over-simplifies the complex dynamics of learning and experience. Priestley and Drew (2016) also draw on Gert Biesta's (2004) approach to preserving and developing teacher agency, something that is at risk in an environment dominated by the aforementioned focus on exchange, outputs and micro-accountabilities facilitated by an over-specific learning outcomes framework.

However, there is another side to that coin, one explored by important research on educational experiences of Irish post-primary students throughout their post-primary education. Smyth *et al.* (2007) conducted an important study with 900 post-primary school students as they made their way through post-primary school. Each year of post-primary school was reported separately and the third year, or 'junior cert' year, report had some interesting interpretations of how assessment had a significant influence on student experience, pedagogy, student outcomes in the junior certificate examination based on ability grouping, differential outcomes based on socio-economic status and increased disengagement from school. Of course, issues such as ability grouping are directly related to the existence of the high stakes externally assessed examination where schools feel compelled to divide students into levels and classes to match the teaching they perceive as appropriate to achievement at that level (higher, ordinary and foundation in the old junior certificate system). Similarly, the report found some decline in student attitudes towards school compared to earlier reports of their experiences of first year and second year in post-primary school (Smyth, McCoy and Darmody, 2004; Smyth *et al.*, 2006). Participants reported that teachers became stricter and created more pressure through an increased focus on the external examination. The aptly named third report in this ESRI series, *Gearing up for the exam?: The experience of junior certificate students* (Smyth *et al.*, 2007), developed findings specific to the experiences and opinions of students on the junior certificate examination. The report found that:

- The junior certificate was viewed as a dry-run for the high stakes leaving certificate.
- Students from working class backgrounds viewed it as more of a high stakes examination as it could be used for entry to apprenticeships.
- More students stated a preference for continuous assessment and 'hands-on' assessment opportunities.
- The examination seemed to make a considerable contribution to schools' decisions to stream students according to ability.

These findings would appear to have borne particular significance in the development of the *Framework for Junior Cycle* (2012; 2015) where considerable efforts were made to address these significant points, most particularly through the reform of assessment practices.

Another expressed fear of the teaching unions would be that teachers will come under unfair and undue pressure from parents and other family members as they go about their daily lives in the communities in which they teach. They argue that they are at risk of being compromised by the local nature of arrangements in Irish society where small rural communities and relatively small urban communities mean that people are more connected to the communities in which they teach. The teacher union argument rests upon the fact that if a teacher is marking junior cycle assessments for their own students that will contribute to external state certification then these teachers are open to influence and undue pressure from other agencies, parents in particular. The union argument extrapolates the sense that middle class populations and schools will maintain higher scores in this system where teachers mark their own students and that students in schools where the cohort come from a less wealthy socioeconomic grouping, where there is less parental influence on school culture, would fall further behind in the assessment 'game', to use Bourdieu's metaphor. This argument is countered by the professionalism stance, stating that teaching is a profession and therefore teachers should be, and are, best-placed to act as the assessors of student work, particularly at junior level where the examination is not high stakes. There is certainly international precedence and evidence of practice where teachers act as the assessors of their students work for the purposes of state certification, some of which will be discussed below. Nevertheless, what is clear is that assessment is a controversial and emotive topic in Ireland and here the country's current assessment dilemmas will be used as a lens to explore some wider debates around assessment.

Looney, Cumming, van Der Kleij and Harris (2018) have undertaken significant work in terms of classifying and constructing teachers as assessors through the concept of teacher assessment identity. This work knits with the Irish context in that there is a recognition of the personal, professional and political context of teachers as assessors. In a sociocultural sense, teachers are made and re-made by their own personal experiences of assessment as students, their professional context and the wider socio-political context. Looney *et al.* (2018) conceptualise teacher assessment identity as a mesh of beliefs, dispositions and professional experiences in terms of how they view and enact assessment practice. In the Irish context, this sense of a social-cultural-historical context from which teacher identities come into being is relevant here also. There is a sense that the teacher may be wedded to the state examination system which rewarded the teacher through recognition of achievement, college entry and a rewarding career. Education has a habit of being reproductive in terms of the people and the kinds of knowledge and skills it has been known to confer with success (Bourdieu and Passerson, 1990; Kennedy and Power, 2010).

There is certainly some related research debate around approaches to pedagogy and its contribution to inequality. Basil Bernstein's influential sociological accounts of restricted codes and elaborated codes are rooted in issues of access, participation and benefit from schooling (Bernstein, 1973). Bernstein, like Bourdieu, emphasised the importance of class-based cultural resources and their contribution to school success. Bernstein referred to 'visible pedagogies' and 'invisible pedagogies' to make a point about the possible latent inequalities in a teacher or school's choice of pedagogy for students (Bernstein, 1975). This is entirely relevant to the space of summative assessment practices such as externally imposed examinations which are open to 'gaming' at the hands of examination candidates and their families. Smyth (2009) emphasised the existence of 'shadow education' amongst privileged state examinations candidates from middle class families who pay for extensive private tuition to improve their performance in the state examinations (most particularly the Leaving Certificate). Bray and Kwo (2013) emphasise how terminal examination systems like that in Ireland facilitate the functioning of this privatised shadow market that feeds off public education system as the middle-classes skew this 'fair' system in their favour. Similarly, the space of classroom-based assessment, where the teacher acts as the primary assessor, is equally open to manipulation by the candidature (as is discussed below).

Mirror, mirror on the wall, who is the fairest of them all?

This shadow education research throws significant question marks over the construction of fairness attached to the externally assessed anonymous state examinations. Gipps and Stobart (2009, p. 31) ask the question:

Can we make an assessment system that is fair to all learners?

They answer their question with a qualified 'no – but we can make it fairer'. Gipps and Stobart (2009, p. 34) suggest that good assessment should be:

- using assessment that supports learning and reflection, including formative assessment with feedback;
- designing assessment that is open and linked to clear criteria (rather than relying upon competition with others);

- including a range of assessment strategies so that all learners have a chance to perform well.

This summation of developing fairer assessment practices is particularly relevant to the discourse surrounding junior cycle reform in Ireland as teacher unions (resistors), political stakeholders (narrators), policy writers (translators) and other stakeholders debate the pros and cons of systemic assessment change in Ireland. We will now shift our attention to the specific case of English as the first subject to change under the junior cycle reform agenda. By focusing on one particular subject area, we hope to crystallise the debate around junior cycle reform through one specific lens.

The case of junior cycle English

Junior cycle reform has made significant movements towards disrupting the traditional culture of assessment in Ireland by moving towards multiple assessment moments which are more situated in practice and experience than had previously been the case. English has been the first subject to be reformed in terms of both curriculum and assessment and therefore it has been the site of much struggle and contestation for the teachers of the subject and at a more macro level of political contestation between teacher unions and the Department of Education and Skills. Indeed, English has blazed a lonesome trail through the re-imagining of junior cycle education in Ireland. It has been to the foreground of debate and industrial action, most particularly with regard to assessment.

In the originating iteration of 2014, the new English assessment was to be configured as follows.

As is evident from Table 4.2 below, this original iteration of assessment in English was a hybrid version of assessment where the State Examinations Commission and the individual teacher would assess different elements of the programme and their results would then be combined to form the overall judgement for the student. However, due to significant industrial action, up to and including withdrawal of service and picketing of schools, a re-negotiation of the assessment process was undertaken. At this point one of the two teaching unions agreed to proceed with

TABLE 4.2 English assessment arrangements, 2014

Type of assessment	Percentage weighting	Assessor
Terminal two-hour examination (higher and ordinary level)	60%	State Examinations Commission
CBA: Oral Communication	15%	Teacher
CBA: Collection of Student's Texts	25%	Teacher

TABLE 4.3 Final version of English assessment arrangements, 2017

Type of assessment	Percentage weighting	Assessor	Reporting
Terminal two-hour examination (higher and ordinary level)	90%	State Examinations Commission	In Junior Cycle Profile of Achievement (JCPA) as grade for English
Assessment task (to be completed in school)	10%	State Examinations Commission	
Oral Communication	n.a.	Teacher	In JCPA under a separate section for CBAs
Collection of Texts	n.a.	Teacher	

the teaching and assessment of English under the above dual assessment configuration.

As is visible from the above (Tables 4.2 and 4.3) there has been a significant re-negotiation of the assessment procedure from the instigation of the curriculum specification to the assessment of the first cohort to complete it and be assessed (a three-year cycle) in 2017. The most significant change is that the CBAs now exist as a separate assessment entity to the state examination paper that will be marked and reported upon using different criteria to those being applied to the externally set and administered examination paper and associated assessment task. Both assessments, by the state and by the school, will be reported in the Junior Cycle Profile of Achievement (JCPA) report to be issued to students upon completion of the junior cycle phase of post-primary education. Table 4.4 below provides an overview of the marks and standards being applied in this dual model of assessment.

Significantly, the classroom-based assessments (CBA) designed in the new English curriculum specification address the re-positioning and foregrounding of oral language through an Oral Communication task. The second CBA addresses the development of process writing opportunities through the Collection of Texts as students have the opportunity to show the processes and revisions involved in the production of two

TABLE 4.4 Grading system for junior cycle

Junior Cycle Grades as marked by the State Examinations Commission	Classroom-based assessments: features of quality
Distinction: 90%–100 %	Exceptional
Higher merit: 75%–89%	Above expectations
Merit: 55%–74%	In line with expectations
Achieved: 40%–54%	Yet to meet expectations
Partially achieved: 20%–39%	
Not graded (NG): 0%–19%	

exemplar texts that they have decided to put forward for assessment. Both of these CBAs address issues that have long exercised teachers of English: rewarding the processes of writing and recognising the centrality of oral communication to English as a subject.

These CBAs are designed to be assessed by the subject teachers in the school, however, there is currently some controversy in this regard with one of the two dominant post-primary teaching unions opting not to engage with the assessment reforms. The argument here centres upon teachers not wishing to examine their own students for certification purposes as they argue it compromises their role as advocate and ally of the student in meeting the challenges of the exam as well as complicating community relationships by putting them in the position of known assessor as opposed to the anonymity of the previous state examination.

The CBAs are still summative assessment moments, however they are far more contextualised in terms of happening within the space of the young people's normal school lives as opposed to being formed as an externalised event which has often been perceived (largely mistakenly) as an abrupt event with life-changing consequences. There is some considerable student agency over the content of the assessment as they choose the topic for their oral communication and the pieces of writing to be submitted as their 'collection of texts' assessment piece. This shift to some level of student agency over assessment is both welcome and necessary and will contribute to shifting the culture of teaching in Irish schools further towards student- centred pedagogies aligned with appropriately chosen curricular materials and assessments. Indeed, the subject of English is well placed for such transitions.

Lenihan, Hinchion and Laurenson (2016) provide a clear rationale and evidence for change in junior cycle English, specifically in relation to the renewed emphasis on oral communication in both classroom experience and assessment. They refer to empirical data generated with 26 teachers of English where support for the inclusion of an oral language assessment is evidenced. Lenihan *et al.* (2016) also note, however, the depth of resistance from a teaching profession demoralised by salary reductions, widespread sectoral cutbacks and a perceived lack of support from ministerial ranks for their practice. Again, as discussed earlier, there is a conflation of issues here where curriculum and assessment decisions are being heavily influenced by the wider socio-political context of the country.

MacPhail, Halbert and O'Neill (2018) point out that the underpinning approach to the reform of assessment at junior cycle level is to turn attention away from the junior cycle as a summative moment and shift it towards a more formative low stakes experience where there would be greater connections between learning and assessment in the classroom. As mentioned earlier, the difficulties here lie in shifting the ingrained cultural expectations of external state assessment as the pre-eminent form of assessment in Ireland. Nevertheless, the junior cycle reform process has now moved forward in a dual assessment system, as mapped through the *Joint Statement on Principles on Principles and Implementation* (2015) where both post-primary teacher unions and the Department of Education and Skills created a co-constructed conciliatory position on assessment. It is this document, primarily, that has led to the dual assessment and reporting system now evident in the Junior

TABLE 4.5 JCPA grade descriptors and CBAs features of quality

JCPA grade descriptors	Classroom-based assessments: features of quality
Distinction (90%–100%)	Exceptional
Higher Merit (75%–89%)	Above expectations
Merit (55%–74%)	In line with expectations
Achieved (40%–54%)	
Partially achieved (20%–39%)	Yet to meet expectations
Not graded (0%–19%)	

Cycle Profile of Achievement (JCPA). Under the JCPA, subject grade descriptors will be used and reported separately from the CBAs. The CBAs also employ a different grading structure (as outlined in Table 4.5 above).

This dual system of reporting on formal assessment, external and school-based does have the potential to be confusing for all parties in the assessment process and is an example of how policy sometimes gets negotiated into complexity because of the requirements to meet the needs of the various actors engaged in the construction process. How this reformed assessment policy comes to be enacted in practice is the next phase of interest for all concerned. Various questions circulate the policy arena, crucially: will school-based and state-based assessments be given parity of esteem by key stakeholders (students, teachers and parents)? It remains to be seen how this tension will play out in the following years as more and more subjects continue to experience reform of curriculum and assessment up to 2020. The initial years of the reformed junior cycle will be important in terms of how new assessment practices are received, translated and enacted by school communities, and indeed by wider audiences.

What junior cycle reform has taught us is that assessment is a complicated, subjective and contested activity that raises more questions about the recognition, quantification and validity of school performance. In fact, assessment continues to be a socioculturally constructed activity that belies easy definition and transaction because it is a complex human activity. This chapter, through the lens of policy analysis, has mapped out the history and present of junior cycle reform in Ireland in order to attempt to unpack the innate messiness of this human activity, as well as to contextualise how various actors representing the state, schools, families and schools are locked in the negotiation of assessment practice. We have attempted to illustrate, through the case of Ireland, how national assessment policy change is slow and complex. It also, as has been demonstrated here, has the potential to be co-opted into agendas, educational and otherwise, as education policy is often less about learning and more about demonstrating performance, accountability and sorting populations for economic purposes. What has yet to emerge from the junior cycle reform saga in Ireland relates to the experiences, and consequences for, the young people who are subject to the assessments. Will they survive assessment policy reform and how will their experiences benefit from the changes discussed here? Barrance and Elwood (2018) have noted the fundamental importance of including and considering student voice in assessment change in Northern Ireland and Wales. Perhaps similar consideration could be given in the Irish context to expand the policy actors to include those most central to the work of assessment, the students themselves.

Prompts for discussion

Teachers assessing their own students raises significant questions about the contextual and relational aspects to assessment. The experiences around policy change outlined in this chapter highlight how assessment is an intensely political act that has far-reaching consequences for students, teachers, systems and the relationships between them. Consider the following prompts for discussion:

- Assessment policy change can be a divisive and contentious process. Discuss what actors have influence over assessment policy change in your area of education. What voices carry more influence? Why might this be the case?
- Discuss the advantages and disadvantages of teacher-based assessment in your context.

5

PERSPECTIVES ON SOCIAL JUSTICE AND ASSESSMENT: TESTING, SOCIAL CLASS AND OPPORTUNITY TO LEARN

Introduction

For the purpose of this chapter, assessment is being taken up as a euphemism for testing. The authors are fully aware of wider interpretations but here the focus is upon how assessment impacts upon issues of social justice and the wider cultural meanings and uses pertaining to the assessment of learning. Assessment can have a significant impact upon opportunities to learn when it is so heavily weighted with comparative import and fixed, insular notions of ability and attainment. Assessment is one of the vehicles through which social and cultural reproduction of inequality in education happens. It can have a significant impact in relation to the experiences and outcomes of education in terms of race, gender, social class, ability and other potentials for marginalisation. Therefore, assessment as a concept needs considered treatment through a social justice lens. This chapter will focus on ways in which assessment practices and social (in)justice issues come to be constituted in education settings. As we have stated earlier in this book, collective and individual meaning making are inseparable and this is absolutely the case when we shine a social justice light upon assessment practice. The primary focus here is upon how socioeconomic status, or social class, impacts upon opportunities to learn and how assessment moments often act as gatekeeping mechanisms to filter these educational opportunities based on performance. The assessment moments used below are primarily moments of testing and summative performance as opposed to assessment of the infused and everyday kind that is the focus of other chapters in this book.

Assessment is often viewed through the triad of reliability, validity and fairness. Significant scholarly work has examined assessment through the lenses of validity and reliability (Carmines and Zeller, 1979; Gronlund, 1998; Kelly, 2009) where the focus has been upon how the construction of assessments is valid (offers a measurement or judgement on what it has been designed to assess) and reliable (offers consistency across participants). Fairness, on the other hand, is often the more neglected leg of the triad and therefore this chapter intends to examine assessment practices in terms of equity, fairness and social justice. Some significant work on fairness and assessment has been produced over recent decades (Gipps and Murphy, 1994; Gipps and Stobart, 2009; Broadfoot 1996; Klenowski, 2014). Klenowski (2014, p. 2) makes the point about the ever-increasing focus on standardised assessment, whilst not necessarily harmful on its own, can also be co-opted by 'second order purposes' where there can be significant unintended consequences in terms of outcome comparisons and aggravated school markets. These issues will also be taken up later in this chapter. Assessment will be treated here through a series of lenses drawing on international education policy statements; data collected through empirical research studies here in Ireland; through an examination of intersections between assessment and tracking (streaming) in post-primary schools; and through a discussion of how school league tables use assessment to create further social justice and distribution issues in education and society. To begin this discussion, this chapter will firstly define social justice through the theoretical lenses of Fraser (1997; 2000) as well as Lynch and Baker (2005). The focus will then shift towards the intersections between social justice and assessment in the various educational settings and contexts outlined above.

What is social justice?

The ideological basis of social justice draws upon theories of equality of opportunity, condition and outcome, equity, theories of equitable redistribution of resources and emphasising recognition for marginalised groups. Groups who are often considered marginalised or underserved are, generally speaking, intersections of socioeconomic inequalities (class), race, ethnicity, gender, disability, sexuality and religion (or no religion). It is often at the various points of intersection between these nominal categorisations that issues of social justice, exclusion or unfairness of treatment emerge within education and assessment spheres. Intersectionality encourages us to view the world from the standpoint of people with a more nuanced understanding of their positions in terms of traditional identity categories such as race, gender, social class and (dis)ability. As a concept, intersectionality, is grounded in black feminist theory where academics and activists struggled to develop nuanced understandings of the intersections between race, class and gender in the oppression of people (Crenshaw, 1991; Collins, 2000). This perspective understands people as multiple and diverse in terms of where we stand in relation to the world and others. The positions we occupy, and the opportunities made available and denied to us, are mutually constructed by our nuanced and multifaceted positions as well as how these positions are understood in the wider discourses of our world. It is important here that we resist, even through the intersectionality perspective, constructing deficited perspectives of cohorts of students. It must also be acknowledged here that the authors are writing from a position of relative privilege in the context of the issues being addressed as we are white-Irish, middle class academics. Nevertheless, our motivation here comes from a desire to develop equity as a lens to view our educational landscapes because the world from which we write has co-opted education (and assessment particularly) as a tool in the unequal distribution of educational capital and wealth. Intersectionality allows us to view the nuanced, positioned experiences and identities of people in their relationship with our education system, and in particular, how assessment is taken up and used in modern society.

In this chapter, Sharon Gewirtz's (1998) and Connie North's (2006; 2008) useful distinctions within social justice theorisation will be used to frame the discussion and analysis of assessment practices. Gewirtz contrasts various social justice definitions, particularly those of Fraser (1997), Young (1990) and Lynch (Lynch and Baker, 2005) in order to create some harmony around the concept. Her concepts of *distributive justice* and *relational justice* will be used here to unpack the actions and consequences of assessment practices from a social justice perspective. *Distributive justice* refers specifically to how wealth, power and privilege are distributed across society. *Relational justice* focuses on how society could function cohesively in terms of disrupting hierarchical relationships based on wealth and moving towards more communitarian perspectives where difference and diversity are valued in our social relations with one another. Such a conceptualisation draws heavily on 'neo-Fabian versions of mutuality' and 'affirmative postmodernist versions of mutuality' (Gewirtz, 1998, pp. 473–475). The relationship to assessment practices is vital across educational contexts. Summative high stakes assessment is one of the key elements of reproducing hierarchies in terms of race, class and gender intersections in twenty-first century education practice. High performance in summative assessment has come to reflect dominant strata of society, particularly in terms of racial and socio-economic differences. This is reflected in progression to third level education, and most particularly in terms of progression to higher education. In Ireland, there are clear socio-economic barriers to accessing universities with far more students from less-privileged backgrounds entering the institute of technology sector. This is mainly accounted for through lower registration fees but also through lower entry thresholds which are decided through attainment in the end of school state examinations (the Leaving Certificate). This issue will be raised later in the chapter.

Nancy Fraser's (1997; 2000) conceptual framework of *redistribution, recognition* and *representation* could also be used to orientate discussion in terms of how educational assessment practices can collide with ambitions for social justice. Redistribution of economic and cultural goods is intrinsic to thinking on social justice and involves spreading the wealth and benefits of society more equitably across the population. The redistributive perspective is particularly relevant when considering social justice from the perspective of social class inequality whilst the recognition perspective may well be more appropriate when considering social justice from perspectives such as sexuality, gender, race and ethnicity. It is relevant here that social justice is a rather broad and contested umbrella term for theorising and disrupting oppression from a variety of perspectives such as social class inequalities, gender, race, ethnicity, disabilities, sexual orientation, religion and the countless intersections of these cultural and positional identity markers in contemporary society. Gewirtz emphasised that Iris Young's work was at odds with Fraser's definitions, particularly in relation to the concept of recognition (see Gewirtz, 1998 for full discussion) and favoured Young's (2009, pp. 55–71) 'five faces of oppression' (exploitation, marginalisation, powerlessness, cultural imperialism and violence) where the various functions and actions of oppressive actions within societies can be viewed more fully from both political-economic and cultural perspectives. This will be important when we analyse assessment as a sociocultural construct within education and society as it functions from both political-economic and cultural perspectives within systems, societies and the identity work of people. Assessment practices in various jurisdictions are culturally produced phenomena that become important sorting devices in hyper-competitive schooling systems, particularly those of developed countries where neoliberal foci on accountability and public representations of school performance are highly valued. In such cultural productions of assessment, there can be significant harm inflicted on those on the margins of society in terms of language, poverty and (dis)ability as of course, every competitive system demands losers in order to create the winners. Similarly, assessment systems are spaces for the production of cultural imperialism where dominant groups (particularly in terms of social class/ socio-economic status) create advantage through creating cultural reproduction in the curriculum and the assessment of that curriculum (Bourdieu and Passeron, 1990). To draw further on Bourdieu, this cultural reproduction could be construed as a form of 'symbolic violence' perpetrated by the tacit reproduction of class power through a collective subconscious. Indeed, in Ireland the 'fairness' of the Leaving Certificate (the summative end of school examination) has become a *doxa* where it is almost sacrilegious to question how it offers the truest possible picture of attainment and ability. Points garnered in this summative examination are then used as the primary data for progression to third level education. In fact, in the vast majority of third level entry criteria, these points are the only gatekeepers for entry. Some programmes and institutions have begun to look at wider criteria such as aptitude testing (Medicine programmes) and portfolio/ performance work (Art/Music programmes).

Lynch and Baker's (2005, p. 143) description of 'lives interpreted through the eyes of the dominant' is particularly pertinent to our interrogation of contemporary assessment practices. It could be argued, that assessment above all other components of education, is the most central to mechanism in producing inequalities of outcome and condition. It is the instantiation or materialisation of difference between people is made most obvious and most damaging in terms of the distribution of economic, cultural and social resources. How we use assessment in our systems of education (and our societies) certainly conforms to the view of an interpretation 'through the eyes of the dominant' as we funnel a particular view of talent and ability (often a narrow one) through various sorting screens that gradually stratify populations from educational perspectives. Problematically, educational opportunities are intrinsically linked to opportunities in terms of employment and personal development. Lynch and Baker's (2005) conceptualisation of *equality of condition* is also useful in terms of framing our discussion around social justice and assessment. In their own words:

> the most general way of defining equality of condition is simply to say that it is the belief that people should be as equal as possible in relation to the central conditions of their lives. Equality of condition is not about trying to make inequalities fairer, or giving people a more equal opportunity to become unequal, but about ensuring that everyone has roughly equal prospects for a good life.
>
> *(Lynch and Baker, 2005, pp. 131–132)*

The resonating point here is about developing the universal availability of 'equal prospects for a good life', which is where how we conceive of, enact, and value our assessment practices comes to play a vital role in the education space.

When considered from the viewpoint of the theories outlined above, uncomplicated meritocratic principles of ability and effort equalling success, although pervasive, are damaging myths impacting upon opportunities for redressing the social justice balance in terms of assessment in education systems throughout the world. In a meritocracy, assessments are the reward for hard work however there is very little, if any, recognition that assessments are designed by and for dominant cultural and economic groups in society and therefore contribute to the perpetuation of inequality. They lack recognition of resources that students bring to schooling and assessment as well as the resources available to them for preparing specifically for assessment moments in their education lives. These resources are economic, cultural, social and familial in nature and all serve to contribute to tilting the table in favour of those representing dominant groups and socioeconomic classes in society. Assessment is the most stubborn area of education practice in terms of breaking down the barriers of cultural and social stratification. Indeed, assessment is often the tool through which stratification, particularly in terms of socio-economic status, is instantiated. This argument is bolstered by various theories of reproduction and resistance in education where performance in school leads to increased opportunities in life (Bourdieu and Passeron, 1990; Willis, 1977). These opportunities, of course, are complicated by the fact that there is very clear unequal distribution across populations. It would appear to be the case in all jurisdictions known to the authors that access to economic capital is readily transferable into cultural and symbolic capital in the guise of educational experiences, opportunities and qualifications. These capitals are circular in the sense that once one garners a place on the wheel then it is self-constituting. Symbolic, social, cultural and economic capital are constitutive of each other in many respects. This is not to say that educational qualifications are the only route to economic capital but they certainly do increase access to economic stability for individuals and families.

How does social justice impact upon assessment?

Throughout the world, school assessment practices serve to separate, select and sort populations of learners. Here in Ireland, the Leaving Certificate is the ultimate terminal examination used as a sieve to stratify the school-leaving population into suitable rank order for third level selection purposes. Similar systems exist throughout the world such as the A-Levels (UK), the High School Certificate (New South Wales, Australia), the High School Diploma (USA). Apart from becoming rites of passage and significant cultural artefacts in the passage through youth into adulthood, these assessments (summative in these cases) act as important measures that have a significant impact on the educational trajectories of students. Results in these organised examinations and assessments are widely accepted as proof of achievement, ability and potential for progression in society. Good results can even become equated with being a good person as we continue to conflate success and moral superiority in our societies. We argue here that assessment is a conduit of cultural hegemony that privileges particular social and cultural practices, and in so doing diminishes and devalues those of 'others'. In other words, issues such as mismatches between the dominant language and culture of the school system against those of the home and out-of-school context creates significant advantages and disadvantages depending upon which cultural position the students are coming from. There are various areas within which such differences would have significant impact. For example, the area of IQ testing is a case in point where many sociocultural researchers and commentators would argue that the IQ test is a cultural artefact which represents the language, values, interests, knowledges and skills of the pre-eminent cultural fractions and therefore the test can become an artefact of stratification and reproduction of inequality (Bourdieu and Passeron, 1990; Gipps and Stobart, 2009). This may have a significant impact when we consider student populations from positions such as racial/ethnic minorities and working-class cultural backgrounds. These groups are, and have been, struggling with oppressive societal and educational arrangements where instruments such as IQ tests, and testing generally, can serve to increase stratification and segregation in education. This is ironic, considering that some of the initial movements in the nineteenth and early twentieth century towards testing as a system of selection was designed to disrupt the practices of appointing people from the dominant culture to positions of power and influence, particularly in the government sector (Gipps and Stobart, 2009). As we will explore later in this chapter, such systems of selection and segregation can also have a significant impact at school level, particularly where practices such as setting and banding are used to organise learning experiences.

What do we mean by fairness in assessment?

From Lynch and Baker's (2005) equality of condition perspective, an examination of assessment practices in school systems is revealing of underlying inequalities from a social justice perspective.

The thrust of this entire book is to deconstruct, and to emphasise, the socio-culturally distributed nature of assessment. This chapter examines some of the effects and affects of current assessment practice in schools where there is both a belief in, and a construction of, the individual as an autonomous being where the weight of success and failure lies entirely within their own abilities and controls. This version of individuality sits well within the contemporary penchant for neo-liberalism and the supremacy of the market as a paradigm of ordering the human world. In fact, as convincingly argued by McGregor (2009), schooling and assessment have become increasingly focused upon sorting human capital for private sector interests. The 'education for education's sake' paradigm has gradually become more marginalised in the neoliberal present of inter-student, inter-school and inter-state competition for supremacy (Francis and Mills, 2012). Within education, the imprint of neoliberal market principles encourages comparison and competition through measurement. Assessment serves the market well in this regard as it facilitates the stratification of children in easily comparable quantitative measures of performance. According to Stephen Ball (2012, p. 132), applying neoliberal market principles to education 'involves the transformation of social relations and practices into calculabilities and exchanges, that is into the market form – with the effect of commodifying educational practice and experience'. In other words, neoliberal perspectives allow for, and encourage, the construction of the competitive individual whose talents and abilities are reified as belonging to, and being produced by, the individual themselves. There is no acceptance or understanding of the social, cultural, historical and intersectional situatedness of assessment. In the neoliberal world, measurement of skills, competences, knowledge and ability have become central elements of global competitiveness and comparisons and therefore the unsuspecting school pupil has been cast into the heady world of attracting global business and doing their national duty through representing their country in these individualised batteries of tests. Of course, such pressures on the education system then encourage and prioritise the practices of assessment over and above the practices of learning. In such environments, the focus is inevitably upon atomised and individualised attainment-driven teaching and testing repertoires. A recent report from the European Agency for Developments In Special Needs Education (recently renamed European Agency for Special Needs and Inclusive Education –EASNIE), Raising Achievement for All Learners (EADSNE, 2012, p. 13) makes clear recognition of the role played by individualisation and choice in the separation of opportunity through methods that 'often increase academic, ethnic and social stratification'. Therefore, the position of the individual in intersectional terms, becomes vital in how educational resources and outcomes are distributed. Assessment becomes, to use Gewirtz's lens, the artefact though which distributional *in*justices and relational *in*justices are transacted.

The questions here then, focus upon the impact of such global shifts in the purposes of education and the concomitant impact for students much of which is transmitted through the assessment moments. Assessment moments take on new significance and responsibility for the students and for their schools. They become cathartic moments of national economic importance and result in the responsibilisation of our young people and our schools with economic positioning and success. Such positionings are evidenced in recent policy statements from various state structures throughout the world. For example, in Ireland, recent and current education policy statements have prioritised the economic outcomes of education, often to the exclusion of other educational outcomes such as artistic, communitarian, emotional, physical and moral learning. The most recent policy statement from the newly formed government, A Programme for a Partnership Government (2016, p. 87) states that:

> Investing in educating improves human capital, thereby generating wider benefits for our economic and jobs growth and competitiveness, as well as ensuring that all our people have opportunities to achieve their potential.

This exclusive focus on a human capital perspective on education draws heavily on a neoliberal paradigm of education where people, and particularly children, are marketised commodities to be developed in the education 'industry'. In such scenarios, assessment and assessment performance is the technology of control deployed over schools, teachers, administrators and students. The economic imperative looms large over the entire document and we are surprised at how all-consuming this economic imperative has become in this national statement on education. Of course, we all realise the centrality of economic stability to providing high quality education (and indeed other services) to the citizens of states. However, in this document the economic value of education is not only highlighted; it is the singular focus. Education is about far more than the production of human capital. Our primary education system is intended to be '—spiritual, moral, cognitive, emotional, imaginative, aesthetic, social and physical' (DES/NCCA, 1999, p. 6). People are not just worker bees buzzing through life; they are far broader people with wide interests and opportunities that need to be developed to provide wide opportunities for holistic development of the person and society. From a social justice perspective, there is certainly a focus on raising standards amongst all students, however, the focus always seems to be trained upon such measures as international league tables rather than the encouragement of a genuinely learner-centred approach to education. This international assessment focus was clearly visible in Ireland's earlier policy statement, *A Programme for National Recovery* (Ireland, 2011, p. 40), where it clearly stated that 'a longer term aim of this Government will be to position Ireland in the top ten performing countries in the OECD Programme for International Student Assessment (PISA)' as well as developing the availability of school assessments in order to provide more choice to parents in terms of choosing schools. From a social justice perspective, there are two key issues here: the focus upon international standards seems driven by economic competitiveness in terms of attracting international industry and business rather than upon the development of life chances and educational pathways for citizens. Second, school choice agendas are generally accepted as central to the neoliberal marketisation of education where the focus is more upon the middle classes garnering and maintaining advantage rather than providing real choice and opportunity for underserved and marginalised sections of society (Cahill and Hall, 2014).

School league tables, assessment and social justice

School results in state assessments and media produced league tables are the central technologies of the 'school market' where there is different opportunities and access to the resources of choice which produces further segregations between schools in terms of key areas such as socio-economic inequalities, race, ethnicity and disability. Courtois (2015) emphasises this point through her examination of fee-paying schools in Ireland and their exclusionary practices. School league tables at primary and post-primary level are firmly entrenched within the English education system. These tables function under the auspices of accountability for schools and teaching as well as providing information for parents when they come to making decisions around school choice for their children (Robinson, 1999). Robinson's (1999) analysis of school league tables remains relevant as it would seem that economists and politicians would appear to be just as important an audience for school league tables and results as any other audience. There is a direct connection between in-country performativity mechanisms and wider global measures of education systems such as PISA, TIMSS and the OECD Universal Basic Skills global league table. The impact of such international comparative measures would appear to be increasingly constraining on the national education policy in individual countries, and consequently on schools and classrooms, as they vie to demonstrate improvement on the narrowest of measures of educational success.

Various assessment-based measures are used as data in the UK to compile these school league tables. Literacy and numeracy scores as well as performance in state examinations such as GCSEs and A-levels are the primary indicators. These performance tables look at student progress while in the school; compare the school against national norms and adjust scores for pupil characteristics (generally referring to poverty indicated by access to free school meals). Similar performance-based league tables exist in the United States based on similar criteria (reading and math results, graduation rates, preparedness for college work, performance of 'disadvantaged' students). Australia uses the *My School* website (www.myschool.edu.au/) where the focus is on offering comparative data on schools serving similar populations. This comparison appears more textured than quantitative testing-based league tables as it purports to compare data concerning 60 schools who serve students with similar backgrounds and who started at a similar point in terms of literacy and numeracy. The website also offers more nuanced data around school attendance, ethos and mission statements as well as the financial resources of the school. However, the data that receives the most attention on the *My School* website is standardised assessment results drawn from the National Assessment Program – Literacy and Numeracy (NAPLAN). Lingard (2010) has warned of the negative impact of high stakes assessment on key areas of schooling, as has been experienced in many other jurisdictions. He makes particular reference to curriculum narrowing and a negative impact on pedagogy as teachers and schools become over-focused on the standardised assessments as measures of performance (not just pupil performance but that of teachers and schools also). Using standardised assessments as neoliberal instruments of marketisation and the commodification of education would seem to have had significant deleterious effects on the educational landscape in Australia (and indeed in England and America). Ragusa and Bousfield (2017) have produced an aptly named ('It's not the test, it's how it's used!') critical analysis of public responses to NAPLAN where they outline some of the key consequences of school comparative data. Issues such as increasing marketisation of education appear to have sparked a narrowing of educational perspectives and school experiences. Curriculum experiences have narrowed due to an increasing focus upon teaching to the test. The curriculum then becomes that which is tested and there can be similar impacts upon pedagogical creativity as teachers feel compelled (or in some instances are compelled) to curb their approaches in favour of meeting the requirements of the standards. Why wouldn't they? Their reputation as a teacher, and that of their school, has become intrinsically dependent upon the performance of their students on the standardised assessments of literacy and numeracy. Critically, from a social justice perspective, the comparative use of NAPLAN data has implications for increasing socio-economic inequalities as those with the cultural and economic resources can maximise access to the 'best' schools as well as provide personal top-ups to student performance through private tuition and the provision of additional resources in the home. As Ragusa and Bousfield (2017, p. 280) comment, education thus becomes 'a commodity that many communities cannot afford'. Education's position as a social and public good becomes completely compromised by the effect of the market and the resulting individualisation of performance and success. Their analysis makes similar comment on the impact of such aggressively marketised policies on the more marginalised sectors of society. Specifically, students with special educational needs and newcomer students become less desirable to schools as they impact upon the overall academic performance of the school. Conversely, students of high ability become more sought after as they boost performance statistics for teachers and schools. Even more worryingly, the Ragusa and Bousfield (2017, p. 280) study suggests that 'maladaptive practices' become part of the agenda for schools as they become more conscious of how data can be manipulated. For instance, they report evidence that certain students (lower performing students) would be requested not to attend on the day of NAPLAN tests in order to skew the results in the school's favour. Clearly, as Klenowski (citing O'Neill, 2013, p. 4) has pointed out, assessment data is susceptible to being redeployed for 'second-order purposes' that often involves contributing to an aggravated market-based version of educational accountability and choice. In such environments, successful students become valued human capital whilst those on the margins risk being jettisoned by the education system. Many countries now bear the evidence of this connection between assessment outcomes and the educational market as schools and districts become polarised in terms of educational success and failure. Unfortunately, these divisions also serve to widen the fault-lines in terms of race, social class and disability. The social justice implications of using assessment outcomes as a signifier of school success has clearly contributed to widening social divides in our societies.

Other nation states, such as Ireland and France, have decided not to use official school league tables, however media agencies have accessed such measures as third level entry statistics in order to compile their own league tables that are published in the national press on an annual basis. Ireland provides one example where the state (through the Department of education and Skills) remain ostensibly opposed to the use of school league tables; yet they do not stop the media from compiling them which does suggest that official resistance to their use is minimal. Therefore the situation exists where several national newspapers produce league tables of post-primary schools based on third level entry figures obtained through freedom of information requests to third level institutions, schools and state departments. It would appear that, regardless of state support or opposition, school performance league tables are a feature of education systems across the globe.

Many of the performance measurement systems deploy a 'value-added' system that attempts to indicate the input of the school in the progress achieved by the student. However, the very human, and qualitative, nature of what schools do is resistant to statistical analysis and therefore we must question the validity of what performance league tables tell us and indeed the raw data on which they are based (Matters, 2009). For example, if we are considering end of school achievement as a measure of a school then we would need to control for parental input, the starting point of the student upon entering the school, private tuition outside of school, the influence of peer effects on the performance of the student, access to cultural capital that would assist the student in deepening understandings of the curricular knowledge being examined and so on. The fact is that performance-based league tables, particularly those focused upon results in examinations and international measures of attainment are far too muddied by the real world of humanity and the messiness of learning and school to be considered accurate.

There are significant entanglements between the world of social justice and school league tables as many countries have experienced significant racial and social class-based segregation of schools, some of which is a direct result of the existence of these tables and the claims made to their veracity by state departments and by media sources. Clearly, the potential for developing more equitable practices and outcomes for people is compromised by aggressive marketisation and commodification of education systems through the drivers of standardised assessments and the ensuing comparisons of data. Students become commodities that can make potential contributions to the success of the school which is an interesting reversal of the notion of education and as a public good, designed to meet the needs of the people and the collective of society. From a distributed justice perspective, the cultural capitals made available through 'succeeding' schools become the commodity and those with less access to money and networks become more excluded and further distanced from the orthodoxies of high-performing school settings. In fact, one consequence of this aggressive marketisation is that schools in marginalised socio-economic districts become further alienated and stereotyped as failing schools. Such appellations then contribute to further reifications of disadvantage and deficit within their respective communities (Reay and Lucey, 2003; Cahill and Hall, 2014). This polarisation of schools and communities serves to function particularly forcefully with regard to issues of race and social class. Economic wealth and access to cultural and social resources is a significant contributor to the inequalities inherent in high stakes assessment. Students with deeper cultural and financial resources to invest in education may have opportunity to garner further advantage through using resources such as parental knowledge, siblings and extra tuition from private sources to prepare for high stakes examinations. Annette Lareau's (2003) cultural distinctions between 'natural growth' and 'concerted cultivation' are relevant here also. Lareau (2003), through her extensive ethnographic work, shows how middle-class parents engage in every opportunity to shape the cultural and social opportunities available to their children whilst less privileged families do not have the opportunity to engage in such a concerted manner. This leads to a difference in terms of access to the cultural resources that have an impact on school performance. Lareau (2003, p. 5) describes how:

> The commitment among working-class and poor families to provide comfort, food, shelter, and other basic support requires ongoing effort, given economic challenges and the formidable demands of child-rearing. But it stops short of the deliberate cultivation of children and their leisure activities that occurs in middle-class families.

Lareau (2003) refers to these different approaches as 'concerted cultivation' and 'natural growth'. They are useful here as they provide us with more evidence of how social class differences impinge upon life opportunities as the advantages conferred by 'concerted cultivation' can be readily cashed in at the table of high stakes school assessments. Students from more middle-class backgrounds will often have access to a wide array of after-school activities including: sports, music, science clubs, language-based residencies, art classes, computer clubs, etc. These activities, all positive in many aspects, do also confer advantage upon children in terms of their engagement with, and knowledge of, various curricular areas. Lareau's research shows us that children from underserved communities and backgrounds are far less likely to have access to such cultural and financial resources. Therefore, they are not coming from an equal position in terms of access to the curriculum, which also has a likely impact upon their performance in high stakes assessments based on the curriculum.

Kathleen Lynch used the example of music (Lynch, 2015, Keynote address) and the weighting towards performance in the Irish Leaving Certificate Examination where students can elect to have fifty per cent of their mark allocated to the performance element of their work. In this sense, success is mediated by: who can afford to buy the instruments? who can pay for the extra classes for performance? Who has the space at home to practice performance? This is but one example of where the cultural and financial resources of the person serve to advantage them in a high stakes examination that contributes in no small part to their opportunities to access higher education in a highly competitive environment.

Competitive and comparative foci in education, particularly in terms of outcomes through summative assessment, are catalysts in creating and emphasising difference. This becomes central from a social justice perspective as marginalised students can often become unwanted by schools in their quest for improving performance averages and assessment outcomes. Consider the following example of how an entrance assessment conducted prior to entry to a post-primary school in Ireland becomes a significant identity moment in the educational trajectories of the young people who are subject to it.

The entrance assessment

The following description is drawn from an ethnographic journal of a recent doctoral study in Portown, a working class urban community in Ireland where students were attending on a Saturday morning for an entrance assessment that the post-primary school used as a ritual to mark entry into the school community and also to stream or track the students into ability-based classes for their first year in post-primary school. The school context is what would be referred to in Ireland as a DEIS school. DEIS is an acronym for Delivering Equality of Opportunity in Schools (DEIS is the Irish language word for opportunity just in case you are searching for opportunity in the acronym). DEIS is the Department of Education and Skills (Ireland) funded intervention to alleviate and address educational disadvantage in areas of socioeconomic marginalisation. The following research journal extract details the event of the 'entrance assessment':

> The test-takers sat in disparate groups along the benches outside the exam hall. There was an uneasy silence pervading the room as they waited with trepidation to be summoned to take their seats in the exam hall. They sat in groups of boys and groups of girls, comfortable in the company of their current classmates in the various primary schools in the area of this post-primary school. They were about to be ripped from the cocoon of the primary school and released into the blackboard jungle of the post-primary world.
>
> Soon, the teachers called for attention and the young people were instructed to sit in alternate columns throughout the exam hall, depending on their school. As they took their seats, the parents who had stayed to sooth the nerves drifted away to let the system 'measure' their children through the various batteries of attainment and ability tests that awaited them within.
>
> As the tests started, the students busied themselves with question after question, some anxiously scribbling their responses on the scripts; others gazed around in search of inspiration; whilst others again fidgeted and shifted in the seats, discomforted and disoriented by the alien world of the post-primary school. Little did they know that their little etchings on these yellowed lined pages were the artefacts of their description and inscription in the world of the

school as able, and indeed disabled. Some were being screened in this moment as bodies of potential, others were being indelibly marked with a fatalistic scrawl of underachievement that would sit with them in the school years ahead and beyond into their adult futures.

(Cahill, 2012)

The entrance assessment, as described above, is both an affective experience for young people whilst also being a significant assessment moment in the technology of the school system. Post-primary schools use assessment as precursors to learning as much as they use it in any formative or summative capacities. In some school settings, particularly schools in areas of poverty, entrance assessments are used to stream or track students despite the vast and convincing catalogue of evidence which outlines the socially and academically reproductive nature of tracking (Oakes, 1985; Reay, Crozier and James, 2011). Moments such as the 'entrance assessment', a rite of passage for entry to Irish post-primary schools, can have significant formative influences on learning trajectories. It can become a milestone identity marker in the lives of children as well as a moment of significant limitation of future experiences as it can be, and often is, ill-used for tracking and setting in the first year of post-primary school. Recent data for Ireland suggest that streaming and tracking is still most present in DEIS schools or schools serving students in poverty. Smyth *et al.*'s (2015) review of provision through DEIS states that forty percent of post-primary DEIS schools still use ability grouping (streaming). They also highlight the educative impact through the fact that 60 per cent of students placed in streamed classes leave school early in comparison to 19 per cent of students placed in mixed-ability classes. There are also significant differences in exam performance evidenced from Smyth *et al.*'s (2015) research showing that students in mixed-ability classes perform better than those in ability grouping situations. Taylor *et al.* (2016) have referred to the wealth of research evidence that reflects the positive outcomes for all students in mixed-ability teaching and learning contexts and yet they also point to the significant resistances and 'fears' amongst schools in moving towards mixed-ability practices. This resistance to mixed-ability became evident in the recruitment process to their study of 'Best Practices in Grouping Students Project' (funded by the Education Endowment Foundation) where the vast majority of schools in their target jurisdiction of England were not willing to engage with the mixed ability end of the study (only 17 out of 137 schools were prepared to participate as mixed- attainment schools). A far larger majority opted to participate as examples of schools practising ability grouping (streaming) (120 out of 137 schools). The researchers concluded from their pilot study that the main factors in resistance to change to mixed-ability grouping were that schools feel 'deterred by a paucity of exemplars and resources and the educational climate is characterised as fearful, risk-averse and time poor' (Taylor *et al.*, 2016, p. 1). An element of the fear in the English context would appear to focus on the increasing emphasis on performance and accountability. In such competitive and comparative educational contexts, schools become fearful of taking perceived risks around performance, despite the existence of a large body of research indicating the contrary (Francis *et al.*, 2017; Ireson, Hallam and Hurley, 2005; Boaler, William and Brown, 2000; Burris and Welner, 2005).

There is important learning for us here in terms of the distributed nature of assessment at the level of performance. These studies show us that assessment performance is in fact distributed and any measure of individual performance cannot be extracted from the sociocultural practices of the group. They also show us that schools are resistant to change, particularly change that might disrupt a comfortable status quo in terms of socioeconomic status, race and ethnicity.

In order to emphasise the social justice focus of this chapter, it is important to remember that the group performs better in mixed- ability settings and therefore the group, as opposed to the individual, would be far more salient as a unit of analysis relevant to the assessment performance. Unpacking the enmeshed world of learning and assessment is messy and complex and not a world that lends itself to simplistic grade point averages as reflections of individual performance despite the temptations of such clear cut and clinical practices (as have become commonplace in the development of contemporary educational outcomes measurement). The purpose of our work here is to problematise these simplistic versions of assessment in the hope of contributing to changes in assessment practices which would be more equitable and framed from a social justice perspective of educational participation and outcomes.

For instance, the entrance assessment can contribute to referral for diagnosis of special educational needs. In such instances, the school reifies the diagnosis and labelling of difference. As Cochran-Smith and Dudley-Marling (2012, p. 240) surmise, 'no one can be disabled on their own' as special educational needs are socially produced and negotiated through normative assessment processes. These assessment moments become significant in the learning trajectories of all people but they become crucial in the closing off of opportunities as result of labelling and concomitant learning expectations of diverse learners (particularly those adjudged as 'having' special educational needs). Stephen O'Brien's book, *Inside Education: Exploring the Art of Good Learning* (2016, p. 16), speaks of the not yet 'marginalised learner' where the world of learning support and special education begins by making micro-inscriptions through various assessment moments and subsequent interventions that can eventually solidify the position of struggling learners on the margins of the education system. The entrance assessment, as instantiated in the extract above is certainly one of these micro-inscriptive moments where an assessment moment creates a particular trajectory for the learner whilst also contributing to their identities as learners within the school. Indeed, this scene serves to emphasise how schools are agents of both inclusion and exclusion and the assessment game is central to who gets included and who gets excluded at various junctures along the way.

As we have seen, assessment is a centrifugal point about which learner-identities become formed and reformed through the practices of schooling. Children become pupils and they are only afforded particular positions and opportunities to interact with the curriculum based upon their performance in assessment. Assessment moments act as gatekeepers to curriculum engagement in tracked (streamed) environments as they delineate who is allowed 'in' to complex curriculum engagements in higher streams as well as, obviously, who is excluded from these supposed complex engagements.

An experience of assessment in a streamed setting

In order to further emphasise the different experiences of assessment discussed above, this section will draw upon data generated by our collaborative project: Adolescent Literacy, Identity and School (ALIAS). This project set out to examine the literacy experiences and identity work of adolescents in post-primary school settings (mainstream and alternative education settings). The project used the lenses of curriculum, pedagogy and assessment to explore these ideas through focus group interviews with students, a curriculum design workshop, qualitative questionnaires and individual interviews.

One of the data collection instruments used in the ALIAS study was based around assessment scenarios (see Box 5.1 below). Twenty-four students from two post-primary schools listened to, and read the two contrasting experiences of assessment and chose a position upon a line between the two experiences to represent their own thoughts and feelings about assessment.

BOX 5.1 ALIAS STUDY SCENARIO RESPONSES

Pat

I don't really like tests. I have always found them just a little bit stressful. I don't do very well in them

And I hate the feeling I get when some of the better students are shouting about their great results. I am always nervous about being asked what I got. We have one teacher who tells everyone their test results out loud. I really don't like this class as it can be embarrassing when you don't do well. If I had a choice, I would have far less tests in school. I would love it if we could find other ways of showing our learning

Sam

I have always loved tests. I can remember back to primary school when we would do spelling tests and table tests every week. I loved the feeling of getting ten out of ten. I look forward to the school reports coming home in school now too. I have always done well in the tests and my parents feel very happy when I do really well. For these reasons, I look forward to the tests in school. I am not afraid of them, in fact see them as a chance to succeed. I think we should have more tests in school.

Locate yourself somewhere along this line between Pat and Sam depending on whose feelings you feel closer to. Be prepared to say why you put yourself at a particular position on the line.

Data analysis revealed a very significant difference in experience amongst students in higher streams and those in lower streams. What follows here is a comparison between Elaine and Barry for the purposes of illuminating the contrasting nature of experiences of assessment evidenced in the study as well as an insight into the societal discourses that permeate the assessment worlds of young people; particularly in terms of how their identities are inscribed with success and failure through the various assessment lenses trained upon them during school.

Students in higher streams looked towards assessment moments with anticipation as they saw it as an opportunity to demonstrate their learning and their ability. For example, consider Elaine's response:

> We had a mid-term French test on verbs and vocab and when I did it I felt confident and ready as I had studied a lot. I thought the test was easy. When I got the test, I got an A which made me feel really great. And my parents felt proud which also made me feel great.

There is evidence of intrinsic and extrinsic motivation here as Elaine offers a lovely account of her assessment success. Elaine, like many of her achieving classmates, sees formal assessment moments as opportunities for success and pride. Elaine is motivated by the pride instantiated by her assessment success both in herself and that conferred upon her by her parents. Elaine is quite representative of many of the succeeding students in the ALIAS study as they offer similar accounts of achievement and success. They are always associated with pride, and in many cases with favourable comparison to their peers. Competition seems intrinsic to the whole experience of school and assessment is just the opportunity for demonstrations of distinction, difference and successful learner identities. Elaine's account of a less successful assessment moment emphasises this competitive focus:

> I had a maths test in first year. I knew I wouldn't get an A but I did study. I did worse than I thought I would. I got a C and I didn't feel great because I did bad. But afterwards I found out that other people didn't [do] great which made feel better.

Interestingly, Elaine's account of not doing well in a test is appeased by the poor performance of others. It is within the comparison and the competition where she experiences success and pride. For Elaine, it is acceptable to perform poorly on a given test as long as others also perform poorly. The focus is certainly not upon the formative aspects of this test, despite it occurring in first year of post-primary school, but on the performative and competitive implications of the event. Therefore personal performance is inextricably linked to the group. In fact, it would appear almost valueless to Elaine without the group and therefore emphasises the necessarily sociocultural construction of success through the paradigm of individual assessment and testing in school. Figure 5.1 shows Elaine's depiction of herself at school. She is content (smiling) and engaged with her work. This self-portrait reflects her positive thoughts about school and assessment, as discussed above.

But what of the others? How does it feel to be unprepared and to fail or perform poorly on the test? Barry is a student from a bottom stream of a post-primary school that organises first year students in terms of ability into three distinct streams: highest, middle and lowest (as defined by performance on standardised entrance assessments of cognitive abilities, literacy attainment and numeracy attainment).

Barry:

> I don't really like tests because I think they are a waste of time and the last test I have done was a maths test and I have done really bad in all of them and I am terrible at Maths as well.

Barry represents a different kind of student and learner identity in the ALIAS study. He does not thrive on the competition and the opportunity to perform, as Elaine does. He experiences failure and inadequacy repeatedly through the maths test regime all of which is reinforcing his deficited view of himself. It would seem that our evidence shows, as we might expect, that regimes of testing reinforce the successful learner identity and also the failing learner identity. Therein lies the case for change and for more equitable, situated and distributed practices. Why would we persist with models of testing that disempower and disengage the majority and only prove successful for the minority?

There has been significant attention paid to the negative impact of testing and particularly on the marginalising and damaging nature of it. For example, Reay and William (1999) emphasised this damaging impact through in their investigation of

FIGURE 5.1 Elaine at school

FIGURE 5.2 Barry working at school

the impact of SAT testing on the identity constructions of 10–11-year-old students in England. The following extract from the interview with Hannah is most affecting:

HANNAH: I'm really scared about the SATs [standard assessment tasks]. Mrs O'Brien [a teacher at the school] came and talked to us about our spelling and I'm no good at spelling and David [the class teacher] is giving us times tables tests every morning and I'm hopeless at times tables so I'm frightened I'll do the SATs and I'll be a nothing.
DIANE: I don't understand Hannah. You can't be a nothing.
HANNAH: Yes, you can 'cause you have to get a level like a level 4 or a level 5 and if you're no good at spellings and times tables you don't get those levels and so you're a nothing.
DIANE: I'm sure that's not right.
HANNAH: Yes it is 'cause that's what Mrs O'Brien was saying.
(Reay and William, 1999, p. 345)

Hannah's dismissal of herself as a nothing because of her anxiety around her performance in the standard assessment tasks (SATs) is most troubling. This small exchange shows Hannah's view of assessment as central, not just to her identity as a learner, but to her identity as a person. In this instance, Hannah sees herself as 'a nothing' and erases any sense of herself as a successful learner in school. From this exchange, the curriculum has narrowed in focus and sent clear signals to the learner in terms of what is of value (spelling and times tables). It is also evident here that these externally imposed assessments are disciplining the work of the teacher (Mrs O'Brien) who is also relaying this message to Hannah and her peers. This research, although conducted almost twenty years ago, resonates with learners today throughout the developed world. The sustained focus on standardised assessments in literacy and numeracy continues to dominate elementary/ primary school landscapes throughout the world. Hannah, and those like her, are often the crunched in the number-crunching games of performance, accountability and national/international comparative league tables where success and failure are meted out disproportionately. Assessment, particularly through the reified cultural script of testing distorts learner identities and creates discourses of value and competitiveness rather than focusing on the learning and development of learners in terms of holistic learners who are being prepared for lives of community, commitments to global sustainability through wider understandings and investigations of their worlds. They are often being reduced to numbers and scores that encourage and reproduce deficit views of those who may already be marginalised from the education game. As Gipps and Stobart (2009, p. 115) have argued, 'different groups being allowed to sit, and be judged by, the same test is a simplistic view. Fairness needs to be linked to equality of opportunity, which includes access to similar resources and curricular opportunities'.

Conclusion

For the students introduced above, particularly Barry and Hannah, every moment is a moment of assessment for students who are struggling to keep up and struggling to succeed. Their personal experience of assessment cannot be untethered from the interpersonal and institutional planes of practice in the Rogoffian sense. Their experiences and emotions, whilst being their own, are also constituted by the wider significance of how assessment is made meaningful between people and through broader institutional understandings of assessment. Sometimes, as evidenced above, silence is the escape route. Silences, written and oral, are powerful statements of disengagement from the processes of school and education. These silences are most often iterated through formal assessment spaces. The emptiness of the exam script is not reflective of the learning of the student; it is a reflection of their disenchantment, disengagement and loss of confidence to express their learning in the form demanded. From a social justice perspective, assessment as instantiated in the above examples, serves to alienate and exclude many groups already considered on the margins of educational experiences. There is a primary focus on socio-economic concerns in this chapter but nevertheless there is an understanding that the intersectional nature of identity is also assumed. The key point remains the same. Assessment moments can and do act as significant actors in the distribution of (in)justice in educational contexts. The distribution of success is significantly influenced by one's social position and the financial, cultural and social resources required for success in formal summative assessments. As Gewirtz (1998) has emphasised in her *distributive justice* definition described earlier in this chapter, this leads to an unequal distribution of the substantial rewards (cultural, economic and symbolic) accruing from exam success and therefore the gap between the winners and losers in the education game widens with every moment. The extremes of competitive high stakes summative assessment militates against opportunities for movement towards the *equality of condition* ambition outlined by Lynch and Baker (2005).

Prompts for discussion

Assessment processes in schools can have a significant impact on people's experiences of education. In the light of this chapter, consider the following questions:

- What are your views on how assessment and social justice intersect in your education context?
- The differences between *equality of opportunity* and *equality of condition* are important in the context of assessment. How do you see these concepts being realised in your educational context?
- What do you think needs to change for assessment to be a more socially just (fair) instrument in your context?

6

THE ASSESSMENT OF PUPILS WITH SPECIAL EDUCATIONAL NEEDS: GIVING EFFECT TO THE PRINCIPLES OF INCLUSIVITY IN PRACTICE

Introduction

Important to all concerned with education, the assessment of pupils serves multiple purposes, both summative and formative. Assessment results are used, for instance, for the purposes of certification or award bearing, accountability, informing instructional activities, and the improvement of pupil learning (Black and Wiliam, 2009; Baker *et al.*, 2016, p. 99; Heitink *et al.*, 2016; Douglas *et al.*, 2016, p. 98). The assessment purpose which is the focus of this chapter, relates to the assessment of pupils with special educational needs arising from identified disabilities and learning challenges. To this end, issues relating to the initial identification of special educational needs, and the subsequent assessment of pupils with special educational needs throughout the course of their formal schooling, are addressed. The influence of particular conceptualisations of learning and attainment on assessment, and the shifts in perspective necessary to develop inclusive assessment practices predicated on inclusive principles, are also addressed.

Assessing special educational needs

Straddling social, cultural and linguistic boundaries, various causes give rise to special educational needs among pupils: physical, emotional, behavioural and cognitive. Internationally, it is widely acknowledged that addressing the special educational needs of particular pupils requires the provision of additional resources and teaching supports. Typically, that provision has been distributed according to assigned categories of special educational need. While the concept of special educational needs is broad, extending beyond categories of disability, to include all children who are in need of additional support, many countries use categorical descriptions of disability to determine eligibility for special education provision.

As a consequence, the history of assessment for pupils with special educational needs has been driven by a particular agenda related to the perceived purpose of that assessment. That is, assessment has been linked to decision-making processes around eligibility for particular educational and support services, access to resources and placement in regular or specialised settings (Keen and Arthur-Kelly, 2010, p. 148). Accordingly, Shevlin *et al.* (2013) state that the complexities and multi-layered processes relating to the assessment of special educational needs are best understood within a broader context of special educational needs provision. Though variable with respect to data collection and data usage processes, in developed economies especially, legally-based assessment procedures seek to identify, categorise and quantify the special needs of pre-enrolment pupils and pupils already enrolled in schools who are experiencing learning challenges of various kinds (Desforges and Lindsay, 2010). As a result, educational provision for pupils with special educational needs has experienced considerable growth in these jurisdictions in recent decades.

Conceptualisations of assessment

Two differing conceptualisations of assessment give rise to particular assessment approaches and practices. With regard to the specific focus of the current chapter, the psycho-medical and biopsychosocial conceptualisations of assessment adopt different approaches toward determinations of special educational needs. In the literature, the terms 'ecological' and 'interactionist' are used interchangeably with the term 'biopsychosocial' to describe similar conceptualisations of assessment.

Psycho-medical conceptualisation of assessment

Historically, the dominant cultural script informing determinations of special educational needs among pupils is one rooted in a psycho-medical conceptualisation of the causation of need. Stressing within-pupil causations of learning needs, and reflective of wider assumptions at the heart of psychometrically-oriented assessment approaches (Elwood and Murphy, 2015), within a psycho-medical conceptualisation of educational need the unit of analysis is the individual pupil. Individual difference in mental capacity or in aptitude is viewed in deficit terms, assessments are activities that take place in isolation, assessment tasks are neutral and stable across pupils, the testing system *per se* does not impact on pupil performance, and pupils responding to test items are isolated from social influences and, consequently, are separately analysable through the test items used (Desforges and Lindsay, 2010). These assumptions apply to psychometrically-oriented assessments administered by a range of professional practitioners, including psychologists, therapists, and teachers.

Dominantly, assessment in special education contexts has been associated with psychological assessment that offers a specific diagnosis for the student. Education and psychology share histories in which, to varying degrees, both have accepted medicalised discourses of the person, invariably in the form of psychopathologies, which have come to restrict the available ways of conceptualising and responding to forms of human difference in our schools and, more specifically, within the realm of special educational needs. Education and psychology have often worked together to propagate such approaches in a shared commitment to constructing assessments of young people which rely, for example, on unproblematic understandings of ability and normalcy (Goodley, 2014).

Though a high percentage of pupils who are targeted for such assessment possess limited test language proficiency (Castro-Villarreal and Nichols, 2016, p. 7; LeRoy *et al.*, 2018, p. 1), commonly, psychological examiners select and administer subtests representing narrow abilities from one or more normative-based cognitive and achievement instruments, to establish significant strengths and weaknesses in broad abilities (McCleary *et al.*, 2013). For instance, the Wechsler Intelligence Scale for Children (WISC V, 2014), is an individually administered intelligence test for pupils aged between six and 16. Generating a 'Full Scale IQ' that represents a student's general intellectual ability, the WISC V instrument also provides five primary index scores: Verbal Comprehension Index, Visual Spatial Index, Fluid Reasoning Index, Working Memory Index, and Processing Speed Index. These indices purport to represent a student's abilities in discrete cognitive domains. Five ancillary composite scores can be derived from various combinations of primary or primary and secondary subtests. Following diagnosis, a determination of the special education provision that is needed is advanced. Diagnostic instruments such as ICD-10 (International Classification of Diseases – 10th edition, 2001 – World Health Organization) and DSM V (Diagnostic Statistical Manual – 5th edition, 2013 – American Psychiatric Association), typically administered by psychologists, therapists and medical professionals, assume that such distinct categories exist and that they can be described coherently. Following diagnosis, viewed from a psycho-medical perspective, needs attributed to particular disability categories are regarded as amenable to remediation with specific treatments or interventions.

Drawing on disciplinary understandings derived from psychology and medicine, in the psycho-medical model the function or purpose of assessment is to determine the correct diagnosis to guide practitioners towards implementing a particular intervention, thus remediating the identified category of need. In doing so, a number of fundamental assumptions are made; first, that the categories used are valid; second, that it is possible to make reliable judgements about which category should be applied to a pupil; third, that particular interventions are differentially effective with different categories of identified need. However, these assumptions are questionable as despite an ongoing debate, many questions on classification, definition, and identification of learning disabilities, as well as on aetiology and effective interventions, remain unsolved (Büttner and Hasselhorn, 2011, p. 75).

Due primarily to problems in technical adequacy for diagnosis (McCleary *et al.*, 2013), no unanimity exits across different countries as to how to determine specific categories of special educational need as criteria determining given categories vary across time and between jurisdictions – even within federally constituted countries – leading to heterogeneous and inconsistent across-region and within-region prevalence rates (Scruggs and Mastropieri, 2002; Büttner and Hasselhorn, 2011, p. 83;

Florian, 2013, p. 11). This leads to suggestions that international classification systems (such as ICD 10 and DSM V) fail to reflect the inherent complexities of special educational needs provision and point to the limited usefulness of categories of disability in many instances. For instance, given that the generality of pupils exhibit a broad spectrum of individual differences, the point at which a difference is delineated as constituting a 'special need' is problematic, thus challenging the validity of discrete categories. It is also unlikely that a similar identified difficulty will have exactly the same aetiology in different pupils, thus challenging the reliability of assessment instruments to place pupils in particular categories. In any case, definitive categories create dilemmas as children can often exhibit a range of difficulties characteristic of more than one category and it may not be readily apparent which one offers the best fit. As a result, similar educational interventions will not be equally successful in each case, as a wide range of ability and disability is represented within each category, with pupils assigned to the same disability category frequently manifesting different needs in terms of school-based learning. In this regard, schools have reported that the actual level of a student's learning need may not necessarily be reflected in their diagnosed category of disability (Kinsella *et al.*, 2014). Furthermore, as no uniformity exists across countries on how categories of disability are defined, or in relation to the particular methods of assessment required in determining the diagnosis, or with respect to the professional groups involved in making the diagnosis, a system of categorisation rooted in a psycho-medical conceptualisation of assessment does not reflect the complexity of the special educational needs of individual pupils, nor does it helpfully inform educational interventions, as the diagnosis of a learning disability frequently does not include any information about how to devise an appropriate form of intervention (Florian *et al.*, 2006, p. 44; Desforges and Lindsay, 2010; Büttner and Hasselhorn, 2011, p. 77).

Teacher-administered norm-referenced tests

An example of a commercially produced, summatively-oriented test administered by teachers is the Cognitive Abilities Test (Fourth Edition – CAT4). The CAT4 provides a standardised measure of cognitive reasoning ability, without reference to curriculum-based material, across four distinct batteries: verbal, non-verbal, mathematical and spatial. In 2011 the CAT4 was standardised on 25,000 primary and secondary pupils across the United Kingdom (UK). Thus, as a norm-referenced test, individual student scores are benchmarked against the UK national average for a given age-group. Age-specific national averages are established via the standardisation process for the particular jurisdiction in question. In the case of the Republic of Ireland, the Drumcondra Reasoning Test (DRT) serves a similar purpose.

Despite assurances, the provision of specific scores on measures of general cognitive ability for assessment of learning difficulties demands interrogation. At a theoretical level, the concept of intelligence, aptitude, or cognitive ability gives rise to much controversy and disagreement. At a transactional level, the reliability of tests generally, and of general cognitive ability in particular, is such that precise boundaries, defined numerically as is currently the case, cannot be meaningfully assessed. All measurements have errors and it is advisable to quote test scores within defined confidence intervals. Given 'the chimaera of reliability' (Elwood and Murphy, 2015, p. 189) the assessment of cognitive abilities is an important element that should be placed in a wider context than the determination of a simple quotient.

The New Group Reading Test (NGRT) is another example of a norm-referenced test that allows teachers, via a Standard Age Score (SAS), to assess reading and comprehension skills benchmarked against the UK national average. Similarly, in the Republic of Ireland, tests such as the Drumcondra Post Primary Test – Reading (DPPT – Read), Drumcondra Post Primary Test – Mathematics (DPPT – Maths) and Mary Immaculate Reading Attainment Test – MICRA-T, are examples of norm-referenced tests that allow the performance of an individual pupil to be compared with that of other pupils nationally at the same age level. However, Fleer (2015) questions why assessment in its dominant form relies on age as a key organising variable in terms of establishing where a student is in terms of achievement and what a student should know. Additionally, while norm-referenced, standardised tests establish how a student is positioned relative to other pupils of a similar age, they do not furnish information on what the student has learned; particularly if utilised for summative purposes, as is dominantly the case, especially when assessment rationale serve accountability purposes.

Assessing for accountability purposes

Notions of accountability can be defined and understood in a multitude of ways. In contemporary globalised education contexts the idea of accountability has become largely synonymous with the use of standardised tests. One of the key aspects of this development is the integral role played by the dissemination and reporting of student scores on large-scale, high-stakes, standardised tests (Crowley and Yu, 2017; Nichols and Castro-Villarreal, 2017, p. 1). What has since become a global testing culture owes much to the inauguration, in the year 2000, of the Programme for International Student Assessment (PISA), on the part of the Organisation for Economic Cooperation and Development (OECD). A sample-based standardised test that allows intercountry comparisons, PISA is administrated in three year cycles. Though the subject of much criticism (e.g. Eivers, 2010; Meyer, 2014; Cosgrove and Cartwright, 2014; Hutt, 2014; Perry and Ercikan, 2015; Anders et al., 2016; Rutkowski and Rutkowski, 2016; Zhao et al., 2018), since its introduction 70 countries (or economies) have participated in the PISA test. PISA differs from most educational assessments in that it examines the capacity of 15-year-olds to use their knowledge and skills in order to meet real-life challenges rather than merely assessing mastery of school curricula. The assessment uses multiple-choice and open-ended questions to assess academic knowledge and skills in the areas of mathematics, reading, science and problem-solving. In addition, information is gathered on the pupils' attitudes and approaches to learning, and pupil and school demographic backgrounds (Sahlberg, 2017; Le Roy et al., 2018, p. 1).

Much has been learned about the intended and unintended consequences of high-stakes testing practices. With respect to intended consequences, high-stakes testing has not had the effect of increasing pupil achievement or decreasing the achievement gap. Negative, unintended consequences include an increased reliance on didactically-oriented instructional practices, a narrowing impoverishment of the curriculum, teaching to the test, an exaggerated emphasis on tests to the exclusion of other educational goals, and compromised pupil-teacher relationships. Thus, the combination of high-stakes consequences with reductive measures of achievement, arising from the use of standardised tests, proves detrimental to the quality of instruction for pupils (Douglas et al., 2012, p. 172; Moss, 2017, p. 62; Nichols and Castro-Villarreal, 2017, pp. 1–2; Crowley and Yu, 2017). Stated succinctly, as debates about instruction cannot be disentangled from the outcomes we aim to achieve, the tendency is 'to treasure what is measured' (Berliner, 2011, p. 299).

Despite these negative effects, high-stakes standardised testing remains a salient component of education reform. In the US, for instance, embracing models of 'accountability' that are designed to hold teachers and administrators liable for their pupils' progress, national efforts at education reform rely largely on the use of standardised testing. This involves regular testing of all pupils, including pupils with special educational needs diagnoses, and demonstrations of adequate yearly progress on tests by all schools (Joyce et al., 2016). Equally, since 2003, PISA has included pupils with special educational needs. Though the percentage of pupils with special educational needs remains low, the number of included pupils has increased with each PISA administration cycle, in response to the interaction between the need to maintain strict sampling criteria and country-level educational mandates to include special educational needs pupils in standardised testing (LeRoy et al., 2018, p. 1).

As the negative effects of high-stakes standardised testing are compounded for pupils (and teachers) in the sphere of special educational needs, a field in which the gaps between system expectations and actual pupil performance can be especially wide, the educational experiences of pupils with special educational needs are of unique concern. Subjecting the rich diversity of pupils who struggle with academic forms of learning to standardised forms of assessment for accountability purposes, creates a difficult state of affairs for educators (Pullin, 2005; Nichols and Castro-Villarreal, 2017, p. 2). In this regard many educators (and parents) believe that participation in large-scale assessments is a critical component of ensuring access to education and equality of opportunity for pupils with special educational needs, not least in respect of promoting access to the general curriculum and academic content knowledge, rather than functional real-life and socialisation skills for pupils with disabilities. Others argue that the participation of pupils with significant or complex educational needs is unnecessarily traumatising and demoralising, or will result in the loss of the individualisation goals of the special education process.

While high stakes accountability regimes, designed with the expressed purpose of equalising outcomes, may make accountability imperatives irrefutable for education systems at national and regional levels, competing beliefs, convictions, professional traditions and the encompassing struggle to engage pupils in learning, regardless of official goals and preferences, demand acknowledgement (Castro-Villarreal and Nichols, 2016, p. 7). The resultant conflict between uniform requirements and expectations and individualised education programming has created a confusing and unrealistic context for general and special education providers. Reflecting wider tensions between a policy commitment to inclusion and raising standards through aggregate performance tables (Norwich and Kent, 2002, p. 60), occupational traditions of differentiation rub uneasily against the system's push for standard and equal treatment (Cohen, Spillane and Peurach, 2018). Resistant realities of pupils' cognitive and emotional needs, enduring value traditions, and claims to professional autonomy and agency create dissonances between accountability obligations, teachers' professional values, and pupil needs (Mintrop and Zane, 2017, p. 5). The push and pull between individualisation and uniform expectations can only be remedied through changes in how we conceptualise pupil learning and academic needs, in order to improve how we address the diversity of these learning needs (Castro-Villarreal and Nichols, 2016, p. 18). This is particularly important since cultural and linguistic minority pupils are often disproportionately represented among special education ranks and therefore at greater risk of suffering from the negative effects of high-stakes testing pressures (Thomas, 2013, p. 476; Nichols and Castro-Villarreal, 2017, p. 2).

Disproportionality: a convoluted, labyrinthine field

As assessment tools serve as a proxy for cultural capital (Kozleski and Waitoller, 2010, p. 663), an association between social and economic inequity and norm-referenced achievement tests, whereby some social and ethnic groupings consistently achieve higher average scores than others, feature as a criticism of standardised test instruments generally (Murchan and Shiel, 2017, p. 39). Similarly, concerns centring on issues of cultural bias and disproportionality attach to the utilisation of normative-based cognitive and achievement instruments in determinations of special educational needs arising from disabilities. In this regard, a wealth of data accumulated over four decades of special education research suggests that minority pupils have been disproportionately represented among special education populations. Therefore, notions of 'specialness' in respect of learning difficulty are constructed to a significant degree out of the disadvantage created by coming from one minority or another (Thomas, 2013, p. 477; Castro-Villarreal and Nichols, 2016, p. 15; Craft and Howley, 2018). Accordingly, within certain categories of disability, significant over- and under-representation of pupils from particular minority ethnic groupings (Strand, Lindsay and Pather, 2006), and socioeconomically marginalised sections of society (Banks, Shevlin and McCoy, 2012; McCoy, Banks and Shevlin, 2012), has been established. Nonetheless, the debate surrounding disproportionality in the special education identification of culturally and linguistically diverse pupils remains highly contentious, particularly as scholars grapple with the meaning and causes of disproportionality (Sullivan, 2017, p. 244).

Several factors point to the complexity characterising the concept and actuality of disproportionality. For instance, with respect to the US, it is unclear whether disproportionate numbers of economically disadvantaged and minority pupils are in special education, or if minority status independent of poverty status is a more accurate predictor. Nonetheless, the high co-occurrence of poverty and minority status underscores minority pupils' cumulative risk for receiving special education services. With respect to achieving competence in English language proficiency, it is exceedingly difficult to assess how many special education pupils are also additional language learners because of the inherent challenges associated with disentangling learning difficulties from language difficulties and nuances in identification and reporting (Castro-Villarreal and Nichols, 2016, pp. 6–7; Jones et al., 2018). Also relevant to the context of the US is that data vary at the national, state, and district levels. Some records reveal clear patterns of disproportionality in special education and some suggest disproportionality as unproven (e.g. Balu et al., 2015, cited in Castro-Villarreal and Nichols, 2016, p. 16). Thus, the scholarship and commentary surrounding disproportionality in special education seems increasingly convoluted, spurred by the divergent interpretations of recent studies. This layer of complexity rests with data that show minorities in some disability categories are overrepresented compared to data that suggest that in some cases they are underrepresented (e.g. Shifrer, Muller and Callahan, 2011; Sullivan, 2011; Sullivan and Bal, 2013; Morgan et al., 2013; Zhang et al., 2014; Morgan et al., 2015; Skiba et al., 2016; Morgan et al., 2017; Umansky et al., 2017; Cooc and Kiru, 2018; Cruz and Rodl, 2018). Where disproportionality exists, in what direction, and for who become critical questions that are difficult to unpack with consistency. It is not surprising that research is inconsistent given the challenges of tracking and identifying special education populations, as well as the varying methodological and statistical approaches used to study these trends (Sullivan 2017, p. 244). Nonetheless, despite the complexities characterising the field, given the consequences of disproportionality, namely the negative outcomes associated with inappropriate placement, access to the general education curriculum, and harsher disciplinary punishment, educators must be mindful of their own referral practices and the ways in which minority pupils are identified, labelled, and treated. As a multitude of factors contribute to disproportionality, it is exceedingly difficult and nuanced to disentangle and therefore 'fix.' Factors such as the cultural bias evident in assessments, a function of the cultural mismatch arising from the linguistic or cultural distance between a student's native language and second language, poverty, special education processes, inequity in general education, issues of behavioural management, are just a few of the possible features of educational systems that contribute to the problem (Zhang et al., 2014, p. 119; Green et al., 2018; Jones et al., 2018).

Questioning psycho-medical principles

A growing body of research, particularly from the US, highlights the increasing psychiatrisation, medicalisation and psychologisation of children and childhood.

While schools and educators play a key role in these processes, the degree to which educators engage in these practices varies internationally (Barker and Mills, 2018, p. 638). A parallel development accompanying enhanced levels of special educational needs-related provision is an increased questioning of those concepts fundamental to how 'special educational needs' have traditionally been conceptualised. Accordingly, the questioning of what 'needs' are, and on what grounds they are deemed 'special', increasingly feature as sources of debate. Equally, assessments of special needs, and related assessment rationales, are also subject to increased levels of interrogative attention (e.g. Vehmas, 2010; Tomlinson, 2015; Florian, 2013; Florian, 2014; Messiou, 2017).

Educational (or school) psychology in practice can be regarded with deep suspicion by some educators, especially by those committed to inclusive practices. Caution is due, at least in part, to the history of educational psychology theory and practice which, it could be argued, has contributed to processes in which generations of pupils have been excluded from various arenas of mainstream educational life. The apparatus of special education, including IQ tests, observations, segregated classrooms and schools, specialised psychologists, service providers, and various therapists, all facilitate the reification of human difference into one of 'disability' that marks individuals from what is deemed normal (Baglieri *et al.*, 2011, p. 2140; Tomlinson, 2012). Given the power of discourses relating to intelligence and hereditability and given also the ways in which they continue to justify many forms of educational and social exclusion, caution is understandable (Chitty, 2007, cited in Billington, 2017). In this regard, the supposed precision of assessment procedures that identify learning 'needs' as discrete 'within-person' problems, is increasingly questioned as learning challenges arise for a host of reasons, most of them unrelated to 'dysfunctions' in the workings of pupils' brains (Thomas, 2013, p. 476).

Contrastingly, counter neuroscientific discourses offer resistance to discriminatory practices in psychology and education which fuel the processes of social exclusion (Billington, 2017). For example, affective neuroscience rejects the kinds of incomplete versions of persons generated by reductionist discourses of deficits, attending, instead, to more complex notions of human experience, emotions and personhoods. Equally, critical neuroscience lifts the neurological or psychological veil to reveal the latest political challenge posed to social and educational inclusion. These counter neuroscientific discourses point to a need in education to maintain a distinction between neuroscientific (or indeed psychological) discourse and the individual pupils who lie at the heart of the educational endeavour. Additionally, neuro-discourses circulating around brain plasticity offer a more dynamic approach to the conceptualisation of learning by demanding that brain development for the vast majority is considered as an interactive process which is responsive to particular environmental conditions and human experience. Thus, the messy interplay which occurs between individuals and their social circumstances, the 'hybrid ontology of nature and culture' (Raikhel, 2012, p. 229, cited in Billington, 2017, p. 874), opens a space in which, as educators, we need not be paralysed but can be emboldened to act, not by replicating deficit or other partial accounts of individuals, but by focusing on the 'conditions' necessary for pupils to achieve learning and change in complex social circumstances (Thomas, 2013). Therefore, the assessment of pupil learning is best served when these 'conditions' are informed by the principles of inclusivity.

Inclusive education

Inclusive education is a contested, ambiguous, dilemmatic domain. Debate on the concept is often characterised by a considerable degree of fractious, disputational engagement, a product of deeply-held perspectives among various protagonists. Given differing emphases, both conceptually and transactionally, achieving consensus has, unsurprisingly, proven elusive. A possible explanation for such disputation is that inclusion is best understood in context. Thus, while some broad principles of inclusion may claim universal appeal, they are, frequently, perceived differently in different contexts, due to the complexities, contradictions and particularities inherent to jurisdictional and school-based contexts of practice. Nonetheless, despite much contestation, a degree of coherence also characterises the domain of inclusive education (Artiles and Dyson, 2005; Thomas and Loxley, 2007; Florian, 2008; Florian and Black-Hawkins, 2011; Baglieri et al., 2011; Florian and Spratt, 2013; Florian, 2014; Douglas et al., 2016; Reindal, 2016; Theoharis et al., 2016; Materechera, 2018).

Sociocultural-informed assessment approaches

Enhancing the educational participation and achievements of pupils with special educational needs, via adoption of particular assessment approaches, is achieved through adherence to particular theoretical conceptualisations of learning and its assessment. To this end, sociocultural theories of learning understand assessment as a historically produced construct. With the passage of time cultural beliefs or 'scripts' about what assessment is and is for become sedimented or reified in expressions of assessments' purposes, uses and practices. These cultural beliefs are embedded in enduring beliefs about learners, learning and assessment and inscribed in assessment routines, practices and behaviours. The value of a sociocultural-informed theoretical approach is that it problematises historically rooted ideas, or enduring cultural scripts, relating to assessment (Elwood and Murphy, 2015). In the absence of exposure to interrogative problematising of this kind, practitioners, be they teachers, assessment developers, or policy-makers, for instance, rely on taken-for-granted cultural legacies about how assessment should be conceived of and transacted within national and international systems.

In contrast to psycho-medical conceptualisations of assessment, which stress within-pupil causations of learning needs, sociocultural theory demands recognition of the essential relationships between learning processes and the assessment of learning. Specifically, sociocultural theory illuminates how that relationship is affected by the social, cultural and historical experiences of pupils, and the political and economic contexts within which assessment occurs. As pupils and teachers are constrained by the cultural traditions, the political and public expectations of education, and the norms of the various institutions within which they operate, the assessment of pupil learning cannot be understood without a consideration of the wider context within which that assessment takes place (Black and Wiliam 2018, p. 20). As there is much to be gained from theory that guides attention towards the student in a situation rather than towards a feature that lies within the student alone, shifting from a focus on the individual self to a focus on the relational or situational self requires a corresponding change of approach in relation to how individual achievement is assessed (Hedegaard and Daniels, 2011; Elwood and Murphy, 2015). Accordingly, four interrelated, sociocultural-informed principles pertaining to learning and its assessment require explanation.

First, as its practices and grading schedules are subject to reification within settings and entire systems, assessment is perceived as a practice that is not neutral. In this regard, human involvement in every aspect of its design and deployment means that the assessment of educational performance is irrevocably a social project and thus subject to all the vagaries of human activity more generally (Broadfoot, 2010, p. vii).

Second, as it occurs within the constructed social practices of historically unique social and cultural settings, learning cannot be viewed as an isolated entity. Instead, learning is a function of constant and ever-changing interactions between the learner, teacher, peers, and parents. As pupils construct themselves and are constructed by a range of others as particular types of learners, these relational interactions offer key insights to any understanding of learning and learners through assessment. One such insight is the perception of learning disability as cultural preoccupation and production (McDermott *et al.*, 2006, p. 12).

Third, though only a relatively recent historical construct, the social and cultural dynamics of classrooms are particularly important, as success criteria regarding learning and achievement are communicated therein, with inevitable implications for which forms of knowledge are most valued. Accordingly, while understandings of identity have evolved in recent decades, what has remained constant is the critical role schooling plays in identity formation. With implications for identities that are carried into adulthood, school norms, practices and expectations relating to assessment provide key symbolic materials that pupils draw on to make sense of their experiences (Reay, 2010, p. 277).

Fourth, with implications for the broadening of assessment outcome criteria, perceiving classrooms as participatory cultural settings necessitates that accomplishments garnered through participation in a myriad of other cultural contexts are incorporated into assessments of pupil achievement (Elwood, 2006; Elwood and Murphy, 2015).

Increased emphases on these four sociocultural-informed principles would help counter the instigation of reform efforts based on statistical correlations derived from national pupil assessment systems and international education databases in the absence of an adequate appreciation of the details that make a difference in schools.

To improve teaching and learning, it behoves reformers to focus more attention on localised, context-based data and the causation they reveal in the present (Sahlberg, 2017).

Biopsychosocial conceptualisation of special educational needs assessment

Informed by sociocultural principles, a biopsychosocial model of assessment is deemed the most appropriate to encapsulate 'the complexities of identifying and providing an appropriate education to pupils with special educational needs' (Desforges and Lindsay, 2010, p. 165). Also termed an 'interactionist' or 'ecological' model, the biopsychosocial model recognises that different factors interplay at different stages of a pupil's life which can affect learning. Thus, the biopsychosocial model takes into account the various forces impinging on the developing student. These form a complex array of stress and support factors that interact at particular times during the life of a pupil to help enhance their life chances or, conversely, to render them especially vulnerable to underperformance in school settings. These factors can be grouped under three dimensions: first, genetic and neurological factors intrinsic to the student that adversely affect sensory, motor and cognitive processes; second, stress and support factors in the student's home and school environment; third, wider socioeconomic factors such as housing, health care, or societal attitudes to disabilities (Desforges and Lindsay, 2010). The interacting, ecological character of all three dimensions means that they are understood as a mutually constitutive continuum rather than as mutually exclusive, trichotomous entities.

While continuing to incorporate individual factors concerning the pupil's abilities, which are the sole focus of assessment under the psycho-medical model, the biopsychosocial model also takes into account home, school, and societal factors, both positive and negative, which impinge on the pupil and affect learning and assessment processes. Therefore, a system of assessment based on the biopsychosocial model requires an approach to assessment which is much broader than those that solely focus on within-pupil factors. Instead, devising a biopsychosocial framework for the assessment of special educational needs requires deployment of a broad range of assessment methods and tools. In this manner assessment is operationalised as an on-going process which is closely linked to intervention and is an integral part of a cycle of assessment, planning, teaching and re-assessment. Such an approach would result in the construction of a comprehensive profile detailing how an individual pupil is interacting with all aspects of the educational environment, and identify barriers to participation, as well as supports required to overcome those barriers.

The inherent limitations of traditionally dominant psycho-medical conceptualisations of special education needs ill-serve those pupils whose inclusion in educational settings frequently proves most challenging to effect (Florian et al., 2006; McLaughlin et al., 2006; Norwich, 2007; Desforges and Lindsay, 2010; Vehmas, 2010; Kinsella et al., 2014). For instance, pupils from culturally and linguistically diverse backgrounds are disproportionately exposed to educational contexts that increase risk of maladaptive behavioural or social-emotional responses. Accordingly, through adoption of a biopsychosocial lens, many disproportionality scholars take a cautious approach and emphasise the need to consider contextual determinants to avoid inappropriately identifying pupils as having a disability when their difficulties result from ineffectual practices or insufficient educational experience (Sullivan, 2017, p. 248). Addressing disproportionality in special education has long been discussed, and methods for addressing it continue to evolve to include better teaching, improved referral processes, greater reliance on data and valid Response to Intervention (RTI) decision-making and philosophical changes to how we view learning problems (Castro-Villarreal and Nichols, 2016, p. 17). Consequently, the development of assessment policies and practices focused on equity, which seek to reduce performance differences among identifiable pupil groups, is necessary. However, it is readily acknowledged that pursuit of equity extends far beyond the development and usage of assessment instruments to the educational and societal structures that affect pupils (Baker *et al.*, 2016, p. 122). But context-based understandings of pupil underperformance often seem to compete poorly with deficit-related explanations. So it is often the longstanding, deficit-related beliefs of the field of special education – beliefs that it is ability and disability, not poverty, difference or life experience – that have succeeded in 'explaining' success or failure (Thomas, 2013, p. 476).

Traditionally in the Republic of Ireland, as in many other countries, the assessment of special educational needs focused on identifying the 'special needs' of individual pupils to inform decision-making on the allocation of resources. Much less attention was paid to how pupils should be supported in schools, on the outcomes of interventions, or on the capacity of the school to deliver appropriate interventions. This led to a concentration on within-pupil deficits rather than to an examination of the pupil's learning environment. A shift from an almost endemic fascination with inputs to a focus on outcomes, challenges the system to take into account both the identified needs of the pupil and the capacity of the learning environment to assist pupils to learn and develop according to their individual potentials. This necessitates adoption of a biopsychosocial-oriented approach where school programmes adapt and change in response to what proves supportive and effective for the pupil and where outcomes are monitored on an ongoing basis in terms of the pupil, the learning task and the learning outcome. Encouragingly, in the context of the Republic of Ireland, recent policy-related developments evidence adoption of a biopsychosocial-oriented approach toward addressing special educational needs in inclusive ways, i.e. NCSE, 2013; NCSE, 2014; DES, 2017a; DES, 2017b; DES, 2017c; DES, 2017d.

Three Wengerian concepts: illuminating inclusive assessment values

Viewed from a sociocultural perspective, three intertwined concepts, derived from the work of Wenger (1998), prove illuminative with regard to how inclusive assessment practices might be developed, especially the assessment of special educational needs. In turn, these three Wengerian concepts refer to community of practice, participation, and reification.

Fostering the development of inclusive assessment practices obliges those who support pupils in schools to engage collaboratively as a community of practice – or collaborative practice team – in the sustained pursuit of shared assessment objectives. Broadening the composition of the community of practice, to include parents and allied professionals, for instance, would further enhance the inclusiveness of assessment practices. Though deemed conceptually deficient (Vandenbussche and De Schauwer, 2018), participation refers to the dynamic character of the interactions, shared experiences and negotiations that occur within purposive communities of practice as, in this instance, inclusive assessment practices are developed. Reification refers to the processes by which communities of practice produce concrete representations of practice. In the present scenario, these representations can include, for instance, assessment resources, policy documents, or systems that monitor pupil progress. As policy documents frequently over idealise practice intentions, it is necessary that the challenges and uncertainties of practice are also acknowledged.

The learning that occurs within a given community of practice is best explained as the intertwining of reification and participation (Wenger, 1998). Mutually constitutive, each concept has the capacity to address ambiguities or uncertainties the other instigates. For instance, when a particular assessment strategy is devised and summarised in a set of guidelines, the guidelines represent a codified reification of practice intentions. However, the practical implications of the assessment strategy only become manifest as it is implemented in schools or other settings and discussed among colleagues. These discussions may lead to the reconceptualisation or modification of the assessment resources in question (Hermansen, 2014). Accordingly, participation leads those in the community of practice towards learning experiences that could not result from reification alone. Nevertheless, the reified articles relating to agreed assessment purposes, such as policy documents, guidelines, materials or tasks, serve as 'guides to action' in the practice setting (Hall et al., 2012, p. 2), thus helping to infuse assessment practices with the values of inclusivity.

While the three Wengerian concepts referred to prove helpful in illuminating the significance of social processes at the heart of change initiatives, assessment-related or otherwise, it is important to stress that instigating and strengthening school-based communities of practice, represents a considerable challenge (Birenbaum et al., 2011). In this regard, attention is drawn to complex, frequently problematic relationships between individuals, and between individuals and communities of practice (e.g. Linehan and McCarthy, 2001; Achinstein, 2002; Graven, 2004; Fuller et al., 2005; Cairns, 2011). Additionally, in stressing the importance of the organisational culture of the school as a mediator of change processes, Ainscow (2008) draws attention to the tension that exists between conserving forces such as, on the one hand, competing exigencies, or prevailing norms of privacy and autonomy amongst staff, and, on the other hand, a desire to explore a more collaborative culture within which teachers support one another in experimenting with new practices. Developing a sustainable assessment regime that is inclusive of pupils for whom existing assessment practices prove marginalising, necessitates long-term, persistent capacity building at school and systems levels. Changing the culture of assessment means developing a shared language regarding goals of learning and teaching as well as shared understandings of the purposes of assessment in meeting such goals through school development plans and staff development initiatives (Elwood, 2006). Schools that have developed inclusive cultures are characterised by the presence of leaders who are committed to inclusive values and to a facilitative leadership style. Though not unproblematic to effect, such schools exhibit a degree of consensus among staff members around values of respect for difference and a commitment to offering all pupils access to learning opportunities. In this manner, assessment practices that are inclusive of pupils with special educational needs, gain traction as 'taken for granted functions that are the culture of a school that is more geared to fostering inclusive ways of working' (Ainscow, 2008, p. 250).

Enhancing inclusivity through conceptually-informed assessment practices

In outlining how inclusion might be understood in the context of achievement, Black-Hawkins (2010, pp. 22–23) draws attention to a shift in the reconceptualisation of inclusion; that is, away from the notion of responding to the identified special educational needs of a small number of individual pupils, and towards that of whole school improvement directed at enhancing the learning experiences and achievements of all pupils. As for achievement, Black-Hawkins (2010, pp. 22–23) calls for the concept to be broadened from the traditionally narrow preoccupation with academic standards, as assessed by tests and examinations, towards a broader conceptualisation of assessment that encompasses, for instance, social, emotional, creative, and physical achievements as well. Accordingly, the assessment of pupils with special educational needs arising from various disabilities is best conceived as predicated on principles or values intended to foster their inclusion through enhancing their participation and achievement in educational settings (Ainscow *et al.*, 2006, p. 25). Therefore, predicated on a socioculturally-informed, biopsychosocial conceptualisation of assessment, and mindful of the opportunities, difficulties and dilemmas involved, three assessment-related concepts, important to enhancing the inclusion of pupils with special educational needs in schools, are now considered. These refer, first, to the concept of Response to Intervention (RTI), second, to the broadening of assessment outcome criteria, and, third, to the concept of assessment accessibility. The sequential order in which these three concepts are considered is not significant. Instead their actual instantiation is to be understood as fluid and iterative, not in linear terms. Within each concept, issues considered have implications for assessment at all levels of educational systems, from large-scale, system-wide standardised testing of pupil achievement, to teacher-designed tests intended for classroom usage.

Response to Intervention (RTI): interrupting failure and progressing success

Historically, as outlined, decisions relating to the provision of educational supports for pupils with special educational needs have been based on IQ-achievement discrepancy systems that rely on the use of standardised assessments. Confined to resource allocation purposes, dominant assessment for identification systems contribute little to removing obstacles to achievement, or to determinations regarding the supports that enable pupils to benefit from school (Shevlin et al., 2013, p. 3). However, in contrast to traditional approaches that conceive of assessment, placement, and intervention as disparate practices, contemporary conceptualisations of assessment emphasise a seamlessly synergistic focus on quality teaching and learning practices. This means that instead of assessment being viewed solely as the principal means whereby evidence for the provision of additional resources is furnished, a phased approach characterises assessment as a 'process' rather than an 'event' and as a critical element in the planning of programmes and interventions designed to meet the needs of the pupils involved. 'Wait to fail' models of assessment and diagnosis are replaced with early identification and compensatory models, where pupils who are at risk for academic or behavioural problems are flagged in timely fashion and provided with research-based services and instruction. As a result, less emphasis is placed on the identification of special educational needs for purposes related to the allocation of additional supports. Instead, emphasis is focused on the early identification of curriculum-based weaknesses, with intervention taking place within the general education classroom. Here teachers embed into their teaching a dynamic review of how their pupils are progressing (Keen and Arthur-Kelly, 2010, p. 142, p. 145, p. 146, p. 149; McCleary et al., 2013, p. 197; Castro-Villarreal and Nichols, 2016, p. 9). Overarchingly, this reconceptualisation involves moving beyond assessment as a means of categorising pupils with special educational needs and allocating finite resources, to understanding assessment as a process that is integral to planning, teaching, and evaluation

The Response to Intervention (RTI) concept is one such early identification and intervention approach. RTI – also known as Multi-Tiered Systems of Support (MTSS) – is an instructional framework delivered as a continuum of three tiers of increasing intensity of support designed to match pupil need. Considering the ecology of pupils' learning experiences rather than solely focusing on academic deficits within the child, RTI involves the regular monitoring of change in a pupil's level or rate of learning through formative (dynamic) assessment. By collecting and interpreting meaningful data from a mastery perspective before proceeding to new, more complex skills, teachers seek to maximise achievement and reduce frustration in their pupils. This allows for a more individualised and flexible approach to assessment because interest is centred on improvement in pupil performance that is linked to instruction. The intensity of instruction must be viewed as a continuum along which pupils may move in either direction as their needs change. The concept of instructional intensity can assist in examining, in a more holistic way, the role and purpose of assessment for pupils with special educational needs (Keen and Arthur-Kelly, 2010, p. 140, p. 146).

In the US, since its introduction in the 2004 reauthorisation of the Individuals with Disabilities Education Act (IDEA), RTI has slowly replaced traditional IQ-achievement discrepancy methods for determining pupils' special education eligibility. Here educators have the option of enacting a programme of research-based instructional services as soon as learning challenges are detected and pupils are considered 'at risk' by some predetermined criteria. Eligibility for special education services for pupils with learning disabilities is subsequently determined in part by how these at risk pupils respond to research-based instruction and intervention.

Within RTI frameworks, pupils who fail to respond to tiered and research-based supports within a specified time frame progress through to formal special education referral processes. Tier 1 incorporates universal benchmark testing or screening into a research-based general education core curriculum. When research-based approaches are in place, most pupils (c. 80 per cent) should thrive in the general education setting. A minority of pupils (c. 15 per cent) identified as at-risk through Tier I screening are provided with supplemental research-based instruction and more frequent progress monitoring at Tier 2. Tier 3 supports are reserved for the smallest minority of pupils (c. 5 per cent) who fail to show adequate response to instruction at Tiers 1 and 2, and usually involve more individualised instruction (individuals or groups of two to three pupils) and even more frequent progress monitoring. Pupils who make progress and respond to intervention require less and less supplemental instruction over time, whereas pupils who fail to respond or show inadequate level change are guided through to formal special education referral processes (Castro-Villarreal and Nichols, 2016, p. 13). Therefore, within RTI frameworks recourse to formal 'psychological' assessment is only undertaken in the interests of identifying pupils whose difficulties are not likely to be catered for adequately within the range of teaching strategies and resources available within the school or who have not responded to the interventions applied (Shevlin *et al.*, 2013, p. 2).

Although currently highly regarded in the field of special education, implementation of RTI-type approaches is not unproblematic. Such actions are not panaceas, nor do they address the full range of concerns with assessment practices. Furthermore, they require careful application to individual contexts (Shaw, 2005, pp. 353–354; Büttner and Hasselhorn, 2011, p. 78). In this regard, educators have struggled with the implementation of RTI in underfunded and understaffed school contexts. In particular, schools that serve higher proportions of culturally and linguistically diverse pupils, higher proportions of economically disadvantaged pupils, have fewer staff, fewer supports, and more pupils who struggle with learning, achievement, and behaviour, find it exceedingly difficult to implement RTI methods with fidelity (Castro-Villarreal and Nichols, 2016, p. 12; Nichols and Castro-Villarreal, 2017, p. 5; Lemons *et al.*, 2018).

Implementation difficulties notwithstanding, RTI initiatives succeed in shifting the discourse from a deficit model of limited expectations for pupils with special educational needs to an empowering model based on the incremental charting of progress through acts of assessment tied closely and intrinsically to instruction and goal setting (Cumming and Wyatt-Smith, 2010, p. 8). While the formative forms of curriculum-based assessment which lie at the heart of RTI initiatives have limited use for system-based data collection, they provide the quality data required for monitoring engagement and progress at individual and school levels (Douglas et al., 2012, p. 172). This is true for all pupils, not just for pupils with special educational needs, thus evidencing the inclusivity of RTI-type approaches to assessment.

Broadening assessment outcome criteria

Roughly sketched, the dominance of academic outcomes as the main focus of schooling received significant impetus in the twentieth century development of testing and the growing sophistication of measurement. The institutionalisation of testing as a mechanism for selection embedded this focus and helped guarantee the hegemony of traditional academic outcomes. Contrastingly, assessments that rely on broad evidence and criteria remain the exception (Ladwig, 2010, p. 117). As a result, the dominant narrative informing assessment design is one of purpose purism, that is, assessment design driven by a single assessment purpose, disposing assessment designers to choose between such purposes or uses (Newton, 2017, p. 5, p. 7). Alternatively, purpose pluralism privileges the principle that assessment design should be driven by a multiplicity of assessment purposes simultaneously.

Espousing a pluralistic approach towards assessment purposes, Newton (2017, pp. 12–13) advises that multipurpose assessment should not be considered an occasional, unavoidable concession, but an organising principle for assessment design. Incorporating multiple indicators of pupil achievement necessitates treating assessment design as a process of negotiation between complementary, and sometimes contradictory, perspectives on assessment purposes. One such negotiative process might relate to how psychometric constraints could be loosened by relaxing particular psychometric 'rules' in some assessment contexts. Unnecessary limitations can be imposed on assessment options by transforming specific rules or models developed in specific contexts and for particular purposes into general principles. By recognising the limited applicability of various rules and rules of thumb, it should be easier to develop assessments that are more educationally relevant and useful. Imposing unnecessary constraints on assessment programmes will not improve their effectiveness, and removing such constraints will not interfere with their effectiveness or defensibility (Kane, 2017, p. 447, p. 452). The flexibility that results from the minimisation of psychometric requirements to those only necessary to the case at hand, allows for the design of assessments that more usefully improve learning.

Official inclusion policy scripts emphasise the raising of pupil achievement levels as the mechanism through which inclusion is to be achieved. However, such policy statements are not neutral, instead reflecting nuanced philosophical and political beliefs about curriculum content, instruction and assessment (Shaw, 2005). Habitually, such policies fail to critically deconstruct notions of what constitutes achievement or question the curriculum and assessment processes that pupils are subjected to. As a consequence, education systems continue to single out pupils and categorise them by their inability to meet a set of norm-related standards. The current focus on performativity marginalises pupils with special educational needs and constructs barriers to their participation and achievement. National testing systems, intended to raise the academic standards of all pupils, may actually impede the progress of some pupils, thus perpetuating inequalities between those who are perceived as high achievers academically and those who are not. The narrowing of the curriculum around topics assessed, most notably literacy and mathematics, may be at the expense of wider curriculum areas that have value for all pupils, but perhaps particular value for those with special educational needs. A consequence of such an omission is a failure to assess (and celebrate) progress in relation to educational outcomes that are relevant to the diverse range of pupils (Glazzard, 2013, p. 186; Black-Hawkins, Florian and Rouse, 2007, p. 25; Douglas *et al.*, 2012, p. 172; Douglas *et al.*, 2016, p. 98).

In arguing that the standards agenda works in opposition to the inclusion agenda, Glazzard (2013, p. 182) emphasises the need to embrace a broader understanding of what constitutes achievement in order to enable all learners to experience success. Educational achievement is deemed to be not limited to academic attainment and, therefore, it seems essential to consider ways of privileging other outcomes. Furthermore, because one type of outcome appears straightforward to 'measure' does not make that particular outcome more valuable than others that are less amenable to evaluation (Black-Hawkins *et al.*, 2007, p. 25). In this regard, Wiliam (2010, pp. 255–256) advises that the traditional preoccupation with the principle of 'assessment adequacy' might be more fruitfully directed toward the 'construct of interest'. In other words, attention should be shifted from how well we measure achievement to what it is that we are measuring (i.e. the construct of interest). In any case, by clearly separating the values issues – what we should be assessing – from the technical issues – how well we are assessing – facilitates greater public engagement in the debate about what should be assessed, as those lacking the necessary technical expertise are not excluded from the debate.

What should be assessed?

A broad distinction usefully groups pupil outcomes into 'attainment-related' outcomes (commonly concerned with academic curriculum areas) and 'wider curriculum-related' outcomes. 'Wider curriculum-related' outcomes commonly include 'additional', non-academic wellbeing and independence-related functional life skills that lie beyond the core curriculum.

For pupils with special educational needs, who may have had a history of failure in the past, opportunities to ignite curiosity and enhance their levels of independence, engagement and self-actualisation, represent central educational goals.

Forming an integral aspect of a broad and balanced curriculum, these so called non-academic, personal and social qualities are diverse and collectively facilitate goal-directed effort (e.g. grit, persistence, diligence, determination, purpose, resilience, optimism, self-regulation, agency, motivation), formation and maintenance of positive social relationships (e.g. gratitude, emotional intelligence, collaboration, social belonging, self-esteem, emotional well-being), and sound judgement and decision making (e.g. curiosity, open-mindedness, independent living skills, executive functioning, successful school transitions). Longitudinal research has confirmed that such qualities powerfully predict academic, economic, social, psychological, and physical well-being (Norwich and Kent, 2002, p. 60; Black-Hawkins et al., 2007, p. 25; Keen and Arthur-Kelly, 2010, p. 144; Douglas et al., 2012, p. 39, p. 168; Douglas et al., 2016, p. 99, p. 102; Duckworth and Yeager, 2015, p. 237; Moore et al., 2015, p. 1; Gustavsson, Kittelsaa and Tøssebro, 2017, pp. 469–483).

'Wider curriculum-related' outcomes, Douglas et al. (2012, pp. 38–39) suggest, may be particular to different special educational needs groups – and as such warrant particular assessment and monitoring. Illustrative examples for a number of such groups, mainly drawing on practice in the UK and Ireland are:

Hearing impairment:
Communication and language skills (in spoken language and sign language, including speech intelligibility); functional hearing ability; personal social functioning, including social inclusion.

Visual impairment:
Mobility and independence, including independent-living skills; social development; Braille proficiency; use of assistive technology.

Autism/autistic spectrum disorders:
Interaction skills, social communication skills (e.g. joint attention), sensory processing, generalisation of learning.

Social, emotional and behavioural difficulties (SEBD):
Assessment of an affective curriculum – personal and social development; developing and maintaining positive relationships with others in the classroom and during wider, extra-curricular activities.

General learning disabilities (mild, moderate, severe and profound):
Curriculum and assessment at a level where all pupils can succeed. A greater focus on functional outcomes and specialist curriculum areas – for pupils with the most profound learning difficulties these specific curriculum areas might include: early thinking skills, early communication, physical and life skills.

Physical disability:
A key thrust of literature on pupils with physical disabilities is linked to curriculum access rather than additional curriculum areas per se. Nevertheless, teaching on specialist equipment to engage fully in certain subjects is common. Motor skills development programmes have been introduced to help pupils draw abreast with their peers in motor learning, and to gain associated learning benefits like improved handwriting and/or keyboard skills.

The inclusion of a diverse range of pupils within education systems means that it is necessary to assess these 'wider' (also termed 'additional', 'broader' or 'expanded') areas of specific relevance to pupils with special educational needs. Assessment regimes should, therefore, attend to the 'wider' aspects of the curriculum as well as those traditionally assessed through examinations and attainment tests, and systems need to be in place to record educational progress on these areas. Different countries gather evidence in relation to these 'wider' outcomes in a variety of ways and to different extents, drawing upon classroom, national and international assessments. In this regard, PISA studies of cognition and content have recently been supplemented by reports centring on self-concept and motivation to pursue scientific studies (Baker et al., 2016, p. 109). However, as country case studies demonstrate (Douglas et al., 2016, p. 102), system-based data collection commonly focuses on 'attainment-related' outcomes regarding specific parts of the curriculum – especially literacy, mathematics and science. These country case examples present a strong case for the importance of conceptualising curriculum assessment in special educational needs as being broader than just areas of a core curriculum, however defined – especially literacy and mathematics. A concern then is that assessments reflect the 'full breath' of a curriculum, rather than just part of it. This 'full breath' includes progress and outcomes identified as appropriate and relevant to pupils with special educational needs, ensuring that their broad and diverse needs are recognised and monitored. An education system concerned with how well pupils with special educational needs are progressing should, logically, monitor progress relating to aspects of the curriculum which fall beyond areas of attainment typically recorded in national assessments. Thus, inclusive assessment should aim to celebrate diversity by identifying and valuing all pupils' individual learning progress and achievements, non-academically as well as academically.

Interest in the 'other side' of the report card is not new. What is new is the expectation that one can measure the 'wider' aspects of the curriculum other than academic ability that contribute to pupil well-being and achievement. While sharing this more expansive view of pupil competence and well-being, Duckworth and Yeager (2015, p. 237) caution that enthusiasm for these factors should be tempered with appreciation for the many inherent limitations of currently available measures. Notwithstanding the importance of 'wider' personal and social qualities, difficulties are encountered by professionals when measuring outcomes which are neither assessed according to numerical scores, nor linear in progression (Black-Hawkins et al., 2007, p. 26). As the frontiers of the measurable lie well beyond conventional testing and academic outcome measures, the field requires much greater clarity about how well it is able to 'count some of the things that count' (Duckworth and Yeager, 2015, p. 237). To find ways to better determine if non-academic educational programmes 'work', both in producing schooling outcomes and in the intended subsequent social effect, there is clearly much more research to be done (Ladwig, 2010, p. 114).

Additionally, difficulties arising with regard to the measurement of 'wider' aspects of the curriculum represent only first-stage challenges, as too little is known about the question of how to act on data regarding the personal qualities of pupils. For instance, if a pupil is assessed as being low in determination or resilience, what should one do? How can one intervene without stigmatising the pupil? Even if one is sure how to proceed, it is widely recognised that areas of cross-curricular development such as personal and social development are not easy to promote in school and require a whole school and integrated commitment (Norwich and Kent, 2002, p. 62). Therefore, while the enlightened use of data on personal and social qualities in educational practice is a topic of increasing importance, it is likely to be just as fraught with difficulty as the collection of that data. Nonetheless, given the advantages, limitations and potential of such measures, quantifying, even imperfectly, the extent to which young people express 'wider curriculum-related' outcomes such as self-control, gratitude, purpose, collaboration, emotional intelligence, and other beneficial personal qualities, has dramatically advanced understanding of pupil development (Duckworth and Yeager, 2015, p. 246; Bryk et al., 2015; Bryk, 2015).

Facilitating assessment accessibility

Accessibility refers to the degree to which pupils are given the opportunity to participate in and engage the curriculum, acquire requisite skills and learn the necessary content, and demonstrate their learning through facilitated access to assessment processes (Beddow, 2012, p. 97). A number of inclusive practices help facilitate the accessibility of assessments for the diverse range of pupils in the education system. Accordingly, four key strategies, used to help overcome access barriers that often deter meaningful participation in assessments by pupils with special educational needs, are now outlined and discussed. In turn, these strategies refer, first, to assessment accommodations, second, to alternative assessments, third, to the concept of 'opportunity to learn', and, fourth, to the application of 'universal design' principles to assessment design.

Accommodations: differentiating assessment practice

Pupils with special educational needs arising from disabilities vary enormously in their capabilities and needs. Even within a particular disability category, considerable variability exists in both the severity of the disability and in the range of disability characteristics across a spectrum, from almost undetectable to almost totally debilitating. Given the variability of pupil needs, concessions are made in the interests of fairness. Such adjustments are officially referred to as accommodations.

Intended to facilitate pupils with special educational needs to demonstrate their knowledge and skills, accommodations are defined as adjustments to the assessment conditions and response methods allowed; they do not change the content of the items tested. Intended to reduce the gap between those pupils receiving the accommodation and those who do not, without providing an unfair advantage to the recipients, key assumptions are that accommodations should be individualised depending on a student's access needs, and are used to equalise the opportunity for each test-taker to perform in such a manner that valid inferences can be drawn from the assessment scores obtained. The concept of differential boost is used to characterise the desired and valid effects of assessment accommodations (Pullin, 2005, p. 205; Shaw, 2005, p. 349; Kettler, 2012, p. 53; Lin and Lin, 2015, p. 774).

Research on accommodations

Constituting a contentious issue in the majority of countries that attempt assessment for all, assessment accommodations are the focus of considerable research attention. In the US, for instance, substantial research has been inspired by federal legislation indicating that all pupils, including those with special educational needs arising from disabilities, need to be included in any large-scale assessment programmes used to evaluate schools and districts. Most studies on accommodations have focused on large-scale or standardised assessments that are more closely linked to summative rather than formative forms of assessment. In this regard, though the large-scale Programme for International Pupil Assessment (PISA) does not officially allow or monitor test accommodations, the issue is on its radar (LeRoy et al., 2018, p. 6). Research has established that appropriate accommodations increase access for many pupils and these accommodations typically have moderate positive effects on the performances of pupils with disabilities. Additionally, appropriate accommodations should permit the same validity of inferences to be made from the results of the test as those from pupils not receiving accommodations. Though the inconsistent use of testing accommodations is problematic, the potential for testing accommodations to meet validity criteria is theoretically founded and well-established in the research literature (Elliott et al., 2012, pp. 8–9, pp. 11–14; Davies and Elliott, 2012, p. 3; Kettler, 2012, pp. 64–65; Beddow, 2012, p. 103–104; Lin and Lin, 2015, p. 774).

Common testing accommodations

Representing variations in the specified procedures for test administration in response to a pupil's special educational needs, accommodations may affect an assessment's environment, content, or format (Wiliam, 2010, p. 276; Beddow, 2012, p. 103; Elliott et al., 2012, pp. 11–14; Hopper, 2001, cited in Douglas et al., 2012, p. 35; Mitchell, 2015, pp. 18–19).

Typical accommodations are those that modify the following assessment features:

(A) **Assessment setting or environment:**

Candidates may be allowed to take their assessment at a location or setting other than the examination centre. For example, to eliminate distractions candidates may be located in a separate room or in a carrel (small recess or enclosed area) or even outside the school in a pupil's home or in a hospital setting.

(B) **Presentation format:**

Common accommodations for test presentation are large-print versions of the test for pupils with visual impairments; versions of the test in Braille; a simplified layout of the examination paper; the use of a scribe or sign language interpreter; the opportunity for the pupil to have instructions read aloud, reread, paraphrased, or clarified; translation of the directions into the pupil's native language; flashcards to assist hearing-impaired candidates in mental arithmetic tests; permitting candidates to use manipulatives in particular assessments.

(C) **Response format:**

Response accommodations relate to how pupils respond to a test question or prompt and include allowing a pupil to respond orally or indicate an answer by pointing or gesturing. Response accommodations also include the use of a scribe to record written answers, permitting test-takers to respond in the test booklet instead of on the answer sheet, use of a brailler, use of technological recording methods, or the provision of typewritten, word-processed or transcribed responses by pupils who are unable to write.

(D) **Timing and scheduling:**

These accommodations are described as changes in the timing or scheduling of testing to suit the pupil, such as extending the length of given time for the assessment to be completed, permitting supervised breaks or rest periods in testing, scheduling test over multiple sessions, or even over multiple days.

(E) **Equipment and materials:**

Equipment and materials accommodations include the permitted use of magnification and amplification equipment, special acoustic conditions, and the use of a calculator.

Alternative assessments

Despite the application of appropriate accommodations, a limited number of pupils who receive most of their instruction in the general curriculum, but experience substantial learning challenges arising from their disabilities, need further support to be effectively included in assessment processes. Alternative or alternate assessments are generic terms for methods used to assess the academic performance of these pupils. Assessing different constructs from the assessments administered to the majority of pupils, alternative assessments are, invariably, based on alternative achievement criteria and performance expectations. However, as with assessments generally, these assessments should have a clearly defined structure, guidelines determining which pupils may participate, and clearly defined scoring criteria and procedures (Davies and Elliott, 2012, p. 4; Elliott *et al.*, 2012, p. 10, pp. 14–16; Mitchell, 2015, pp. 18–19; Wiliam, 2010, pp. 276–277).

Addressing different standards from the tests taken by pupils without disabilities, alternative assessments can take very different forms. These include the collection of classroom work products, portfolios of work, digital video recordings, interviews, structured observations, and pupils' responses to on-demand tasks. Requiring pupils to construct rather than select responses, portfolio assessment, for example, is an organised collection or documentation of pupil generated or pupil focused work, typically depicting the range of individual pupil skills. Evidence samples derived from various forms of alternative assessment, are assessed either by reference to the grade-level expectations and achievement level descriptors specified for all pupils in that grade or relative to pupils' Individual Education Plans (IEPs), rather than to relevant national or state standards. Nonetheless, there is little doubt that alternative assessments (as with accommodations) have had the effect of altering the content of special education away from the low-level functional-life skills approaches, traditional for pupils with more severe disabilities, in favour of a richer, more academic curriculum associated with the standards articulated for general education (Pullin, 2008, p. 123, cited in Wiliam, 2010, p. 276).

Opportunity to learn (OTL)

In focusing attention on the teaching and learning of important knowledge and skills for pupils with special educational needs, inclusive assessment-based accountability systems represent a potentially powerful lever for improving classroom instruction and pupil performance. However, a key barrier to assessments that measure what pupils with special educational needs have learned is limited 'opportunity to learn' the intended curriculum. As a result, test score inferences are often based on unverified assumptions of alignment between curricular content and assessment constructs. As virtually all pupils with special educational needs should be afforded an equitable opportunity to access the intended curriculum, the goal of improved educational opportunities and outcomes requires the development of a variety of assessment and instructional strategies. Though difficult to measure (Elliott, 2015, p. 58), 'opportunity to learn' (OTL) is one such strategy that aims to ensure that all pupils have access to the general curriculum, or at least the curriculum on which they are assessed.

As the validity of test score inferences depend on pupils' opportunity to learn the intended curriculum, curricular access provides the context for interpreting test scores and thus should be understood when making claims about pupils' achievement levels based on assessment results. 'Opportunity to learn' (OTL) research, in particular research on alignment between what is taught and what is assessed, has confirmed its importance in relation to promoting and understanding pupil achievement. In the context of the US, OTL is of critical importance for the majority of pupils with special educational needs who participate in the same large-scale achievement tests (with or without accommodations) as pupils without disabilities. By virtue of being administered the same assessments, pupils with special educational needs have to be afforded a comparable opportunity to learn the content they are expected to know on these assessments, regardless of where or by whom they receive their instructional content. Failure to do so undermines educational equity, fairness in assessment, and the validity of certain test score uses and interpretations (Elliott et al., 2012, pp. 8–9, pp. 10–11; Kurz et al., 2012, p. 37, pp. 49–50; Elliott et al., 2018).

Universal design of assessments

A rich literature describes the modification of assessments to accommodate pupil diversity. However, assessment practices internationally continue to be influenced by dated standards and limited conceptualisations of item modification. Additionally, challenges and controversies have arisen related to the administration and interpretation of accommodated results, as accommodations may alter an assessment to the extent that accommodated and non-accommodated items are no longer comparable. Consequently, there has been a shift in thinking toward the universal design of assessments, where the underlying principle is that the design of an assessment should be accessible to the largest number of pupils possible, thereby reducing the need for accommodations or other adaptations.

Defined as a form of proactive differentiation, 'universal design' stands in binary opposition to retrospective forms of adjustment. Therefore, in contrast to the retrofitting nature of accommodations, application of the concept of 'universal design' takes the diversity of the pupil population into consideration from the outset. Universally designed assessments are designed and developed from the beginning to allow participation of the widest possible range of pupils, and to result in valid inferences about performance for all pupils who participate in an assessment. A universal assessment design incorporates seven elements: inclusive assessment population; precisely defined constructs; accessible, non-biased items; amenability to accommodations; simple, clear, and intuitive instructions and procedures; maximum readability and comprehensibility; and maximum legibility (Shaw, 2005, p. 350). Accordingly, rather than modifying assessments designed for the general pupil population, the application of universal design principles results in a single assessment that is suitable for all pupils (Abedi et al., 2012, p. 82; Beddow, 2012, p. 97; Elliott et al., 2012, p. 9, p. 15; Thurlow and Kopriva, 2015; Douglas et al., 2016, pp. 101–102; Capp, 2017, pp. 793–795). Though research to increase test accessibility by applying 'universal design' principles to assessment design is relatively new, nonetheless, 'universalising' assessments to their most fundamental and simple formats, presents potential solutions to the challenges of facilitating assessment accessibility and interpreting score data derived from modified assessments. However, to this end, further research needs to be undertaken on the consequences for the validity and reliability of assessment data of the application of elements of universal design.

Accessibility overview

The four accessibility strategies outlined – i.e. assessment accommodations, alternative assessments, 'opportunity to learn', and the application of 'universal design' principles to assessment design – can be implemented at all levels of the education system to ensure that there is equitable assessment for all pupils. Accordingly, schools can apply accessibility strategies to ensure that those who might remain outside of large-scale assessments are provided with valid small-scale assessment systems, thus ensuring the benchmarking and monitoring of all pupils. Equally, national and regional assessment authorities can apply pressure to ensure that there is equity for all pupils in the application of accessible assessment (Elliott et al., 2012, pp. 16–17). Although discourse on assessment accessibility has improved, we are still far from creating the degree of access necessary (Castro-Villarreal and Nichols, 2016, p. 12). However, the cumulative contribution of research and practice relating to accommodations, alternative assessments, 'opportunity to learn', and 'universal design', can do much in the way of alleviating educators' concerns with standardisation and the provision of accessible assessments (Shaw, 2005, p. 350). In time, further research and development efforts on these issues with national and regional assessment systems, can contribute to the improvement of internal, school-based assessment practices.

Concluding summary remarks

With specific reference to the assessment of special educational needs amongst pupils, this chapter discussed the influence of particular conceptualisations of learning and attainment on the assessment of those needs. Also discussed were the shifts in perspective necessary to develop inclusive assessment practices predicated on inclusive principles. Evident from the discussion throughout is that differing conceptualisations of assessment give rise to particular assessment approaches and practices. In this regard, a psycho-medical conceptualisation of assessment stresses within-pupil causations of learning needs, while a sociocultural-informed, biopsychosocial conceptualisation of assessment demands recognition of the inextricable relationships between context-dependent learning processes and the assessment of learning. Also evident from the chapter discussion is that the assessment of special educational needs is a complex, multi-layered process. Not least among these complexities are concerns centring on issues of cultural bias and disproportionality, arising from the utilisation of normative-based cognitive and achievement instruments in determinations of special educational needs. As a result, a parallel development accompanying enhanced levels of special educational needs-related provision is an increased questioning of those concepts fundamental to how 'special educational needs' have traditionally been conceptualised, assessed, and addressed. In drawing attention to the need for a reorientation of assessment practices, yet mindful of the opportunities, difficulties and dilemmas involved, three assessment-related concepts, important to enhancing the inclusion of pupils with special educational needs in schools, were discussed. These were adoption of a response to intervention approach, the broadening of assessment outcome criteria, and the enhancement of assessment accessibility. As subjecting the rich diversity of pupils to psychometrically-oriented, standardised forms of assessment, to satisfy categorisation and accountability-oriented purposes, creates a range of difficulties for educators and pupils, the case for significantly increasing the adoption of inclusive assessment practices predicated on a socioculturally-informed, biopsychosocial conceptualisation of special educational needs is irrefutable.

Prompts for reflection and discussion

- Reflect on how taken-for-granted cultural legacies may inform how assessment is conceived of and transacted in your context.
- Does a psycho-medical conceptualisation of assessment adequately account for the complex nature of the special educational needs of individual pupils?
- Should the full diversity of pupils, including pupils who struggle with academic forms of learning, be assessed for accountability purposes using standardised forms of assessment?
- What are the implications for assessment practices of shifting from a focus on the individual self to a focus on the relational or situational self?
- Negative consequences of disproportionality can include inappropriate placement and restricted access to the general education curriculum. With reference to your context, consider how referral, assessment, and placement practices, impact on the educational participation and achievement of pupils from minority backgrounds.
- When conceived of as constituting a 'process' rather than an 'event', consider how assessment can best serve the needs of pupils with special educational needs in your context.
- Consider the advisability of embracing broader understandings of what constitutes achievement in order to enable all learners to experience success.
- With respect to your context, reflect on how pupils with special educational needs can be helped to overcome access barriers that deter their meaningful participation in assessments.

CONCLUSION: DISRUPTING NORMATIVE THINKING ON ASSESSMENT

This chapter brings together some of our thinking around assessment policy and practice against the backdrop of international policy and principles of inclusive assessment practice. We invite the reader to formulate your own questions around the implications for a shift in an understanding of assessment which takes into account the many different worlds and arenas which shape and are shaped by assessment policy and practice.

Dominant discourses of assessment, teaching and learning

The OECD's Synergies for Better Learning: An International Perspective on Evaluation and Assessment (2013) reports on an international review of evaluation and assessment policies across 28 countries, including Ireland. Larger in scale than our international policy analysis within this text we conclude with it here in summary as representative of dominant discourses and voices of assessment in policy and practice worldwide.

The OECD report suggests in summary that increased demands for quality, equity and effectiveness have resulted in assessment being positioned in international policy documents across a wide range of countries as a tool for improvement, accountability and educational planning. Accountability itself is further positioned as a purpose of assessment as assessment discourses centre around measurement and learning outcomes. In Ireland this move towards greater accountability at national, local and classroom level can be seen in, for example, the introduction of whole school inspection of post primary schools in 2003, the publication of school inspection reports since 2006 and the introduction of mandatory standardised testing in primary schools in 2007.

With this language of outcomes and accountability comes a focus nationally and internationally on quality and standards, which is reflected in for example the previously mentioned standardised assessments for students in many countries in ways which tie to an agendum of monitoring and accountability. National indicator frameworks and international benchmarking are also becoming more and more a feature of assessment practice as results are being used to hold policy makers, school leaders and teachers accountable.

Countries are deploying more resources to invest in development of their assessment and evaluation strategies with a particular emphasis on whole school evaluation, but this is resulting in a greater variety in assessment activities reported across the 28 countries involved in the study. What remains common to much of these assessment activities is the need to keep the student at the centre of the assessment process. Classroom based assessment is understood as having a formative role and there is an emerging recognition that data on assessment can be collected in classrooms and other sites to improve how we, nationally and internationally, do assessment. The development in Ireland of national standards of student achievement alongside the collection of national data as a result of the development of The National Strategy for Literacy and Numeracy (2011) align with the wider international policy context and focus on assessment as central to any reforms in education practice.

Assessment emerges from this report as an international business becoming ever more public, with national and international comparisons now so readily available, alongside the recognition of the importance of education in a global world. Findings suggest that greater technological sophistication should allow for more individualised assessments and greater school autonomy. Commercial and media interest in education is nationally and internationally at an all time high, consumed by more educated parents and expectant students, against a backdrop of a demanded efficiency and care in the use of public resources and teacher professionalism. Despite this discourse of change and expectation the Irish education system and in particular the Junior and Leaving Certificate assessments have remained until current proposed reforms a relic of bygone years and as stated by the OECD in an earlier report, 'the face that the Irish school presents to the world is thus quite recognisably that of previous generations' (OECD, 1991, p. 55).

Understanding assessment as sociocultural practice

Throughout this book, we have endeavoured to unpack some of the stories and effects of current assessment practices. A common thread running through many of the chapters is the sense that assessment can often emerge as a damaging instrument that often serves to solidify failure and lack of achievement as much as it rewards success and endeavour. Indeed, assessment is often at the sharp edge of what Becky Francis and Martin Mills (2012) have referred to as the damage of schooling whereby the system becomes far too invested in the school as an elaborate sorting mechanism in thrall to the demands of national and global industrial and economic demands through a human capital orientation. Indeed, performance on standardised state-imposed assessments of literacy, numeracy and subject-specific areas have become the dominant mechanisms, not just of student selection and stratification, but also of school, teacher and area accountabilities. An alternative view would see schools and assessment as processes linked to the lifelong development of creativity, understanding and creativity amongst people that would serve to assist the development of sustainable lifepaths for humans and humanity. Of course, this social justice perspective on education conflicts with the human capital demands of late capitalism and also disrupts long-standing relationships between social class and race privilege within the education system.

Our view is that international and national perspectives on assessment have become far too invested in the normative nature of assessment, that is in terms of its construction of comparative numerators used to stratify and categorise populations. As we draw to a conclusion in this volume we would like to engage in some imaginative 'blue-skies thinking' whereby we consider how things might be rather than how things are in the present moment. This means calling into question the narrow human capital approach to education where students are viewed almost entirely as outputs and products in terms of their potential contributions to the economy. It means considering education and schooling in terms of their potential for personal, social, cultural and environmental transformation; rather than continuing to fuel the current system of reproduction and stratification.

Is it possible, in a world of competences, that assessment would no longer be time-bound and students could repeat to achieve higher grades to demonstrate increased 'competence'? After all, in development terms, age is just a number and it is in fact the school system that places normative age-related standards and expectations on learning and performance. In many countries, performance in terminal state-imposed assessments exist as a rite of passage and as a significant milestone in the life trajectories of people. Here in Ireland, the Established Leaving Certificate has become the pre-eminent qualification for higher education entry, without very little additional requirements or displays of proficiency. Other jurisdictions have similar systems whereby terminal school examinations contribute all or most of the entry requirements for courses in higher education institutions (O'Donnell, 2018).

If we were to conceptualise assessment practice in schools as criterion-referenced and developmental (beyond age-related norms) then we would create possibilities to free people from the restricted pressure cooker situation that has evolved into terminal school examinations. Perhaps, by harnessing the potential allowed by global digitisation, people could view their educational trajectories as life-long and incremental portfolios to be filled and re-filled *ad infinitum*. Imagine learning as truly continuous and assessment as dynamic, lifelong and fluid. In such a world, a student is free to build and develop their portfolio of knowledge and skills throughout their lives without being limited by the sitting of terminal examinations at given moments in their educational trajectories. Their learner identities also become more dynamic in that the individual has the opportunity to define their own pathways through flexible and genuinely student-centred education systems.

In such a system, people could reach the criteria for university entry at any stage over their life trajectory and thus allow the education system to escape from the inflexibility and imprisonment imposed by a terminal examination of extreme high stakes. When learning is viewed from a sociocultural perspective, it becomes clear that learning happens anywhere and everywhere and it not entirely bound by linear or stage-based transitions through cognitive development. It is also the case that learning is less of an individual and product-oriented experience but rather a communal activity that is inextricably linked to cultural, historical and social contexts. When we take these views, then we become less enamoured with individualised terminal examinations and more open to flexible and situated understandings of learning and the performance of learning. Criterion-based approaches to assessment practices in schools could allow for the required freedom and flexibility that would allow students pursue their own learning goals without being hamstrung by systemic, globally-imposed restraints around what should be learned and when it should be learned. Of course, as has been the experience throughout the history of schooling, every change or development in the system of assessment is open to colonisation and co-option by the wealthy and educationally-invested classes in western society. As long as educational credentials hold potential for capitalisation as a positional good then they will be sought-after and attained by any means necessary by those who desire them. It seems unlikely that assessment can ever be disentangled from the personal, public, cultural, political, economic and ability driven worlds that both sustain it and need it, however, our proposition is that we should always act to de-emphasise the external human capital orientated view of assessment, in favour of more person-centric forms and modes of assessment practice. However, as mentioned previously, any collective actions that we can take to provide greater opportunities for equality of condition amongst engagement with education then there will be wide societal/ communal benefits accruing for humanity.

Understanding the complex sociocultural interactions of the worlds of assessment explored in this text has the potential to unlock new worlds for assessment practice, perhaps for example like some of the 'blue skies thinking' begun here in this concluding chapter. Reconceptualising assessment practice within and without of these worlds opens new worlds and ways for assessment as it is mediated and negotiated by individuals in every new and unique assessment setting and situation. While we cannot remove assessment from the very many worlds which make up its specification, enactment and experience as it is through these worlds that assessment comes to be, understanding how these complex worlds function to mediate assessment policy and practice allows new opportunities to question, critique and understand the practice of assessment in individual settings. We conclude with a consideration of some sample key assessment issues from this perspective.

Student progress and individual needs

The practical challenges of tracking student progress and identifying individual needs in typically diverse heterogeneous classrooms are immense (Keen and Arthur-Kelly, 2010, p. 150). As assessing pupil learning is a complex, multi-faceted process, assessment capability, traditionally conceived as assessment literacy, is considered a fundamental competency for all teachers (Poskitt, 2014; DeLuca and Johnson, 2017). Three significant shifts have occurred in the assessment landscape over recent decades (Brookhart, 2011). These refer, first, to the increased reliance on assessments for accountability purposes, including large-scale and standardised measures administered within classroom contexts; second, to increased usage of formative assessment approaches; and, third, to the enactment of assessments within highly diverse teaching contexts. These shifts foreground the necessity of attending to the assessment capabilities of teachers as a matter of priority.

Despite widespread calls for assessment capable teachers, research indicates that teachers generally maintain low levels of assessment knowledge and skills. As a result, teachers struggle to interpret assessment policies and to implement assessment practice in alignment with contemporary mandates and assessment theories. Beginning teachers are particularly unprepared for assessment in schools, as assessment has historically been a neglected area of study in teacher education programmes. Moreover, current teacher education models prove challenging with respect to supporting teacher candidates' and initial teachers' developing conceptions and practices of assessment. Post-graduation, beginning teachers work to establish confidence across their practice with explicit professional learning in assessment not always accessible or available. Instead, practising teachers tend to learn about assessment through collaboration and discussions with colleagues, and adapt to in-school assessment routines and cultures. However, how effective this learning is, how similarly and how consistently teachers are able to apply criteria-based standards of judgement when evaluating evidence of student learning and achievement is rarely systematically researched (DeLuca and Johnson, 2017, p. 121). As a result, despite the compelling arguments for assessment capability, many teachers are often involved in assessment-related decision-making without sufficient background or professional development in assessment. Moreover, researchers have noted that there is comparatively little research on teachers' current assessment practices from which to construct responsive professional learning structures aimed at promoting teacher assessment capability. Cumulatively, these issues give rise to concerns about how to enhance teachers' enactment of assessment in the complex realities of the classroom. Notwithstanding the challenges involved, an emerging trend toward assessment education is increasingly evident, a deliberate focus within professional learning communities to enhance and support teachers' assessment capabilities (Poskitt, 2014; DeLuca et al., 2016a).

Reconceptualising teacher assessment capability

In contrast to how professional development opportunities were traditionally conceptualised – i.e. short-term, pre-prepared, one-off courses, delivered in similar format with minimal adaptation to individual needs – DeLuca et al. (2016b, p. 264) assert the need to reconceptualise teacher assessment capability as a socially and contextually dependent developmental process. Occurring in social, political, economic, cultural, educational, and human contexts, assessment is subject to multiple, dynamic influences. Therefore, influenced by national and regional policies, curricular and pedagogical emphases, and community expectations, teacher assessment capability is a complex structure rather than a simple set of delineated skills that can be implemented in any context. As a result, building teacher capability in assessment requires school leaders, teacher educators and policy advisers, as well as teachers themselves, to understand its interrelationship with other key aspects in educational change processes, including the wider policy context and the social, cultural and professional contexts in which they work (Looney et al., 2018, p. 445; Livingston and Hutchinson, 2017, p. 291; Poskitt, 2014). In response, Xu and Brown (2016) propose moving the field beyond a focus on the knowledge base, towards consideration of a situated, dynamic, and evolving system in which teachers constantly make compromises among competing tensions. This suggests that the improvement of teacher assessment capability is a systematic, communal enterprise that depends on joint efforts from relevant stakeholders. It also helps to dispense with dichotomous conceptualisations of capability, moving, instead, towards conceiving of assessment capability as on a continuum, with different levels of mastery contingent upon the context in which assessment is conducted.

Conceiving of teacher assessment capability as being context specific, and subject to reinterpretation over time in particular socio-cultural settings, has implications for how that capability is most effectively developed among teachers. Mockler (2011, cited in Looney et al., 2018, p. 446) states that that effectiveness is predicated on attending equally to three domains of practice: personal teacher experience; professional context; systemic factors. Though mutually constitutive, nonetheless each domain possesses its own particular focus. Consideration is now given to how each of the three domains proves influential with respect to the enhancement of teachers' assessment capabilities.

Personal teacher experience

That long-held views can inhibit change in professional thinking and practice, is well understood. Yet support for teachers to uncover and confront their prior beliefs and reflect on the impact they have on their practices, is seldom an integral element of their professional development. Enabling teachers to understand that their assumptions can act as a filter or indeed a block, to adaptive ways of thinking and acting in the classroom, serves as a professional development priority. With respect to assessment reforms, teachers who find that their beliefs are consistent with envisaged reforms support the changes proposed. On the other hand, teachers fail to implement proposed reforms if their pre-existing, rooted beliefs conflict with the ideals of the reforms. There is also evidence, Choi (2017) established, that different teachers respond to a particular reform differently, frequently implementing superficial aspects but disregarding more fundamental aspects of the reform.

As teachers' understandings, beliefs and values influence the extent to which changes to assessment practices are enacted, particularly at a fundamental level, personal experiences, including teachers' historical experiences of assessment, are significant and demand acknowledgement in the design of professional development endeavours. Predetermined professional learning opportunities, designed without consideration of teachers' learning needs, will not develop their assessment capabilities, particularly as teachers as individual learners are likely to have different understandings of assessment in relation to their pupils' learning needs, the curriculum and their own pedagogical choices. Consequently, they will need more tailored professional learning opportunities throughout their career as the contexts within and across schools change and as their own and their pupils' learning needs change (Livingston and Hutchinson, 2017; Choi, 2017).

Professional context

A range of contextual factors help determine assessment practices in school settings. These include curricular principles, pedagogical practices, organisational culture, collegial relationships, and dominant dispositions toward reform. To engage in reflective and challenging conversations about assessment, teachers need to recognise their practice as ongoing enquiry. Accordingly, what can facilitate transformative, sustainable change is building not only teachers' knowledge and skills in assessment but also their capacity to enquire and to engage in quality learning conversations with peers, within supportive, trusting, collegiate school cultures (Livingston and Hutchinson, 2017, p. 296). The conditions that enable and facilitate meaningful teacher dialogue must therefore be understood if challenging conversations, supportive of an enquiry stance towards assessment practices, are to be valued by teachers and school leaders.

Systemic factors

Complex and interconnected, a range of systemic factors prove central to the enhancement of teachers' assessment capabilities. These systemic factors relate, for instance, to the roles of national agencies, local authorities, teacher education programmes, reform agendas, high stakes testing practices, and national (even regional) teaching and learning cultures. Inherently political, other 'external' influences include media commentary and debates about teachers and their work, including the assessment practices of teachers.

Single initiatives, implemented in fragmented ways, do not result in long-term, sustainable and effective assessment-related change. Instead, transforming the enactment of assessment requires establishing partnerships within, across and beyond the education sector into the community and political realms, thus rendering it necessary that all those involved in enhancing teacher assessment capability, are responsive to the full breadth of considerations arising from these 'wider' contexts. In this regard, to reduce the chasm between intended reforms and enacted reforms, as evidenced by classroom practices (Cuban, 2013), policy makers, for instance, should appreciate the challenges teachers face when they attempt to implement assessment reforms. More generally, as enhancing the assessment capabilities of teachers on a sustainable, system-wide basis is complex and difficult, a positive outcome is contingent on the establishment of shared understanding and identification of priorities among partners (Wylie and Lyon, 2009; Poskitt, 2014; Choi, 2017; Livingston and Hutchinson, 2017).

Implications for a research agenda on assessment capability development

How teachers extend their knowledge and practice on assessment once they are integrated into the teaching profession is relatively unknown (Poskitt, 2014, p. 543). The need for well-conceived and well-conducted research into the area of teacher assessment capability is therefore generally acknowledged. Encouragingly, over recent decades, teacher assessment capability has been a growing area in assessment research. As assessment capability is increasingly promoted as a fundamental competency for teachers, how teachers develop fluency in assessment, based on their context of practice and exposure to responsive teacher education, must feature as research foci. In this regard, areas prioritised for future capability-related research include: determining best-practice models for universities and colleges to build meaningful learning partnerships with local schools, education bodies and accreditation agencies in the service of teacher assessment capability enhancement; the design of coherent teacher education programmes that position assessment capability as a priority vis-à-vis other fundamental teacher competencies; identifying diverse pedagogical approaches to engage teachers in assessment capability development; motivating teacher candidates' and teachers' to prioritise assessment capability within their own professional development. Researching how teachers' orientations to assessment shift from preservice to in-service, and across years of experience, will also provide important information on the development of teachers' assessment capability over their careers (DeLuca *et al.*, 2016b; DeLuca and Johnson, 2017). Combined, these aspects will not only direct what teachers need to learn to enhance their assessment capabilities but also provide important information on preferred modes for professional development.

Assessment practice and policy: the eye and the storm

In this book we have sought to redefine assessment as a sociocultural practice through an exploration of what we understand as assessment within and without the personal, public, cultural, political, economic and ability driven worlds that simultaneously shape and are shaped by it. Each chapter focuses in on one key area of assessment and exemplifies central concepts, policies and experiences for practice from this perspective. In our discussion assessment emerges as a complex entity with varying far reaching and often unperceived effects for everyone involved in the act.

Returning now to our introductory chapter and our Rogoffian approach outlined here, the challenge for ourselves and for the reader is to understand assessment as a contested space for learning, itself an entity but continually evolving in and emerging from all of these worlds at once with a fierce energy and unstoppable momentum. We understand and the chapters in this book exemplify how the practice of assessment exists within tempestuous spaces bringing with it both opportunities and challenges. As we come to reflect on and develop our assessment practice we need to do so in ways that recognise this while also prioritising context and individual specific and inclusive definitions and practices of assessment. Our definitions of assessment matter and allow us to mediate assessment policy and practice in meaningful ways.

Somewhat like the eye at the heart of the storm assessment sits at the heart of continually emerging complex debates across a large number of sites and arenas. We are reminded of Sylvia Plath here and her image of the eye of a tornado. We hope that some of the discussion, ideas and questions in this book will help ourselves and readers get closer to what assessment is, what it looks at feels like at the centre of individual and context specific practices and that it is not experienced by students and teachers as Sylvia imagines as:

> …very still and empty, the way the eye of the tornado must feel, moving dully along in the middle of the surrounding hullabaloo.
>
> *(Sylvia Plath, The Bell Jar)*

BIBLIOGRAPHY

Abedi, J., Bayley, R., Ewers, N., Mundhenk, K., Leon, S., Kao, J., and Herman, J. (2012) Accessible reading assessments for students with disabilities. *International Journal of Disability, Development and Education*, 59(1), 81–95.
Achinstein, B. (2002) Conflict amid community: The micropolitics of teacher collaboration. *Teachers College Record*, 104(3), 421–455.
Acquah, D. (2013) *School Accountability in England: past, present and future*. AQA Centre for Education Research and Policy. www.cerp.org.uk.
Agnew, J. (2005) Space: Place. In P. J. Cloke (Ed.) *Space of Geographical Thought: Deconstructing Human Geography*. London: Sage. 81–96.
Ainscow, M. (2008) Teaching for diversity – The next big challenge. In Connelly, F. M., He, M. F., and Phillion, J. (Eds) *The Sage handbook of curriculum and instruction*. London: Sage. 240–258.
Ainscow, M., Booth, T., and Dyson, A. (2006) *Improving schools, developing inclusion*. Abingdon: Routledge.
Ainscow, M., Dyson, A., Hopwood, L., and Thomson, S. (2016) *Primary Schools Responding to Diversity: barriers and possibilities*. A Report for the Cambridge Review Trust.
Anders, J., Jerrim, J., and McCulloch, A. (2016) How much progress do children in Shanghai make over one academic year? Evidence From PISA. *AERA Open*, Sage Journals, 2(4), doi: doi:2332858416678841.
Artiles, A. J., and Dyson, A. (2005) Inclusive education in the globalization age: The promise of comparative cultural historical analysis. In Mitchell, D. (Ed.) *Contextualizing inclusive education*. London: Routledge. 37–62.
ASTI (2017) *Reform not Harm* (leaflet). Dublin: ASTI. www.asti.ie/fileadmin/user_upload/Documents/Campaigns/ASTI_Junior_Cycle_A5.pdf (accessed 07. 11. 2017).
ASTI, DES, TUI (2015) *Junior cycle reform: Joint statement on principles and implementation and appendix to the joint statement*. www.asti.ie/fileadmin/user_upload/Documents/Campaigns/16pp_ASTI_Joint_Statement___Appendix.pdf.
Australia Education Union – AEU (VIC) (2012) *Submission to the Victorian Competition and Efficiency Commission: Inquiry into School Devolution and Accountability*. Australia.

Australian Curriculum, Assessment and Reporting Authority (ACARA) (2013) *Revised draft Australian curriculum: The arts foundation to year 10*. www.acara.edu.au/verve/_resources/Draft_Arts_Curriculum _22_February_2013.pdf (accessed 27. 06. 2013).

Baglieri, S., Bejoian, L. M., Broderick, A. A., Connor, D. J. and Valle, J. W. (2011) [Re]claiming 'Inclusive Education' toward cohesion in educational reform: Disability studies unravels the myth of the normal child. *Teachers College Record*, 113(10), 2122–2154.

Baird, J.*et al*. (2013) *Predictability in the Irish Leaving Certificate*. Oxford University Centre for Educational Assessment Report, Oxford.

Baker, J., Lynch, K., Cantillon, S., and Walsh, J. (2016) *Equality: From theory to action*. London: Springer.

Ball, S. J. (1993) What is policy? Texts, trajectories and toolboxes. *The Australian Journal of Education Studies*, 13(2), 10–17.

Ball, S. J. (2009) Academies in Context: Politics, Business and Philanthropy and Heterarchical Governance. *Management in Education*, 23(3), 100–103.

Ball, S. J. (2012) *Foucault, power, and education*. London: Routledge.

Ball, S. J., Maguire, M., and Braun, A. (2012) *How schools do policy: Policy enactments in secondary schools*. London: Routledge.

Ballou, D., and Springer, M. (2015) Using student test scores to measure teacher performance: some problems in the design and implementation of evaluation systems. *Educational Researcher*, 44(2), 77–86.

Banks, J., Shevlin, M., and McCoy, S. (2012) Disproportionality in special education: Identifying children with emotional behavioural difficulties in Irish primary schools. *European Journal of Special Needs Education*, 27(2), 219–235.

Barker, B., and Mills, C. (2018) The psy-disciplines go to school: psychiatric, psychological and psychotherapeutic approaches to inclusion in one UK primary school. *International Journal of Inclusive Education*, 22(6), 638–654.

Barrance, R., and Elwood, J. (2018) National assessment policy reform 14–16 and its consequences for young people: student views and experiences of GCSE reform in Northern Ireland and Wales. *Assessment in Education: Principles, Policy and Practice*, 1–20. https://doi.org/10.1080/0969594X.2017.1410465.

Beddow, P. A. (2012) Accessibility theory for enhancing the validity of test results for students with special needs. *International Journal of Disability, Development and Education*, 59(1), 97–111.

Benjamin, S., Nind, M., Hall, K., Collins, J., and Sheehy, K. (2003) Moments of inclusion and exclusion: pupils negotiating classroom contexts. *British Journal of Sociology of Education*, 24(5), 547–558.

Berliner, D. (2011) Rational responses to high stakes testing: The case of curriculum narrowing and the harm that follows. *Cambridge Journal of Education*, 41(3), 287–302.

Bernelius, V. (2013) Street numbers as educational outcomes? Segregation and school effects in comprehensive schools in Helsinki (Osoitteenmukaisia oppimistuloksia? Kaupunkikoulujen eriytymisen vaikutus peruskoululaisten oppimistuloksiin Helsingissä). In V. Bernelius (Ed.) *Eriytyvät Kaupunkikoulut. Helsingin peruskoulujen oppilaspohjan erot, perheiden kouluvalinnat ja oppimistuloksiin liittyvät aluevaikutukset osana kaupungin eriytymiskehitystä*. Research Series 2013, 1, 135–149.

Bernelius, V., and Kauppinen, T. (2011) School outcomes and neighbourhood effects: A new approach using data from Finland. In M. Van Ham, D. Manley, N. Bailey*et al*. (Eds) *Neighbourhood Effects Research: New Perspectives*. New York: Springer. 225–247.

Bernstein, B. (1973) *Class, codes and control*. Vol. 2. London: Routledge and Kegan Paul.

Bernstein, B. (1975) Class and pedagogies: Visible and invisible. *Educational studies*, 1(1), 23–41.

Biesta, G. J. (2004) Education, accountability, and the ethical demand: Can the democratic potential of accountability be regained?. *Educational theory*, 54(3), 233–250.

Bildungsbericht (2014) *Bildung in Deutschland 2014*. www.bildungsbericht.de/daten2014/bb_2014.pdf.

Billington, T. (2017) Educational inclusion and critical neuroscience: friends or foes?. *International Journal of Inclusive Education*, 21(8), 866–880.

Birenbaum, M., Kimron, H., and Shilton, H. (2011) Nested contexts that shape assessment for learning: School-based professional learning community and classroom culture. *Studies in Educational Evaluation*, 37(1), 35–48.

Black, P., and Wiliam, D. (2009) Developing the theory of formative assessment. *Educational Assessment, Evaluation and Accountability*, 21(1), 5–31.

Black, P., and Wiliam, D. (2018) Classroom assessment and pedagogy. *Assessment in Education: Principles, Policy and Practice*, 25(6), 551–575.

Black-Hawkins, K. (2010) The framework for participation: a research tool for exploring the relationship between achievement and inclusion in schools. *International Journal of Research and Method in Education*, 33(1), 21–40.

Black-Hawkins, K., Florian, L., and Rouse, M. (2007) *Achievement and Inclusion in Schools*. London: Routledge.

Bloomer, M. (1997) *Curriculum making in Post-16 education: The Social Conditions of Studentship*. London: Routledge.

Bloomer, M. (2001) Young lives, learning and transformations: some theoretical considerations. *Oxford Review of Education*, 27(3), 429–449.

Blume, H. (2016) Charter Schools. *LA Times*, 4 October 2016.

Boaler, J., William, D., and Brown, M. (2000) Students' Experiences of Ability Grouping-disaffection, Polarisation and the Construction of Failure. *British Educational Research Journal*, 26(5): 631–648.

Bogason, P. (2000) *Public Policy and Local Governance: Institutions in Postmodern Society*. Cheltenham, UK: Edward Elgar.

Borland, R. (2005) Ruth Borland in *The Irish Times*, 27 September 2005.

Boud, D. (2000) Sustainable Assessment: Rethinking Assessment for the Learning Society. *Studies in Continuing Education*, 22: 151–167.

Bourdieu, P., and Passeron, J. C. (1990) *Reproduction in education, society and culture*, Vol. 4. London and New York: Sage.

Boyd, W. L., Kerchner, C. T., and Blyth, M. (2008) *The transformation of great American school districts: How big cities are reshaping public education*. Cambridge, MA: Harvard Education Press.

Bradbury, A. (2014a) Phonics test: changing pedagogy through assessment, IOE London Blog, 30 September 2014. https://ioelondonblog.wordpress.com/2014/09/30/phonics-test-changing-pedagogy-through-assessment/.

Bradbury, A. (2014b) Slimmed down assessment or increased accountability: teachers, elections and UK government assessment policy. *Oxford Review of Education*, 40(5), 610–627.

Brancaleone, D., and O'Brien, S. (2011) Educational commodification and the (economic) sign value of learning outcomes. *British Journal of Sociology of Education*, 32(4), 501–519.

Bray, M., and Kwo, O. (2013) Behind the façade of fee-free education: Shadow education and its implications for social justice. *Oxford Review of Education*, 39(4), 480–497.

Broadfoot, P. (1996) *Education, assessment and society: A sociological analysis*. Open University Press.

Broadfoot, P. (2010) Signs of change: Assessment past, present and future [Foreword]. In Wyatt-Smith, C., and Cumming, J. (Eds) *Educational assessment in the 21st century - Connecting theory and practice*. London: Springer. v–xi.

Brookhart, S. (2011) Educational assessment knowledge and skills for teachers. *Educational Measurement: Issues and Practice*, 30(1), 3–12.

Brown, M., Askew, M., Millett, A. and Rhodes, V. (2003) The key role of educational research in the development and evaluation of the National Numeracy Strategy. *British Educational Research Journal*, 29(5), 655–672.

Bruner, J. (1996) *The Culture of Education*. Cambridge, MA: Harvard University Press.

Bryk, A. S. (2015) 2014 AERA distinguished lecture: Accelerating how we learn to improve. *Educational Researcher*, 44(9), 467–477.

Bryk, A. S., Gomez, L. M., Grunow, A., and LeMahieu, P. G. (2015) *Learning to improve: How America's schools can get better at getting better*. Harvard Education Press.

Buchanan, I. (1992) *Extraordinary Spaces in Ordinary Places: De Certeau and the Space of Postcolonialism*. www. mcc.murdoch.edu.au/readingroom/litserv/span/36/jabba.html.

Burris, C. C., and Welner, K. G. (2005) Closing the Achievement Gap by Detracking. *Phi Delta Kappan*, 86(8), 594–598.

Büttner, G., and Hasselhorn, M. (2011) Learning disabilities: Debates on definitions, causes, subtypes, and responses. *International Journal of Disability, Development and Education*, 58(1), 75–87.

Byrne, D., and Smyth, E. (2010) *No Way Back? The Dynamics of Early School Leaving*. Dublin: Liffey Press/ESRI.

Cahill, K. (2012) *What class are you in? A critical ethnography of school choice, social class and student identity in an Irish urban post-primary school*. Unpublished PhD thesis, Cork: University College Cork.

Cahill, K., and Hall, K. (2014) Choosing schools: Explorations in post-primary school choice in an urban Irish working class community. *Irish Educational Studies*, 33(4), 383–397.

Cahill, K., Curtin, A., Hall, K., and O'Sullivan, D. (2017) Adolescent Literacy, Identity and School (ALIAS): positions, pedagogies and spaces for learning. In Culligan, B. and Mehigan, G. (Eds) *Exploring the Literacy Landscape: Celebrating 40 Years of Research and Practice*. Dublin: Literacy Association of Ireland, 32–39. https://cora.ucc.ie/bitstream/handle/10468/6910/ALIAS_LAI_CORA.pdf?sequence=1and isAllowed=y.

Cahill, K., Curtin, A., Hall, K., and O'Sullivan, D. (2018) Views from the margins: teacher perspectives on alternative education provision in Ireland. *International Journal of Inclusive Education*, 1–18. https://doi.org/10.1080/13603116.2018.1492643.

Cahill, K., O'Sullivan, D., Hall, K., and Curtin, A. (2018) *ALIAS Project*.

Cairns, L. (2011) Learning in the Workplace: Communities of Practice and Beyond. In Malloch, M., Cairns, L., Evans, K., and O'Connor, B. N. (Eds) *The SAGE Handbook of Workplace Learning*. London: Sage, 73–85.

California Department of Education (2016) *Charter Schools CalEdFacts – CalEdFacts*.

California Head Start Association and CCR Analytics (2015) *California Head Start Family Outcomes Bulletin 2015*.

Californian Educational Data (2016) www. ed100.org (accessed 04. 09. 2016).

California Teachers' Association (CTA) (2016) *Common Core Standards*. www.cta.org/en/Issues-and-Action/Testing-and-Standards/Common-Core-State-Standards.aspx.

Capp, M. J. (2017) The effectiveness of universal design for learning: a meta-analysis of literature between 2013 and 2016. *International Journal of Inclusive Education*, 21(8), 791–807.

Carmines, E. G., and Zeller, R. A. (1979) *Reliability and validity assessment*. California, London and New Delhi: Sage.

Castro-Villarreal, F., and Nichols, S. L. (2016) Intersections of Accountability and Special Education: The Social Justice Implications of Policy and Practice. *Teachers College Record*, 118(14).

Choi, J. (2017) Understanding Elementary Teachers' Different Responses to Reform: The Case of Implementation of an Assessment Reform in South Korea. *International Electronic Journal of Elementary Education*, 9(3), 581–598.

Clarke, J., and Baxter, J. (2014) Satisfactory progress? Keywords in English school inspection. *Education Inquiry*, 5(4).

Clarke, J., and Ozga, J. (2011) *Governing by Inspection? Comparing School Inspection in Scotland and England Paper for Social Policy Association Conference.* University of Lincoln, 4–6 July 2011.

Clarke, J., Grek, S., and Ozga, J. (2013) *Governing by Inspection (2) Redesigning School Inspection in England and Scotland.*

Cochran-Smith, M., and Dudley-Marling, C. (2012). Diversity in teacher education and special education: The issues that divide. *Journal of Teacher Education*, 63(4), 237–244.

Coffield, F., and WilliamsonB. (2011) *From Exam Factories to Communities of Discovery: the democratic route.* Bedford Way Papers. London: Institute of Education.

Cognitive Abilities Test Fourth Edition (CAT4) *GL Assessment.* www.gl-assessment.co.uk/products/cognitive-abilities-test-cat4.

Cohen, D. K., Spillane, J. P., and Peurach, D. J. (2018) The dilemmas of educational reform. *Educational Researcher*, 47(3), 204–212.

Collins, P. H. (2000) Gender, black feminism, and black political economy. *The Annals of the American Academy of Political and Social Science*, 568(1), 41–53.

Common Core State Standards Initiative (2010) *Common Core Standards.* www.corestandards.org/read-the-standards/ (accessed 07. 08. 2016).

Cooc, N., and Kiru, E. W. (2018) Disproportionality in Special Education: A Synthesis of International Research and Trends. *The Journal of Special Education*, doi: doi:0022466918772300.

Cosgrove, J., and Cartwright, F. (2014) Changes in achievement on PISA: the case of Ireland and implications for international assessment practice. *Large-scale assessments in education*, 2(1), 1–17.

Courtney, S. (2016) Post-panopticism and school inspection in England. *British Journal of Sociology of Education*, 37(4), 623–642.

Courtois, A. (2015) 'Thousands waiting at our gates': moral character, legitimacy and social justice in Irish elite schools. *British Journal of Sociology of Education*, 36(1), 53–70.

Cowie, B. (2005) Student commentary on classroom assessment in science: a sociocultural interpretation. *International Journal of Science Education*, 27(2), 199–214.

Craft, E., and Howley, A. (2018) African American Students' Experiences in Special Education Programs. *Teachers College Record*, 120(10).

Crenshaw, K. (1991) Mapping the margins: Intersectionality, identity politics, and violence against women of color. *Stanford Law Review*, 1241–1299.

Crowley, C. B., and Yu, M. (2017) The global testing culture. *Teachers College Record* (Review Article), 19 December 2017. www.tcrecord.org, ID No.: 22213.

Cruz, R. A., and Rodl, J. E. (2018) An Integrative Synthesis of Literature on Disproportionality in Special Education. *The Journal of Special Education*, 52(1), 50–63.

Cuban, L. (2013) Why so many structural changes in schools and so little reform in teaching practice?. *Journal of Educational Administration*, 51(2), 109–125.

Cumming, J., and Wyatt-Smith, C. (2010) Framing assessment today for the future: Issues and challenges. In Wyatt-Smith, C., and Cumming, J. (Eds) *Educational assessment in the 21st century – Connecting theory and practice.* London: Springer. 1–16.

Davies, M., and Elliott, S. N. (2012) Inclusive assessment and accountability: Policy to evidence-based practices. *International Journal of Disability, Development and Education*, 59(1), 1–6.

Dedering, K., and Müller, S. (2010) School improvement through inspections? First empirical insights from Germany. *Journal of Educational Change*, 12(3). Springer. 301–322.

DeLuca, C., and Johnson, S. (2017) Developing assessment capable teachers in this age of accountability. *Assessment in Education: Principles, Policy and Practice*, 24(2), 121–126.

DeLuca, C., LaPointe-McEwan, D., and Luhanga, U. (2016a) Teacher assessment literacy: A review of international standards and measures. *Educational Assessment, Evaluation and Accountability*, 28(3), 251–272.

DeLuca, C., LaPointe-McEwan, D., and Luhanga, U. (2016b) Approaches to classroom assessment inventory: A new instrument to support teacher assessment literacy. *Educational Assessment*, 21(4), 248–266.

Department for Education (DfE) (2010) *The Importance of Teaching (The Schools White Paper)*. London: DfE.

Department for Education (DfE) (2011) Record number of under-performing schools to become academies. Press Release, 5 September. London: DfE.

Department for Education (DfE) (2013) *Primary Assessment and accountability under the new national curriculum*.

Department for Education (DfE) (2014) *Reforming Assessment and Accountability for Primary Schools: Government response to consultation on primary school assessment and accountability*.

Department for Education (DfE) (2016) *Intervening in failing, underperforming and coasting schools: Government Consultation Response*.

Department for Education (DfE) (UK) (2016) *Educational Excellence Everywhere*. London: Government Publications.

Department of Education and Early Childhood Development (2009) *Supporting School Improvement: Transparency and Accountability in Victorian Government Schools Blueprint Implementation Paper*. Victoria.

Department of Education and Early Childhood Development (2011) *The Accountability and Improvement Framework for Victorian Government Schools*. Victoria.

Department of Education and Early Childhood Development (2013) *Professional Practice and Performance for Improved Learning – school accountability*. Victoria.

Department of Education and Skills (DES) (2011) *Literacy and Numeracy for Learning and Life: The National Strategy to Improve Literacy and Numeracy among Children and Young People 2012–2020*.

Department of Education and Skills (DES) (2012) (2015) *A Framework for Junior Cycle*. Dublin: Government Publications.

Department of Education and Skills (DES) (2017a) *Circular No 0013/2017, Special Education Teaching Allocation, Circular to the Management Authorities of all Mainstream Primary Schools*. Dublin: Stationary Office. www.education.ie/en/Circulars-and-Forms/Active-Circulars/cl0013_2017.pdf.

Department of Education and Skills (DES) (2017b) *Circular No 0014/2017, Special Education Teaching Allocation, Circular to the Management Authorities of all Post Primary Schools: Secondary, Community and Comprehensive Schools and the Chief Executive Officers of the Education and Training Boards*. Dublin: Stationary Office. www.education.ie/en/Circulars-and-Forms/Active-Circulars/cl0014_2017.pdf.

Department of Education and Skills (DES) (2017c) *Guidelines for Primary Schools Supporting Pupils with Special Educational Needs in Mainstream Schools*. Dublin: Stationary Office. www.education.ie/en/The-Education-System/Special-Education/Guidelines-for-Primary-Schools-Supporting-Pupils-with-Special-Educational-Needs-in-Mainstream-Schools.pdf.

Department of Education and Skills (DES) (2017d) *Guidelines for Post-Primary Schools Supporting Students with Special Educational Needs in Mainstream Schools*. Dublin: Stationary Office. www.education.ie/en/The-Education-System/Special-Education/Guidelines-for-Post-Primary-Schools-Supporting-Students-with-Special-Educational-Needs-in-Mainstream-Schools.pdf.

Desforges, M., and Lindsay, G. (2010) *Procedures used to diagnose a disability and to assess special educational needs: An international review*. Trim, County Meath, Ireland: National Council for Special Education. http://ncse.ie/wp-content/uploads/2014/10/5_NCSE_Diag_Ass.pdf.

DES/NCCA (1999) *Primary School Curriculum*. Dublin: Government Publications.

Diagnostic Statistical Manual (DSM V) (2013) 5th edition. American Psychiatric Association. www.psychiatry.org/psychiatrists/practice/dsm.

Donaldson, G. (2015) *Successful Futures: Independent Review of Curriculum and Assessment Arrangements in Wales*. OGL, Crown Copyright.

Dore, R. (1997) *The Diploma Disease: Education, Qualification and Development*. London: Institute of Education, University of London.

Douglas, G., Travers, J., McLinden, M., Robertson, C., Smith, E., Macnab, N., Powers, S., Guldberg, K., McGough, A., O'Donnell, M., and Lacey, P. (2012) *Measuring educational engagement, progress and outcomes for children with special educational needs: A review*. Trim, County Meath, Ireland: National Council for Special Education. http://ncse.ie/wp-content/uploads/2014/10/Outcomes26_11_12Acc.pdf.

Douglas, G., McLinden, M., Robertson, C., Travers, J., and Smith, E. (2016) Including pupils with special educational needs and disability in national assessment: Comparison of three country case studies through an inclusive assessment framework. *International Journal of Disability, Development and Education*, 63(1), 98–121.

Drumcondra Post Primary Test – Mathematics (DPPT – Maths) Educational Research Centre. www.erc.ie/test-sales/achievement-tests-post-primary.

Drumcondra Post Primary Test – Reading (DPPT – Read) Educational Research Centre. www.erc.ie/test-sales/achievement-tests-post-primary.

Drumcondra Reasoning Test (DRT) Educational Research Centre. www.erc.ie/test-sales/ability-and-aptitude-tests/drumcondra-reasoning-test-drt.

Duckworth, A. L., and Yeager, D. S. (2015) Measurement matters: Assessing personal qualities other than cognitive ability for educational purposes. *Educational Researcher*, 44(4), 237–251.

Dustmann, C. (2004) Parental background, secondary school track choice and wages. *Oxford Economic Papers*, 56, 209–230.

Education and Training Inspectorate (ETI) Northern Ireland. etini.gov.uk.

Education and Training Inspectorate (ETI) (2013) *Together Towards Improvement*.

Education Scotland (2015) *How Good is Our School?*. 4th edition. Livingston: Crown Copyright.

Education Scotland (2016) *Assessment for Curriculum for Excellence: Strategic Vision, Key Principles*. www.gov.scot/Topics/Education/Schools/curriculum/assessment.

Education Scotland (n.d.) *Curriculum for Excellence*. www.curriculumforexcellencescotland.gov.uk.

Education Week Research Center (2016) *Quality Counts 2016 – Called to Account. New Directions in School Accountability*.

Eivers, E. (2010) PISA: Issues in implementation and interpretation. *The Irish Journal of Education*, 38, 94–118.

Elliott, S. N. (2015) Measuring opportunity to learn and achievement growth: Key research issues with implications for the effective education of all students. *Remedial and Special Education*, 36(1), 58–64.

Elliott, S. N., Davies, M., and Kettler, R. J. (2012) Australian students with disabilities accessing NAPLAN: Lessons from a decade of inclusive assessment in the United States. *International Journal of Disability, Development and Education*, 59(1), 7–19.

Elliott, S. N., Kurz, A., and Yel, N. (2018) Opportunity to Learn What Is on the Test and Performance on the Test. *The Journal of Special Education*, doi: doi:0022466918802465.

Ellison, S. (2012) Intelligent Accountability: Re-Thinking the Concept of "Accountability" in the Popular Discourse of Education Policy. *Journal of Thought*, Summer 2012 2012, 19–41.

Elwood, J. (2006) Formative assessment: possibilities, boundaries and limitations. *Assessment in Education: Principles, Policy and Practice*, 13(2), 215–232.

Elwood, J., and Murphy, P. (2015) Assessment systems as cultural scripts: A sociocultural theoretical lens on assessment practice and products. *Assessment in Education Principles Policy and Practice*, 22(2), 182–192.

Emirbayer, M., and Mische, A. (1998) What is agency?. *American Journal of Sociology*, 103, 962–1023.
Entorf, H., and Minoiu, N. (2005) What a difference immigration policy makes: A comparison of PISA score in Europe and traditional countries of immigration. *German Economic Review*, 6(3), 355–376.
Esteban-Guitart, M., and Moll, L. C. (2014) Funds of Identity: A new concept based on the Funds of Knowledge approach. *Culture and Psychology*, 20(1), 31–48.
Estyn Inspection System *Wales Common Inspection Framework from September 2010.* estyn.gov.wales.
EU Education and Training Monitor (2015) *Germany*. https://ec.europa.eu/education/tools/docs/2015/monitor2015-germany_en.pdf.
European Agency for Development in Special Needs Education (EADSNE) (2012) *Raising Achievement for All Learners – Quality in Inclusive Education*. Odense, Denmark: European Agency for Development in Special Needs Education.
Eurydice (2007) *School Autonomy: Policies and Measures*. Brussels: Eurydice European Unit.
Eurydice (2010) *Organisation of the Educational System in Germany*. Brussels: European Commission.
Fleer, M. (2015) Developing and assessment pedagogy: the tensions and struggles in re-theorising assessment from a cultural-historical perspective. *Assessment in Education: Principles, Policy and Practice*, 22(2), 224–246.
Florian, L. (2008) Inclusion: special or inclusive education: future trends. *British Journal of Special Education*, 35(4), 202–208.
Florian, L. (2013) Reimagining special education: Why new approaches are needed. In Florian, L. (Ed.) *The SAGE handbook of special education*. 2nd edition. London: Sage. 9–22.
Florian, L. (2014) What counts as evidence of inclusive education?. *European Journal of Special Needs Education*, 29(3), 286–294.
Florian, L., and Black-Hawkins, K. (2011) Exploring inclusive pedagogy. *British Educational Research Journal*, 37(5), 813–828.
Florian, L., and Spratt, J. (2013) Enacting inclusion: A framework for interrogating inclusive practice. *European Journal of Special Needs Education*, 28(2), 119–135.
Florian, L., Rouse, M., and Black-Hawkins, K. (2016) *Achievement and inclusion in schools*. London: Routledge.
Florian, L., Hollenweger, J., Simeonsson, R. J., Wedell, K., Riddell, S., Terzi, L., and Holland, A. (2006) Cross-cultural perspectives on the classification of children with disabilities: Part I. Issues in the classification of children with disabilities. *The Journal of Special Education*, 40(1), 36–45.
Foucault, M. (1977) *The archaeology of knowledge*. London: Tavistock.
Foucault, M. (1980) in Gordon, C. (Ed.) *Power/Knowledge: selected interviews and other writings, 1972–1977*. New York: Pantheon Books.
Francis, B., and Mills, M. (2012) Schools as damaging organisations: Instigating a dialogue concerning alternative models of schooling. *Pedagogy, Culture and Society*, 20(2), 251–271.
Francis, B., Archer, L., Hodgen, J., Pepper, D., Taylor, B., and Travers, M. (2017) Exploring the relative lack of impact of research on 'ability grouping' in England: a discourse analytic account. *Cambridge Journal of Education*, 47(1), 1–17, doi: doi:10.1080/0305764X.2015.1093095.
Fraser, N. (1997) *Justice interruptus: Critical reflections on the "postsocialist" condition*. New York and London: Routledge.
Fraser, N. (2000) Rethinking recognition. *New Left Review*, 107–120.
Frymier, J. (1996) *Accountability in Education: still and evolving concept*. Bloomington, Indiana: Phi DeltaKappa Educational Foundation.

Fuller, A., Hodkinson, H., Hodkinson, P., and Unwin, L. (2005) Learning as peripheral participation in communities of practice: a reassessment of key concepts in workplace learning. *British Educational Research Journal*, 31(1), 49–68.
Gee, J. P. (2003) Opportunity to learn: a language-based perspective on assessment. *Assessment in Education*, 10(1), 27–46.
Gewirtz, S. (1997) Post-Welfarism and the reconstruction of teachers' work in the UK. *Journal of Education Policy*, 12(4), 217–231.
Gewirtz, S. (1998) Conceptualizing social justice in education: Mapping the territory. *Journal of Education Policy*, 13(4), 469–484.
Gipps, C. (1999) Socio-Cultural aspects of assessment. *Review of Research in Education*, 24, 355–392.
Gipps, C. V., and Murphy, P. (1994) *A fair test? Assessment, achievement and equity*. Open University Press.
Gipps, C., and Stobart, G. (2009) Fairness in assessment. In C. Wyatt-Smith, and J. Cumming (Eds) *Educational assessment in the 21st century: Connecting theory and practice*, 105–118. Dordrecht, Heidelberg, London and New York: Springer.
Glatter, R. (2012) Persistent Preoccupations: the rise and rise of school autonomy and accountability in England. *Educational Management, Administration and Leadership*, 40(5), 559–575.
Glatter, R. (2014) The academies model: fragmentation, favouritism and failure. *The Guardian*, 7 January 2014. London.
Glazzard, J. (2013) A critical interrogation of the contemporary discourses associated with inclusive education in England. *Journal of Research in Special Educational Needs*, 13(3), 182–188.
Golding, J. (2017) Policy critics and policy survivors: who are they and how do they contribute to a department policy role typology?. *Discourse: Studies in the Cultural Politics of Education*, 38(6), 923–993.
Goodley, D. (2014) *Dis/ability studies. Theorising disablism and ableism*. London: Routledge.
Graven, M. (2004) Investigating mathematics teacher learning within an in-service community of practice: The centrality of confidence. *Educational studies in mathematics*, 57(2), 177–211.
Green, A. L., Cohen, D. R., and Stormont, M. (2018) Addressing and preventing disproportionality in exclusionary discipline practices for students of color with disabilities. *Intervention in School and Clinic*, 54(1) 241–245.
Gronlund, N. E. (1998) *Assessment of student achievement*, 6th edition. Massachusetts: Allyn & Bacon Publishing.
Gustavsson, A., Kittelsaa, A., and Tøssebro, J. (2017) Successful schooling for pupils with intellectual disabilities: the demand for a new paradigm. *European Journal of Special Needs Education*, 32(4), 469–483.
Hacking, I. (2006) Kinds of People: Moving Targets, The Tenth British Academy Lecture. www.britac.ac.uk (accessed 05. 05. 2017).
Hall, K., and özerk, K. (2010) *Primary Curriculum and Assessment: England and other Countries*. In The Cambridge Primary Review Research Surveys. London: Routledge.
Hall, K., Allan, C., Dean, J. and Warren, S. (2003) Classroom Discourse in the Literacy Hour in England. *Language, Culture and Curriculum*, 16(3), 284–297.
Hall, K., Collins, J., Benjamin, S., Nind, M., and Sheehy, K. (2004) Saturated modles of pupildom: assessment and inclusion/exclusion. *British Educational Research Journal*, 30(6), 801–817.
Hall, K., Conway, P. F., Murphy, R., Long, F., Kitching, K., and O'Sullivan, D. (2012) Authoring oneself and being authored as a competent teacher. *Irish Educational Studies*, 31 (2), 103–117.
Hall, K., Curtin, A., Kitching, K., Connolly, T., and Ni Laoire, C. (2013) *The VIP Project Final Report*. IRCHSS.

Hall, K.Curtin, A., and Rutherford, V. (2014) *Networks of Mind: Learning, Culture, Neuroscience*. Routledge: London.

Hall, S. (1996) Introduction: Who Needs Identity?. In Hall, S., and du Gay, P. (Eds) *Questions of Cultural Identity*. London: Sage.

Hansen, J. B. (1993) Is educational reform through mandated accountability an Oxymoron?. *Measurement and Evaluation in Counseling and Development*, 26(1), 11–21.

Hanson, F. A. (1994) *Testing Testing: Social Consequences of the Examined Life*. Berkeley, CA: University of California Press.

Harlen, W., and Deakin Crick, R. (2002) *A systematic review of the impact of summative assessment and tests on students' motivation for learning*. EPPI Centre Review in Research Evidence in Education Library, Issue 1. London: EPPI-Centre, Social Science Research Unit, Institute of Education.

Hattie, J. (2012) *Visible learning for teachers: Maximising impact on learning*. New York: Routledge.

Hedegaard, M., and Daniels, H. (2011) Introduction. In Daniels, H., and Hedegaard, M. (Eds) *Vygotsky and Special Needs Education – Rethinking Support for Children and Schools*. London: Continuum. 1–8.

Heinrich, M. (2015) Metamorphoses of pedagogical autonomy in German school reforms: continuities, discontinuities and synchronicities illustrated by empirical studies on school development planning, school profiling and school inspection. Open access article.

Heitink, M. C., Van der Kleij, F. M., Veldkamp, B. P., Schildkamp, K., and Kippers, W. B. (2016) A systematic review of prerequisites for implementing assessment for learning in classroom practice. *Educational Research Review*, 17, 50–62.

Herman, J., and Ing, M. (2008) State testing. In T. L. Good *21st century education: A reference handbook*, Vol. 2, (II-) 410–418. Thousand Oaks, CA: SAGE Publications Ltd. Doi: doi:10.4135/9781412964012.n93.

Hermans, H. J. M. (2001) The dialogical self: towards a theory of personal and cultural positioning. *Culture and Psychology*, 7(3), 243–281.

Hermansen, H. (2014) Recontextualising assessment resources for use in local settings: Opening up the black box of teachers' knowledge work. *Curriculum Journal*, 25(4), 470–494.

Hochschild, J., and Scovronick, N. (2003) *The American Dream and the Public Schools*. Oxford, MA: Oxford University Press.

Holden, L. (2005) Interview with Ruth Borland in *The Irish Times*. 20 September 2005.

Hussain, I. (2013) The School Inspector Calls. *Education Next*, 13(3). http://educationnext.org/the-school-inspector-calls/.

Hutchings, M. (2018) *Exam Factories: The impact of accountability measures on children and young people*. Research commissioned by the National Union of Teachers.

Hutt, E. L. (2014) The GED and the rise of contextless accountability. *Teachers College Record*, 116(9), 1–20.

International Classification of Diseases (2001) 10th edition [ICD10]. World Health Organization. www.who.int/classifications/icd/ICD10Volume2_en_2010.pdf.

Ireland, Government of (2011) *Programme for National Recovery 2011–2016*. Dublin: Government Publications.

Ireland, Government of (2016) *A Programme for a Partnership Government*. Dublin: Government Publications.

Ireson, J., Hallam, S., and Hurley, C. (2005) What are the Effects of Ability Grouping on GCSE Attainment?. *British Educational Research Journal*, 31(4), 443–458.

Itkonen, T., and Jahnukainen, M. (2007) An Analysis of Accountability Policies in Finland and the United States. *International Journal of Disability, Development and Education*, 54(1), 5–23, doi: doi:10.1080/1034912060114966.

Ivinson, G., and Murphy, P. (2003) Boys don't write romance: the construction of knowledge and social gender identities in English classrooms. *Pedagogy, Culture and Society*, 11(1), 89–111.

Jeffrey, B. and Woods, P. (2002) The reconstruction of primary teachers' identities. *British Journal of Sociology of Education*, 23(1), 89–106.

Jones, C. D., Priestley, K. L., and Ding, G. (2018) An Overview of Four Challenges for English Learners Experiencing Learning Difficulties. *Teachers College Record*, 3 December 2018. www.tcrecord.org. ID No.: 22588.

Joyce, J., Harrison, J. R., and Murphy, D. (2016) Evaluating Students with Disabilities and Their Teachers: Use of Pupil Learning Objectives. *Teachers College Record*, 118(14).

Kane, M. T. (2017) Loosening psychometric constraints on educational assessments. *Assessment in Education: Principles, Policy and Practice*, 24(3), 447–453.

Keddie, A. (2015a) Matters of autonomy and accountability in the English schooling policy context: constraints and possibilities. *Journal of Educational Administration and History*, 47(1).

Keddie, A. (2015b) New modalities of state power: Neoliberal responsibilisation and the work of academy chains. *International Journal of Inclusive Education*, 19(11), 1–16.

Keddie, A. (2016) Academisation, school collaboration and the primary school sector in England: a story of six school leaders . *School Leadership and Management*, June.

Keen, D., and Arthur-Kelly, M. (2010) Assessment, disability, student engagement and responses to intervention. In Wyatt-Smith, C., and Cumming, J. (Eds) *Educational assessment in the 21st century – Connecting theory and practice*. London: Springer. 137–155.

Keillor, G. (1985) *Lake Wobegon Days*. New York: Viking.

Kelly, A. V. (2009) *The curriculum: Theory and practice*. London andNew York: Sage.

Kennedy, M., and Power, M. J. (2010) 'The smokescreen of meritocracy': Elite education in Ireland and the reproduction of class privilege. *Journal for Critical Education Policy Studies*, 8, 222–248.

Kerchner, C. T., and Özerk, K. (2014) Teaching Language Minority Students in Los Angeles and Oslo – A Metropolitan Perspective nr 1. *International Electronic Journal of Elementary Education*, 6(2), 315–332.

Kettler, R. J. (2012) Testing accommodations: Theory and research to inform practice. *International Journal of Disability, Development and Education*, 59(1), 53–66.

Kinsella, W., Murtagh, L., Senior, J., and Coleman, M. (2014) *Review of NCSE resource allocation process and evaluation of deployment of resources in schools*. Trim, County Meath, Ireland: National Council for Special Education. http://ncse.ie/wp-content/uploads/2014/10/NCSE-Resource-Allocation-No18finalwebaccessibleversion26.01.15.pdf.

Klenowski, V. (2014) Towards fairer assessment. *The Australian Educational Researcher*, 41(4), 445–470.

Klumpp, L.et al. (2014) *Education Policy Outlook*. Germany: OECD.

Kozleski, E. B., and Waitoller, F. R. (2010) Teacher learning for inclusive education: Understanding teaching as a cultural and political practice. *International Journal of Inclusive Education*, 14(7), 655–666.

Kupari, P., Välljärvi, J., Andersson, L.,Arffman, I. Nissinen, K., Puhakka, E., and Vettenranta, J. (2013) PISA12 Ensituloksia [PISA12 First Results]. Opetus- ja kulttuuriministeriön julkaisuja.www.minedu.fi/export/sites/default/OPM/Julkaisut/2013/liitteet/okm20.pdf?lang=en (accessed 09.09.2016).

Kurz, A., Talapatra, D., and Roach, A. T. (2012) Meeting the curricular challenges of inclusive assessment: The role of alignment, opportunity to learn, and student engagement. *International Journal of Disability, Development and Education*, 59(1), 37–52.

Ladwig, J. G. (2010) Beyond academic outcomes. *Review of Research in Education*, 34(1), 113–141.

Lantolf, P. J. (2000) *Socio-cultural theory and second language learning*. Oxford: Oxford University Press.

Lareau, A. (2003) *Unequal childhoods: Class, race, and family life*. Berkeley and Los Angeles: University of California Press.

Lave, J. (1988) *Cognition in practice: Mind, mathematics and culture in everyday life*. New York: Cambridge University Press.

Lave, J. (1996) Teaching, as learning, in practice. *Mind, Culture and Activity*, 3(3), 149–164.

Lemke, T. (2001) 'The birth of bio-politics': Michel Foucault's lecture at the Collège de France on neo-liberal governmentality. *Economy and society*, 30(2), 190–207.

Lemon, N., and Garvis, S. (2013) What is the Role of the Arts in a Primary School?: An Investigation of Perceptions of Pre-Service Teachers in Australia. *Australian Journal of Teacher Education*, 38(9). http://dx.doi.org/10.14221/ajte.2013v38n9.7.

Lemons, C. J., Vaughn, S., Wexler, J., Kearns, D. M., and Sinclair, A. C. (2018) Envisioning an improved continuum of special education services for students with learning disabilities: Considering intervention intensity. *Learning Disabilities Research and Practice*, 33(3), 131–143.

Lenihan, R., Hinchion, C., and Laurenson, P. (2016) A changing assessment landscape in Ireland: the place of oral language . *English in Education*, 50(3), 280–296.

LeRoy, B. W., Samuel, P., Deluca, M., and Evans, P. (2018) Students with special educational needs within PISA. *Assessment in Education: Principles, Policy and Practice*. 1–11.

Lewis, C., Enciso, P., and Moje, E. B. (Eds) (2007) *Reframing Sociocultural Research on Literacy: Identity, Agency and Power*. Mahwah, New Jersey: Lawrence Erlbaum Publishers.

Lin, P. Y., and Lin, Y. C. (2015) Identifying Canadian teacher candidates' needs for training in the use of inclusive classroom assessment. *International Journal of Inclusive Education*, 19 (8), 771–786.

Linehan, C., and McCarthy, J. (2001) Reviewing the "community of practice" metaphor: An analysis of control relations in a primary school classroom. *Mind, culture, and Activity*, 8 (2), 129–147.

Lingard, B., and Sellar, S. (2012) A policy sociology reflection on school reform in England: from the 'Third Way' to the 'Big Society'. *Journal of Educational Administration and History*, 44(1), 43–63.

Livingston, K., and Hutchinson, C. (2017) Developing teachers' capacities in assessment through career-long professional learning . *Assessment in Education: Principles, Policy and Practice*, 24(2), 290–307.

Lohmar, B., and Eckhardt, T. (2015) *The Education System in the Federal Republic of Germany 2013/2014. A description of the responsibilities, structures and developments in education policy for the exchange of information in Europe*. Secretariat of the Standing Conference of the Ministers of Education and Cultural Affairs of the Länder in the Federal Republic of Germany.

Looney, A., Cumming, J., van Der Kleij, F., and Harris, K. (2018) Reconceptualising the role of teachers as assessors: Teacher assessment identity. *Assessment in Education: Principles, Policy and Practice*, 25(5), 442–467.

Luginbuhl, R., Webbink, D., and de Wolf, I. (2009) Do inspections improve primary school performance?. *Educational Evaluation and Policy Analysis*, 31(3), 221–237.

Lynch, K. (2015) 'There is no view from Nowhere', Ideology, Social Justice and Teacher Education, 13th annual SCoTENs conference 'Teacher Education for Social Justice', Strand Hotel, Limerick, 15–16 October 2015.

Lynch, K., and Baker, J. (2005) Equality in education: An equality of condition perspective. *Theory and Research in Education*, 3(2), 131–164.

MacPhail, A., Halbert, J., and O'Neill, H. (2017) Introducing school-based teacher-led assessments in the Irish school context: challenging the practice of favouring centralized, externally-conducted assessment. *Revista Infancia, Educación y Aprendizaje*, 3(2), 8–13.

MacPhail, A., Halbert, J., and O'Neill, H. (2018) The development of assessment policy in Ireland: a story of junior cycle reform. *Assessment in Education: Principles, Policy and Practice*, 1–17, doi: doi:10.1080/0969594X.2018.1441125.

Mannion, G. (2007) Going Spatial: Why 'listening to children' and children's participation needs reframing. In *Discourse*, 28(3), September 2007. Special Issue on Pupil Voice in Educational Research, 405–420.

Mansell, W. (2016) *Academies: autonomy, accountability, quality and evidence*. Research Report for the Cambridge Primary Review Trust.

Martin, P. C. (2016) Test-Based Education for Students with Disabilities and English Language Learners: The Impact of Assessment Pressures on Educational Planning. *Teachers College Record*, 118(14).

Mary Immaculate Reading Attainment Test (MICRA-T) www.cjfallon.ie/books/micra-t.

Materechera, E. K. (2018) Inclusive education: why it poses a dilemma to some teachers. *International Journal of Inclusive Education*, 1–16.

Matters, G. (2009) A problematic leap in the use of test data: From performance to inference. In C. Wyatt-Smith, and J. Cumming (Eds) *Educational assessment in the 21st century: Connecting theory and practice*. Dordrecht, Heidelberg, London and New York: Springer. 209–225.

McCleary, D. F., Rowlette, E. F., Pelchar, T. K., and Bain, S. K. (2013) Interventions for Learning Disabilities: Does a Journal-Based Change in Focus and Article Type Reflect or Influence Legal Mandates?. *Review of Educational Research*, 83(2), 196–210.

McCoy, S., Banks, J., and Shevlin, M. (2012) School matters: How context influences the identification of different types of special educational needs. *Irish Educational Studies*, 31(2), 119–138.

McDermott, R. (1996) The acquisition of a child by a learning disability. In S. Chaiklin, and J. Lave (Eds) *Understanding practice: Perspectives on activity and context*. Cambridge: Cambridge University Press. 269–304.

McDermott, R., Goldman, S., and Varenne, H. (2006) The cultural work of learning disabilities. *Educational Researcher*, 35(6), 12–17.

McGregor, G. (2009) Educating for (whose) success? Schooling in an age of neo-liberalism. *British Journal of Sociology of Education*, 30(3), 345–358. doi: doi:10.1080/01425690902812620.

McKinsey (2007) *How the world's best-performing school systems come out on top*. McKinsey and Co. http://mckinseyonsociety.com/downloads/reports/Education/Worlds School Systems Final.pdf.

McLaughlin, M. J., Dyson, A., Nagle, K., Thurlow, M., Rouse, M., Hardman, M., Norwich, B., Burke, P. J., and Perlin, M. (2006) Cross-cultural perspectives on the classification of children with disabilities: Part II. Implementing classification systems in schools. *The Journal of Special Education*, 40(1), 46–58.

Messiou, K. (2017) Research in the field of inclusive education: time for a rethink?. *International journal of inclusive education*, 21(2), 146–159.

Meyer, H. D. (2014) Imagining PISA's Policy Futures: a postscript and some extensions to the Open Letter to Andreas Schleicher. *Policy Futures in Education*, 12(7), 883–892.

Mintrop, H., and Zane, R. (2017) When the Achievement Gap Becomes High Stakes for Special Education Teachers: Facing a Dilemma With Integrity. *Teachers College Record*, 119(9).

Mitchell, D. (2015) Inclusive education is a multi-faceted concept. *Center for Educational Policy Studies Journal*, 5(1), 9–30.

Moll, L. C., Amanti, C., Neff, D., and Gonzalez, N. (1992) Funds of knowledge for teaching: Using a qualitative approach to connect homes and classrooms. *Theory into practice*, 31(2), 132–141.

Moore, K. A., Lippman, L. H., and Ryberg, R. (2015) Improving outcome measures other than achievement. *AERA Open*, 1(2).

Morgan, P. L., Staff, J., Hillemeier, M. M., Farkas, G., and Maczuga, S. (2013) Racial and ethnic disparities in ADHD diagnosis from kindergarten to eighth grade. *Pediatrics*, 132(1), 85–93.

Morgan, P. L., Farkas, G., Hillemeier, M. M., Mattison, R., Maczuga, S., Li, H., and Cook, M. (2015) Minorities are disproportionately underrepresented in special education: Longitudinal evidence across five disability conditions. *Educational Researcher*, 44(5), 278–292.

Morgan, P. L., Farkas, G., Hillemeier, M. M., and Maczuga, S. (2017) Replicated Evidence of Racial and Ethnic Disparities in Disability Identification in US Schools. *Educational Researcher*, 46(6), 305–322.

Moss, G. (2017) Assessment, accountability and the literacy curriculum: reimagining the future in the light of the past. *Literacy*, 51(2), 56–64.

Mullis, I. V. S., Martin, M. O., Gonzalez, E. J., and Kennedy, A. M. (2003) *PIRLS 2001 International Report: IEA's study of reading literacy achievement in primary schools*. Chestnut Hill, MA: Boston College. http://isc.bc.edu/pirls2001i/PIRLS2001_Pubs_IR.html.

Munns, G., and Woodward, H. (2006) Student engagement and student self assessment: The REAL framework. *Assessment in Education*, 13(2), 193–213.

Murchan, D., and Shiel, G. (2017) *Understanding and applying assessment in education*. London: Sage.

Murray, C., and Herrnstein, R. (1994) The bell curve. *Intelligence and Class Structure in American Life*. New York: Free Press.

Musset, P. (2012) *School Choice and Equity: Current Policies in OECD Countries and a Literature Review*. OECD Education Working PapersNo. 66. Paris: OECD.

National Council for Special Education (NCSE) (2013) *Supporting Students with Special Educational Needs in Schools*. NCSE Policy Advice Paper No. 4. Trim, County Meath, Ireland: National Council for Special Education. http://ncse.ie/wp-content/uploads/2014/09/Supporting_14_05_13_web.pdf.

National Council for Special Education (NCSE) (2014) *Delivery for Students with Special Educational Needs – A better and more equitable way. An NCSE Working Group Report*. Trim, County Meath, Ireland: National Council for Special Education. http://ncse.ie/wp-content/uploads/2014/09/Allocating_resources_1_5_14_Web_accessible_version_FINAL.pdf.

Nelson, R., and Ehren, M. (2014) *Review and synthesis of evidence on the (mechanisms of) impact of school inspections*.

New Group Reading Test (NGRT) *GL Assessment*. www.gl-assessment.co.uk/products/new-group-reading-test-ngrt.

Newton, P. E. (2017) There is more to educational measurement than measuring: The importance of embracing purpose pluralism. *Educational Measurement: Issues and Practice*, 36(2), 5–15.

Nichols, S. L., and Berliner, D. (2008) Testing the joy out of learning. *Educational Leadership*, 65(6), 14–18.

Nichols, S. L., and Castro-Villarreal, F. (2017) Introduction to the Special Issue: The Social (In) justice of Labeling in a High-Stakes Testing Era: Implications for Teachers and School Psychologists. *Teachers College Record*, 119(9).

Nind, M., Curtin, A., and Hall, K. (2016) *Research Methods for Pedagogy*. UK: Bloomsbury.

No Child Left Behind Act (NCLB) (2001) *The Elementary and Secondary Education Act (The No Child Left Behind Act) of 2001*. Pub. L. 107–110, 115 Stat. 1425, enacted 8 January 2002.

North, C. E. (2006) More than words? Delving into the substantive meaning (s) of "social justice" in education. *Review of Educational Research*, 76(4), 507–535.

North, C. E. (2008) What is all this talk about "social justice"? Mapping the terrain of education's latest catchphrase. *Teachers College Record*, 110(6), 1182–1206.

Northern Ireland Assembly (2013) *Approaches to School Inspection by Caroline Perry for the NIA Research and Information Services*.

Northern Ireland Assembly (2016) *Oral Answers to Questions – Education in the NI Assembly*, 11 October 2016.
Norwich, B. (2007) *Dilemmas of difference, inclusion and disability: International perspectives and future directions*. London: Routledge.
Norwich, B., and Kent, T. (2002) Assessing the Personal and Social Development of Pupils with Special Educational Needs: wider lessons for all. *Assessment in Education: Principles, Policy and Practice*, 9(1), 59–80.
Oakes, J. (1985) *Keeping track: How schools structure inequality*. New Haven and London: Yale University Press.
O'Brien, S. (2016) *Inside Education: Exploring the Art of Good Learning*. London and New York: Routledge.
O'Donnell, S. (2018) *Upper secondary education in nine jurisdictions. Overview report: Desktop study for the National Council for Curriculum and Assessment*. Dublin: NCCA. www.ncca.ie/media/3337/scoping-report-online-2.pdf (accessed 03. 01. 2019).
O'Donoghue, T., Gleeson, J., and McCormack, O. (2017) National newspaper-reporting on state examinations: An historical exposition of the exceptional case of the Irish Leaving Certificate. *Encounters in Theory and History of Education*, 18, 134–149.
OFSTED (2012) *The Pupil Premium: how schools are using the pupil premium funding to raise achievement for disad vantaged pupils*. London: OFSTED.
OFSTED (2014) *The Pupil Premium: an update*. London: OFSTED.
OFSTED (2016) *Guidance for inspecting schools under the common inspection framework, with a myth buster document on common misconceptions*. London: OFSTED.
O'Neill, O. (2013) Intelligent accountability in education. *Oxford Review of Education*, 39(1), 4–16.
Organisation for Economic Co-operation and Development (OECD) (1991) *Reviews of National Policies for Education: Ireland*. https://unesdoc.unesco.org/ark:/48223/pf0000170934.
Organisation for Economic Co-operation and Development (OECD) (2007) *Improving School Leadership: Country Background Report for Northern Ireland*.
Organisation for Economic Co-operation and Development (OECD) (2008) OECD Economic Surveys, Germany.
Organisation for Economic Co-operation and Development (OECD) (2010) *Viewing the UK school system through the prism of PISA*. www.pisa.oecd/dataoecd/33/846624007.pdf (accessed 04. 10. 2016).
Organisation for Economic Co-operation and Development (OECD) (2013) *Synergies for better learning: An international perspective on evaluation and assessment*.
Organisation for Economic Co-operation and Development (OECD) (2014) *Improving Schools in Wales: an OECD Perspective*.
O'Sullivan, J. (2015) Minister for Education and Skills, Jan O'Sullivan TD, Private Member's Bill on Junior Cycle Reform, 20 January 2015. www.education.ie/en/Press-Events/Speeches/2015-Speeches/SP-%202015-%2001-%2021.html#sthash.M4FxJwCG.dpuf (accessed 05. 05. 2017).
Özerk, K. (2010) *Pedagogikkens hvordan 1. Lærerens rolle, kompetanse og betydning* (The methodological aspect of pedagogy – The role of the teacher and teacher competency). Oslo: Cappelen Damm Akademisk Forlag.
Page, E., and Goldsmith, M. (Eds) (1987) *Central and Local Relations*. London: Sage.
Perry, N., and Ercikan, K. (2015) Moving beyond Country Rankings in International Assessments: The Case of PISA. *Teachers College Record*, 117(1).
Plath, S. (2006) *The Bell Jar*. Harper: London.
Poskitt, J. (2014) Transforming professional learning and practice in assessment for learning. *Curriculum Journal*, 25(4), 542–566.

Power, S. (2016) The politics of education and the misrecognition of Wales. *Oxford Review of Education*, 42(3), 285–298.
Powers, J. M. (2004) High-stakes accountability and equity: Using evidence from California's public school Accountability Act to address the issues in Williams v. State of California. *American Educational Research Journal*, 41(4), 763–795.
Priestley, M., and Drew, V. (2016) Teachers as agents of curriculum change: closing the gap between purpose and practice. In European Conference for Educational Research, Dublin, 23–26 September 2016. http://dspace.stir.ac.uk/bitstream/1893/24179/1/Teachers%20as%20agents%20of%20curriculum%20change_ECER2016_full%20paper.pdf (accessed 02. 04. 2018).
Programme for International Student Assessment (PISA) [OECD] www.oecd.org/pisa/.
Pullin, D. (2005) When one size does not fit all – The special challenges of accountability testing for students with disabilities. *Yearbook of the National Society for the Study of Education*, 104(2), 199–222.
Ragusa, A. T., and Bousfield, K. (2017) 'It's not the test, it's how it's used!' Critical analysis of public response to NAPLAN and MySchool Senate Inquiry. *British Journal of Sociology of Education*, 38(3), 265–286.
Reay, D. (2010) Identity Making in Schools and Classrooms. In Wetherell, M., and Mohanty, C. T. (Eds) *The SAGE Handbook of Identities*. London: Sage. 277–294.
Reay, D. (2017) "The power of tests". In Katznelson, N., Sørensen, N. U., and Illeris, K. *Understanding learning and motivation in youth: Challenging policy and practice*. London: Routledge. 48–56.
Reay, D., and William, D. (1999) 'I'll be a nothing': structure, agency and the construction of identity through assessment. *British Educational Research Journal*, 25(3), 343–354.
Reay, D., and Lucey, H. (2003) 'The Limits of Choice' Children and Inner City Schooling. *Sociology*, 37(1), 121–142.
Reay, D., Crozier, G., and James, D. (2011) *White middle-class identities and urban schooling*. Basingstoke: Springer.
Reindal, S. M. (2016) Discussing inclusive education: An inquiry into different interpretations and a search for ethical aspects of inclusion using the capabilities approach. *European Journal of Special Needs Education*, 31(1), 1–12.
Review of the Australian Curriculum *Final Report 2015*. Australian Government.
Roberts-Holmes, G., and Bradbury, A. (2016) Governance, accountability and datafication of early years education in England. *British Education Research Journal*, 42(4), 600–613.
Robinson, P. (1999) The Tyranny of League Tables: international comparisons of educational attainment and economic outcomes. In A. Alexander, P. Broadfoot, and D. Phillips (Eds) *Learning from Comparing: new directions in comparative education research: Contexts, classrooms and outcomes*, Vol. 1. Oxford: Symposium Books. 217–236.
Rogoff, B. (1995) Observing sociocultural activity on three planes: Participatory appropriation, guided participation, and apprenticeship. In Murphy, P., Hall, K., and Soler, J. *Pedagogy and Practice: Culture and Identities*. Sage: London. 58–74.
Rogoff, B. (1998) Cognition as a collaborative process. In W. Damon (Ed.) *Handbook of child psychology*. New York: John Wylie. 679–744.
Rutkowski, L., and Rutkowski, D. (2016) A call for a more measured approach to reporting and interpreting PISA results. *Educational Researcher*, 45(4), 252–257.
Sahlberg, P. (2011) *Finnish Lessons: What Can the World Learn from Educational Change in Finland?*. Foreword by Andy Hargreavas. The series on School reform. Forward by Ann Lieberman. New York: Teachers College, Colombia University.
Sahlberg, P. (2017) The global testing culture: shaping education policy, perceptions, and practice [Review Article], W. C. Smith (Ed.) *Educational Review*, 69(1), 135–137.
Sayer, A. (2005) *The moral significance of class*. Cambridge: Cambridge University Press.

Scruggs, T. E., and Mastropieri, M. A. (2002) On babies and bathwater: Addressing the problems of identification of learning disabilities. *Learning Disability Quarterly*, 25(3), 155–168.

Shanker, A. (1988) Exams fail the test. *New York Times*, E. p. 7.

Shaw, J. M. (2005) Getting things right at the classroom level. *Yearbook of the National Society for the Study of Education*, 104(2), 340–357.

Shevlin, M., Winter, E., and Flynn, P. (2013) Developing inclusive practice: teacher perceptions of opportunities and constraints in the Republic of Ireland. *International Journal of Inclusive Education*, 17(10), 1119–1133.

Shifrer, D., Muller, C., and Callahan, R. (2011) Disproportionality and learning disabilities: Parsing apart race, socioeconomic status, and language. *Journal of Learning Disabilities*, 44(3), 246–257.

Skiba, R. J., Artiles, A. J., Kozleski, E. B., Losen, D. J., and Harry, E. G. (2016) Risks and consequences of oversimplifying educational inequities: A response to Morgan et al. (2015). *Educational Researcher*, 45(3), 221–225.

Smith, K. (2011) Professional development of teachers—A prerequisite for AfL to be successfully implemented in the classroom. *Studies in educational evaluation*, 37(1), 55–61.

Smyth, E. (2009) Buying your way into college? Private tuition and the transition to higher education in Ireland. *Oxford review of education*, 35(1), 1–22.

Smyth, E., McCoy, S., and Darmody, M. (2004) *Moving up: The experiences of first-year students in post-primary education*. Dublin: Liffey Press.

Smyth, E., Dunne, A., McCoy, S., and Darmody, M. (2006) *Pathways through the Junior Cycle: the experience of second year students*. Economic and Social Research Institute Research Series. Dublin: ESRI.

Smyth, E., Dunne, A., Darmody, M., and McCoy, S. (2007) *Gearing up for the exam?: The experience of junior certificate students*. Economic and Social Research Institute Research Series. Dublin: ESRI.

Smyth, E., McCoy, S., and Kingston, G. (2015) *Learning from the evaluation of DEIS*. Dublin: ESRI.

Stobart, G. (2008) *Testing Times: The uses and abuses of assessment*. London: Routledge.

Stobart, G. (2010) Assessment fit for the future. Lecture at IAEA Annual Conference 2010, Bangkok, Thailand.

Strand, S., Lindsay, G., and Pather, S. (2006) *Special educational needs and ethnicity: Issues of over- and under-representation*. Research Report No. 757. Centre for Educational Development, Appraisal and Research, Institute of Education, University of Warwick. www.naldic.org.uk/Resources/NALDIC/Research%20and%20Information/Documents/RR757.pdf.

Sullivan, A. L. (2011) Disproportionality in special education identification and placement of English language learners. *Exceptional Children*, 77(3), 317–334.

Sullivan, A. L. (2017) Wading through quicksand: making sense of minority disproportionality in identification of emotional disturbance. *Behavioral disorders*, 43(1), 244–252.

Sullivan, A. L., and Bal, A. (2013) Disproportionality in special education: Effects of individual and school variables on disability risk. *Exceptional Children*, 79(4), 475–494.

Taylor, B., Francis, B., Archer, L., Hodgen, J., Pepper, D., Tereshchenko, A., and Travers, M. C. (2016) Factors deterring schools from mixed attainment teaching practice. *Pedagogy, Culture and Society*, 1–16.

Theoharis, G., Causton, J., and Tracy-Bronson, C. P. (2016) Inclusive reform as a response to high-stakes pressure? Leading toward inclusion in the age of accountability. *Teachers College Record*, 118(14), 1–30.

Thomas, G. (2013) A review of thinking and research about inclusive education policy, with suggestions for a new kind of inclusive thinking. *British Educational Research Journal*, 39(3), 473–490.

Thomas, G., and Loxley, A. (2007) *Deconstructing special education and constructing inclusion*. 2nd edition. Maidenhead, UK: McGraw-Hill.

Thurlow, M. L., and Kopriva, R. J. (2015) Advancing accessibility and accommodations in content assessments for students with disabilities and English learners. *Review of Research in Education*, 39(1), 331–369.

Tomlinson, S. (2012) The irresistible rise of the SEN industry. *Oxford Review of Education*, 38 (3), 267–286.

Tomlinson, S. (2015) Is a sociology of special and inclusive education possible?. *Educational Review*, 67(3), 273–281.

Torrance, H. (2017) Blaming the victim: assessment, examinations, and the responsibilisation of students and teachers in neo-liberal governance. *Discourse: Studies in the Cultural politics of Education*, 38(1), 83–96.

Troman, G. (1997) Self management and school inspections: complementary forms of surveillance and control in the primary school. *Oxford Review of Education*, 23(3), 345–384.

Umansky, I. M., Thompson, K. D., and Díaz, G. (2017) Using an Ever–English Learner Framework to Examine Disproportionality in Special Education. *Exceptional Children*, 84(1), 76–96.

Vandenbussche, H., and De Schauwer, E. (2018) The pursuit of belonging in inclusive education–insider perspectives on the meshwork of participation. *International Journal of Inclusive Education*, 22(9), 969–982.

Varjo, J., and Kalalahti, M. (2015) The conceivable benefits of being comprehensive – Finnish Local Education Authorities on recognizing and controlling the social costs of school choice. *European Educational Research Journal*, 14(3–4), 312–330.

Vasagar, J., and Shepherd, J. (2011) National curriculum review puts emphasis on facts. *The Guardian*, 20 January 2011.

Vehmas, S. (2010) Special needs: a philosophical analysis. *International Journal of Inclusive Education*, 14(1), 87–96.

Victorian Curriculum and Assessment Authority (VCAA) (2010) *Victorian Curriculum F–10 Revised curriculum planning and reporting guidelines*. Victoria. vcaa.vic.edu.au.

Victorian Curriculum and Assessment Authority (VCAA) (2013) *Report 2012–2013*. Victoria. vcaa.vic.edu.au.

Vincent, C., Braun, A., and Ball, S. (2010) Local links, Local Knowledge: Choosing case settings and schools. *British Educational Research Journal*, 36(2), 279–298.

Waldergrave, H., and Simons, J. (2014) *Watching the Watchmen: the future of school inspections in England*. London: Policy Exchange.

Wales, Government of (2015) *Successful Futures: independent review of curriculum and assessment arrangements in Wales*. Cardiff: Welsh Government.

Walsh, P. (2008) Effects of school choice on the margin: The cream is already skimmed. *Economics of Education Review*. Doi: doi:10/1016/j.econedurev.2007.11.005.

Waslander, S., Pater, C., and van der Weide (2010) *Markets in Education: an analytical review of empirical research on market mechanisms in education*. www.oecd.org/officialdocuments/public displaydocumentpdf (accessed 02. 10. 2016).

Wechsler Intelligence Scale for Children (WISC V) (2014) www.iupui.edu/~flip/wiscde scription.pdf.

Weir, S., McAvinue, L., Moran, E., and O'Flaherty, A. (2014) *A Report on the evaluation of DEIS at the second level*. Dublin: Educational Research Centre.

Wenger, E. (1998) *Communities of Practice: Learning, Meaning and Identity*. Cambridge: Cambridge University Press.

Wenger-Trayner, E., Fenton O'Creevy, M., Hutchinson, S., Kubiak, C., and Wenger-Trayner, B. (2015) *Learning in Landscapes of Practice: Boundaries, Identities, and Knowledgeability in Practice Based Learning*. New York: Routledge.

West, A. (2010) High stakes testing, accountability, incentives and consequences in English schools. *Policy and Politics*, 38, 23–29.

West, A., Mattei, P., and Roberts, J. (2011) Accountability and Sanctions in English Schools. *British Journal of Educational Studies*, 59(1), 41–62.

Whitby, K. (2010) *School inspections: recent experiences in high performing education systems.* Reading, England: CfBT Education Trust.

Wiggins, A., and Tymms, P. (2002) Dysfunctional effects of league tables: a comparison between English and Scottish primary schools. *Public Money and Management*, 22(1), 43–48.

Wiliam, D. (2010) What counts as evidence of educational achievement? The role of constructs in the pursuit of equity in assessment. *Review of Research in Education*, 34(1), 254–284.

Wilkins, C. (2011) Professionalism and the post-performative teacher. *Professional Development in Education*, 37(3), 389–409.

Willis, P. (1977) *Learning to Labour: How Working Class Kids Get Working Class Jobs.* Farnborough: Gower.

Wylie, C., and Lyon, C. (2009) What schools and districts need to know to support teachers' use of formative assessment. *Teachers College Record*, 3 August 2009. www.tcrecord.org. ID No.: 15734.

Xu, Y., and Brown, G. T. (2016) Teacher assessment literacy in practice: A reconceptualization. *Teaching and Teacher Education*, 58, 149–162.

Young, I. M. (1990) *Justice and the Politics of Difference.* New Jersey: Princeton University Press.

Young, I. M. (2009) Five faces of oppression. In G. W. Henderson, and M. Waterstone (Eds) *Geographic thought: A praxis perspective.* New York andLondon: Routledge. 55–71.

Zhang, D., Katsiyannis, A., Ju, S., and Roberts, E. (2014) Minority representation in special education: 5-year trends. *Journal of Child and Family Studies*, 23(1), 118–127.

Zhao, Y., Harris, A., and Jones, M. (2018) PISA vs. PISA: What Works May Hurt. *Teachers College Record*, 29 August 2018. www.tcrecord.org. ID No.: 22486, www.tcrecord.org/Content.asp?ContentId=22486.

Zipin, L. (2009) Dark funds of knowledge, deep funds of pedagogy: Exploring boundaries between lifeworlds and schools. *Discourse: Studies in the Cultural Politics of Education*, 30(3), 317–331.

INDEX

Page numbers in **bold** refer to figures, page numbers in *italic* refer to tables.

ability 9
ability grouping 74
absolute achievement 45
academic outcomes, dominance of 120
academic practice, visitors to 16
accessibility 124–129
accommodations: alternative assessments 126–127; assessment setting 125; common 125–126; equipment and materials 126; presentation format 126; research 125; response format 126; special educational needs 124–127; timing and scheduling 126
accountability 2, 4–5, 8, 20, 62–63, 107–109, 131, 135; Australia 55–57; California 48–49, 49–53; cultural legacies 58–59; datafication 58; England 30, 33, 34–37; Finland 48; Germany 41–43, 43, 58; hierarchical 41, 43, 48, 59; intelligent 59; language 33, 34; market 41, 43, 48, 59; neoliberal 58; Northern Ireland 39; public 55–56; Scotland 38–39, 58; teachers 52; United States of America 57–59, 108; Victoria 55–57; Wales 38–39
accuracy 30
achievement: expectations for 4; individual responsibility 45; standards of 59; types of 45
achievement gap 71
acquisitionist discourse 62
administrative workload 55

Adolescent Literacy, Identity and School (ALIAS) 5–6, 97–101, **99, 100**
agency 22, 63
Ainscow, M. 116–117
Alex (student) 10–11, 17, 18, 26, 27
alternative assessments, special educational needs 126–127
A Nation at Risk 49
assessment: definition 12, 23; understanding of 1, 7, 9, 26–27, 132–134; uses 103
assessment approaches, traditional 4–5
assessment bubbles 67
assessment capability, teachers 135; personal teacher experience 136–137; professional context 137; reconceptualising 135–136; research agenda 137–138; systemic factors 137–138
assessment design 120
assessment discourses 9
assessment moments 15, 82, 88–89, 95–97, 98; multiple 77
assessment outcome criteria, broadening 117, 120–121
assessment outcomes, broadening 9
assessment performance, distributed nature of 95–96
assessment policy 2, 8, 9, 23, 25, 138–139; actors 67, 68–70, *69*; adapters 68; adopters 68; critics 73; as discourse 68; intentions 64; Ireland 66–81; Junior Cycle curriculum 66; messages 63–64;

production 68; resistors 68, 73; as text 68; unintended effects 64; wider imperatives 3
assessment practice 85, 133–134, 138–139; boundaries 16–17, 21; conceptually-informed 117–118; Finland 44–45; Germany 41–43; special educational needs 124–127; successful participation 11; variability 124
assessment reforms, Ireland 14
assessment regimes 4: Ireland 71; special educational needs 123–124
assessment resources, students 26
assessment setting, accommodations 125
assessment settings 18; reconceptualisation of 21; spatial and temporal aspects 11–12, 12–16
assessment worlds, engagement with 5–7
assessor identity 23–26
Association of Secondary Teachers of Ireland 68, 73–74
attainment-related outcomes 121
attainment targets 31–32
Australia 29, 53–57, 91; accountability 55–57, 57–59; National Assessment Program 56–57; National Assessment Program – Literacy and Numeracy (NAPLAN) 56–57; school choice 54, 57
Australian Council for Educational Research 54
Australian Curriculum Framework 53–54
Australian Education Act 2013 56
autonomy 40–41, 54–55, 57; teachers 43

Baker, J. 83, 84, 85–86, 101
Ball, S. J. 66, 67, 67–68, 88
Barrance, R. 81
Barry (student) 99, **100**, 101
Basic Education Act, 1999, Finland 46–47
beliefs 2, 3, 62, 64, 75, 106, 112, 115, 121, 136
benchmarking 119, 132
Bernstein, B. 76
best-performing school systems 59
Best Practices in Grouping Students Project 95–96
Biesta, G. 74
biopsychosocial model 104, 114–115
Black-Hawkins, K. 117
Boud, D. 26
boundaries 11, 27–28; assessment practice 16–17, 21; brokers 27; communities of practice 19–20; focus on 26–27; as learning assets 18–23, 28; negotiating 12, 16–17, 21–22; and reflection 27

boundaries of practice, learning across 15–16
boundary activity 27
boundary practices 7, 11–12; negative 10–11, 13
boundary spaces 14
Bourdieu, P. 76, 85
Bousfield, K. 91
Brancaleone, D. 74
Braun, A. 67, 68
Bray, M. 76
Brown, G. T. 136
Bruner, J. 63
Bush, George W. 49–50

Cahill, K. 94–95
California 29, 48–53; accountability 48–49, 49–53, 57–59; Classroom Instructional Improvement and Accountability Act, 1988 49, 50; Common Core State Standards (CCSS) 51–52, 53; education. policy 49; funding strategy 49; privatisation 50; quality assurance 53; State Board of Education 48
California Teachers' Association 52
Cambridge Primary Review Trust 35
capitalisation 134
Centre for International Large-Scale Assessment (*Zentrum für Internationale Bildungsvergleichsstudien* – ZIB), Germany 41
certification 103
child centred approach 42–43
Choi, J. 136
Chris (student) 18–19, **19**, 20–21, 21–22, 26, 27
Clarke, J. 38
classroom-based assessments 71–72, 76, 78–79, *78, 80*, 132
Classroom Instructional Improvement and Accountability Act, 1988, California 49, 50
classroom level 4
classrooms: competitive ethos 62; dynamics 113; space 13; teacher talk domination 20
Cochran-Smith, M. 96
cognitive abilities, assessment of 106–107
Cognitive Abilities Test 106
collaboration 39, 40, 55
collective meaning-making 2
collective responsibility 44, 47
commodification 92–93
communities of practice 11, 12, 17, 116–117; boundaries 19–20; and identity 22–23; trajectories 21
comparative examinations 42

competences 133
competition 40, 44, 45, 53, 57, 70, 70–71, 88, 94, 98
conceptually informed assessment 9, 117–118
concerted cultivation 93
Courtois, A. 90
criterion-referenced assessment 133–134, 135
cultural analysis 8
cultural bias 129
cultural capital 86, 109–110
cultural imperialism 85
cultural legacies 2, 58–59
cultural reproduction 85
cultural resources 2, 76
cultural scripts 8, 61–65, 104
cultural tools 2–3
cultural traditions 112–113
Cumming, J. 75–76
curriculum 91; breadth 123; design 6, 36, 74; enactment 3, 4; reform 67, 71–76, 77–80, 77, 78
Curtin, A. 13

datafication 58
data generation 6
DeLuca, C. 135
Department of Defense Education Activity (DoDEA) (USA) 48
developmental concepts 5–6
differential boost 125
differential practices, focus on 20
differentiation 109
disabilities: *see* special educational needs
disenchantment 101
disproportionality 109–110, 115, 129
dissonances, in practices 20–21
distributive justice 84, 101
dominant discourses 131–132
Donaldson, G. 38
Donaldson Review 39
Dore, R. 17
Douglas, G. 122
Drew, V. 74
Drumcondra Post Primary Test – Mathematics 107
Drumcondra Post Primary Test – Reading 107
Drumcondra Reasoning Test 106
Duckworth, A. L. 123
Dudley-Marling, C. 96

economic capital 86
economic imperative 89

economic outcomes 89
educational psychology 111
education outcomes 82
education policy 80
Education Reform Act, 1988 (UK) 31
Education Training Inspectorate (ETI) 39–40
effectiveness 131
Ehren, M. 36
Elaine (student) 98–99, **99**
Elwood, J. 4–5, 81, 104
enactments 3, 4
Enciso, P. 21
engagement 3, 27; with assessment worlds 5–7
England 29, 30–37, 40, 91; accountability 30, 33, 34–37, 57–59; assessment 31–33, 61; concerns 36–37; datafication 58; Education Reform Act, 1988 31; funding strategy 36; legislative and policy context 31; Local Education Authorities 33; national curriculum 31, 36; Office for Standards in Education (OFSTED) 34; policy documents 30; school autonomy 35; school choice 58; school inspection system 34; school types 34, 35; summative assessment 30–31
entrance assessment 9, 94–97
environment 4, 43
equality 44, 83, 134
equality of condition 86, 87–88, 101
equality of opportunity 101, 108
equipment and materials, accommodations 126
equity 84, 115, 131
Esteban-Guitart, M. 5–6
Estyn's Common Inspection Framework 39
European Agency for Developments In Special Needs Education 88
Every Student Succeeds Act (USA) 51
exclusion 83, 96, 101, 111

failure 99; assessment moment as source of 6; definitions of 9
fairness 82–83, 85–86, 87–90, 101
fairness tracking 9, 76–77
feedback 13, 45
Finland 29, 29–30, 63; accountability 44–45, 57–59; assessment practice 44–45; Basic Education Act, 1999 46–47; collective responsibility 44, 47; comprehensive school system 45–46; National Core Curriculum 47; school choice 47, 48
Fleer, M. 4
flexible learning opportunities 5
floor standards 32, 33

Fok tree, the 5–6
formative assessment 120
Foucault, M. 22
Framework for Junior Cycle (2015) 8, 66–67, 72, 73, 75
France 92
Francis, B. 132
Fraser, N. 83, 84, 84–85
funding strategy: England 36; Scotland 38; United States of America 49; Victoria 53
Funds of Assessment 6
Funds of Identity 5–6
Funds of Knowledge perspective 5–6
Funds of Pedagogy 5

Gearing up for the exam?: The experience of junior certificate students (Smyth et al) 74–75
Gee, J. P. 14
Germany 29, 30; accountability 43, 58; assessment practice 41–43; autonomy 40–41; Basic Law 41–42; comparative examinations 42; Ministry of Education and Cultural Affairs 41; quality assurance 42–43, 44; school evaluation 41–42; tracking 40–41
Gewirtz, S. 84, 85, 101
Gipps, C. 76–77, 101
Glazzard, J. 121
Gleeson, J. 67
Golding, J. 68
group performance 96
guided participation 4

Hacking 11–12
Halbert, J. 79
Hall, K. 13, 62
Hannah (student) 100–101, 101
Harris, K. 75–76
Hattie, J. 20
headline measures 33
health care support workers 16
Heinrich, M. 40–41
hierarchical accountability 41, 43, 48, 59
higher education, barriers to access 84
Hochschild, J. 45, 50
Holden, L. 16
human action 2–3
human capital 89, 91

identity: assessment 75–76; assessment as 16–18; assessor 23–26; categories 83; and communities of practice 22–23; constructions 100; as a failure 18; intersectional nature of 101; negotiating 18; teachers 23–26

identity development 10–28, 21, 22–23, 27, 27–28; spatial aspects 12–16
identity-formation 2, 11–12, 113; trajectories 21
inadequacy 99
inclusion 9, 63, 64, 96, 109, 115–118; *see also* special educational needs
inclusion policy scripts 120–121
inclusive assessment values 115–117
inclusive education 112
independence 57–58
Individual Education Plans 127
individualisation 88, 109
individualism 71
individuality 88
individual meaning-making 2
individual needs 134–135
individual responsibility 45
inequality 76, 82, 90, 91
informal spaces 14
intelligent accountability 59
interactive computerised assessment system 37
interdependence 57–58
international benchmarking 132
international case studies 8, 29–59; Australia 29, 53–57, 57–59; California 29, 48–53, 57–59; cross-case comparison 57–59; England 29, 30–37, 40, 57–59; Finland 29, 29–30, 44–48, 57–59; Germany 29, 30, 40–44, 58; key messages 40; methodological approach 30; Northern Ireland 39–40, 40; Scotland 37–38, 40, 57–59, 58; United States of America 29, 48–53, 57–59; Victoria 29, 53–57, 57–59; Wales 38–39, 40
international metrics 29
interpersonal plane 4
interviews 6
invisible pedagogies 76
Ireland 8, 76–77, 92; assessment policy 66–81; assessment reforms 14; assessment regimes 71; bell-curve approach 69; educational trajectory 72; entrance assessment 94–97; entrance examinations 9; Established Leaving Certificate 133; fairness tracking 76–77; Junior Cycle curriculum reform 67, 71–76, 77–80, 77, 78; Junior Leaving Certificate 132; Leaving Certificate 67, 72, 85, 87; National Strategy for Literacy and Numeracy 132; shadow education 76; summative assessment 66
Irish Department of Education and Skills 72

Irish Research Council for the Humanities and Social Sciences 7
Irish Times 16
Itkonen, T. 44, 45
Ivinson, G. 10–11

Jahnukainen, M. 44, 45
Joint Statement on Principles on Principles and Implementation 79
Junior Cycle curriculum 66; classroom-based assessments 78–79, *78, 80*; English 77–80, 77, 78; features of quality *80*; grade descriptors *80*; grading system *78*; reform 67, 71–76, 77–80
Junior Cycle Profile of Achievement 72, 79–80

Kalalahti, M. 45, 46, 47
Keddie, A. 58
Keillor, Garrison 28
Klenowski, V. 83, 91
knowledge 3
knowledge exchange meetings 24
Kwo, O. 76

labelling 96
language proficiency 104–105
Lantolf, P. J. 15
Lareau, A. 93
Laurenson, P. 79
league tables 40, 70, 90–94, 101; negative impact 36
learner identities 6
learners: responsibilisation 70; subjectivities 63
learning: acquisitionist discourse 62; across boundaries of practice 15–16; and agency 22; complexity of 3; process-based 26; sociocultural definition 17; sociocultural theories 112; sociocultural theory of 17
learning outcomes, shift towards 74
learning trajectories 11, 16, 21
Lenihan, R. 79
Lewis, C. 21
lifepaths 133
lifeworlds 6
Lingard, B. 90–91
literacy 6
Local Education Authorities, England 33
Looney, A. 75–76
looping effect, the 11–12
Lynch, K. 83, 84, 85–86, 93–94, 101

McAvinue, L. 71
McCormack, O. 67

McDermott, R. 2, 15, 20
McGregor, G. 88
MacPhail, A. 79
Maguire, M. 67, 68
maladaptive practices 91
Mannion, G. 12–13
Mansell, W. 35
marginalisstion 70, 83, 94, 99–100, 121
market accountability 41, 43, 48, 59
marketisation 92–93
Mary Immaculate Reading Attainment Test 107
meaning-making 82; collective 2; individual, the 2
mediation 15, 25; subtle 3
medicalisation 110–111
methodology 6
Mills, M. 132
Ministry of Education and Cultural Affairs, Germany 41
moderation guides 37
Moje, E. B. 21
Moll, L. C. 5–6
moment-by-moment processes 3
motivation 98
Multi-Tiered Systems of Support 118–120
Munns, G. 18, 20
Murphy, P. 13, 104
mylocalschool 39

National Assessment Program, Australia 56–57
National Assessment Program – Literacy and Numeracy (NAPLAN) 90–91; Australia 56–57
National Assessment Resource 37
national standards 37
National Strategy for Literacy and Numeracy 132
natural growth 93
negative impact 99–100, 108
negotiation 3
neighbourhood school principle 45
Nelson, R. 36
neoliberal accountability 58
neoliberalisation 70, 88, 89–90
neuro-discourses 111–112
neutrality 113
New Group Reading Test 107
Newton, P. E. 120
Nind, M. 13
No Child Left Behind Act, 2001 (USA) 49–50, 51
non-academic educational programmes 123
non-formal assessment 14

Nord Anglia International School, Dublin 73
normative thinking 9
norm-referenced tests 106
North, C. 84
Northern Ireland 39–40, 40

O'Brien, S. 74, 96
observations 25
O'Donoghue, T. 67
OECD 29, 30, 39, 42, 43, 44, 50, 54, 57, 58, 59, 89, 90, 107, 131, 132
Office for Standards in Education (OFSTED) 34, 36, 39
O'Flaherty, A. 71
O'Malley, D. 69–70
O'Neill, H. 79
opportunity to learn (OTL) 127–128, 129
oppression 83, 85
organisational culture 116–117
O'Sullivan, J. 14, 23
outcomes 9, 74, 82, 89, 120, 121, 123–124
Overall Performance Scores 71
Ozga, J. 38

parents 75
parent teacher meetings 25
participation 22, 25, 26, 116–117; level of 16–17; patterns of 12; research 12–13
participatory appropriation 8, 21, 26
pedagogy 6, 63, 91
performance assessment tables 33, 37
performance data 34
performance descriptors 31–32
performance measurement systems 90–94
personal plane 7–8, 10–28; assessment as identity 16–18; assessor identity 23–26; boundaries as learning assets 18–23; identity-formation 11–12; spatial aspects 12–16
personal qualities 124
Plath, S. 139
pluralistic approach 120
policy analysis toolbox 67–68
poverty 110
power, relations of 22
practices 3; dissonances in 20–21
presentation format, accommodations 126
pressures 6
Priestley, M. 74
privatisation 50
privilege 43, 83
process-based learning 26
profilisation 47, 48

Programme for a Partnership Government 89
Programme for International Student Assessment (PISA) 43, 44, 89, 107–108, 123, 125
Programme for National Recovery (Ireland) 89
progress 32
Progress in International Reading Literacy Study (PIRLS) 43
progression 43
project, research questions 5
psychiatrisation 110–111
psychological assessment 104–105
psychologisation 110–111
psycho-medical approaches 104–112, 114–115
psychometrically-oriented assessments 104
psychometric constraints 120
public accountability 55–56
public opinion 67

quality assurance 43, 44, 53, 56, 57, 131
questionnaires 6
Quinn, R. 72–73

Ragusa, A. T. 91
Reay, D. 70–71, 99–100
redistribution 84–85
reflection 7, 27
reification 116–117
relational justice 84
reliability 9, 82–83
response format, accommodations 126
Response to Intervention 117–118, 118–120
responsibilisation 70
responsibility 59; sharing 55
rigidity 62–63
rigour 55
Robinson, P. 90
Rogoff, B. 1, 2, 3, 8, 21, 26
Rogoffian approach 1, 2, 3, 7
Ruth (student) 16–18, 22, 26, 27

school autonomy 35, 132
school evaluation, Germany 41–42
school inspection 34
schools 3
school worlds 6
Scotland 37–38, 40; accountability 57–59, 58
Scottish National Party 38
Scovronick, N. 45, 50
self-accountability 42–43
settings problems 14–15

shadow education 76
silence 101
Smyth, E. 71, 74–75, 76, 95
snapshot assessment 26
social background factors 57
social class 70, 71, 75, 76, 82, 93, 133
social context, moment-by-moment 3
social/institutional plane 3–4
social justice 9, 82, 101; definition 83, 83–86, 101; entrance assessment 94–97; equality of opportunity 101; fairness 85–86, 87–90, 101; impacts 87; and performance measurement systems 90–94; streaming experience 97–101, **99, 100**
socially practiced places 13
social order 2–3, 63, 64–65; of assessment 8; importance of 1
social order messages: Australia 57–59; California 53, 57–59; cross-case comparison 57–58, 57–59; England 57–59; Finland 47–48, 57–59; Germany 44, 58; Scotland 57–59, 58; United States of America 57–59; United Kingdom 40; Victoria 53–57, 57–59
social practices 20, 113
social purpose 9
social stratification 86, 88
sociocultural-informed approaches 112–120
socioculturalists 3
sociocultural perspective 1–9, 15, 26, 64
sociocultural practice 1; assessment as 132–134
sociocultural space 7–8
sociocultural theory, of learning 17
spatial aspects 11–12, 12–16; classrooms 13; identity development 12–16
special educational needs 9, 96, 103–130; accommodations 124–127; and accountability 107–109; agenda 104; alternative assessments 126–127; assessment 103–109; assessment accessibility 123, 124–129; assessment outcome criteria 117, 120–121; assessment practice 124–127; assessment regimes 123–124; assessment setting 125; benchmark testing 119; biopsychosocial model 104, 114–115; conceptually-informed assessment practice 117–118; definition 103; diagnostic instruments 105; disproportionality debate 109–110, 115; educational goals 121–122; equality of opportunity 108; groups 122–123; guides to action 116; identification 118;

inclusion 115–118, 124, 129–130; inclusion policy scripts 120–121; inclusive education 112; individual differences 106; individualised instruction 119; international classification systems 105–106; opportunity to learn (OTL) 127–128, 129; outcomes 121, 123–124; progress monitoring 119; psycho-medical approaches 104–112, 114–115; Response to Intervention 117–118; sociocultural-informed approaches 112–120; teacher-administered norm-referenced tests 106–107; universal assessment design 128
special needs 115
standard assessment tasks (SATs) 100–101
standardised assessment 83, 91, 92, 100–101, 107–109, 109, 132
standards, raising 64
Standing Council on School Education and Early Childhood (SCSEEC) 56–57
State Examinations Commission 71, 72, 73–74, 77
Stobart, G. 15, 26, 28, 76–77, 101
streaming 9, 95–96; experience of 97–101, **99, 100**
students, assessment resources 26; experiences 14, 20; negative experiences 10–11, 13; progress 134–135
success 58; collective responsibility 44, 47; constructions of 15; definitions of 9; distribution of 101
summative assessment 30–31, 36–37, 66, 79, 84
sustainable assessment 8, 26
symbolic capital 86
symbolic violence 85
Synergies for Better Learning: An International Perspective on Evaluation and Assessment (OECD) 131–132

Taylor, B. 95–96
teacher-administered norm-referenced tests 106–107
teacher assessment 31–32, 38–39
teacher education 135
teachers 3, 59; accountability 52; agency 63; assessment capability 135, 135–138; assessment identity 75–76; assumptions 136; autonomy 43, 57; beginning 135; definition of assessment 23; identity 75–76; identity as assessors 23–26; innovation 24; professional context 137; professionalism 75–76; professional

learning opportunities 137; successful 63; understanding of assessment 23–26
teacher talk 20
Teaching Councils 40
technological sophistication 132
temporal aspects 11–12
testing, assessment as euphemism for 82
test score inferences 127–128
theoretical justification 1
timing and scheduling, accommodations 126
Torrance, H. 64, 70
tracking 40–41, 95
transparency 50, 55–56
Trends in International Mathematics and Science Study (TIMSS) 43
trust 59
Tymms, P. 37

under-achievement 44–45
unintended consequences 108
United States of America 29, 48–53, 91; accountability 57–59, 108; Common Core Standards Initiative 51–52, 53; Common Core State Standards Initiative 48; Department of Defense Education Activity (DoDEA) 48; disproportionality debate 110; education policy assumptions 49; Every Student Succeeds Act 51; funding strategy 49; ideology 50; Individuals with Disabilities Education Act 119; No Child Left Behind Act, 2001 49–50, 51; opportunity to learn (OTL) 127–128
universal assessment design 128

validity 9, 62, 82–83
value-added system 92
value, and assessment 13–14
values, inclusive 9
van Der Kleij, F. 75–76
Varjo, J. 45, 46, 47

Victoria 29, 53–57; accountability 55–57, 57–59; Accountability and Improvement Framework for Victorian Government Schools 55–56; autonomy 54–55, 57; funding strategy 53; National Assessment Program 56–57; quality assurance 56, 57; school choice 54, 57; social background factors 57
Victorian Competition and Efficiency Commission 54
Vincent, C. 36
VIP (Voice, Identity, Participation) Project 7, 23, 25
visible pedagogies 76
voice, young people's 12–13

Wait to fail models 118
Wales 38–39, 40
Wechsler Intelligence Scale for Children 105
Weir, S. 71
Welsh Assembly 39
Wenger, E. 11, 17, 21, 22, 115–117
Wenger-Trayner, E. 16, 19–20, 26, 26–27, 27
wider curriculum-related outcomes 121
Wiggins, A. 37
Wiliam, D. 121
William, D. 99–100
Woodward, H. 18, 20
workshops 6

Xu, Y. 136

Yeager, D. S. 123
Young, I. 84, 85

Zentrum für Internationale Bildungsvergleichsstudien 41
Zipin, L. 5